Voices in the Wind

Stories, Thoughts and Reflections
Along a Contemporary Christian Pilgrimage

Forward by Bishop D. Max Whitfield

Rodney Aist

Cover Art by Pat Maines
Cover Design by Joan Addison

Printed in the United States of America. *1ˢᵗ Edition*

Published by Cross Cultural Publications, Inc. Cross Roads Books

Library of Congress Catalog Number: 2002116152

ISBN: 0-940121-76-X

Voices in the Wind

Stories, Thoughts and Reflections
Along a Contemporary Christian Pilgrimage

Forward by Bishop D. Max Whitfield

Rodney Aist

Cross Cultural
PUBLICATIONS, INC.

We had the experience but missed the meaning.

-T.S. Eliot
Four Quartets: The Dry Salvages, line 93

Contents

Foreword

Spiritual pilgrimages are very common. These are the experiences that renew us and put us in touch with the God who transforms and remakes our lives. Most of my pilgrimages are not to far away places but rather are those short journeys to sites for study, retreat and spiritual renewal.

For me, these pilgrimages have occurred when I knew that my relationship with Jesus Christ was strained by my lack of sensitivity to the presence of Christ within me. I took my relationship with Jesus for granted and neglected those basic spiritual disciplines of Bible study, prayer, and acts of mercy. Then it would dawn upon me that my spiritual well was dry, and if I expected to continue providing leadership, I had to care for my own soul. I would set out on an intentional journey to renew my relationship with my Creator, Sustainer, and Redeemer.

In this marvelous book, you will discover a pastor who sets out on a much longer journey as a positive response to a calling. Rev. Rodney Aist is constantly searching for and discovering the presence and power of God in some of the most unexpected and unusual people and places. Rodney has that unique ability to capture and share his insights and experiences.

Rodney and I became well acquainted while he was serving two United Methodist churches in Calico Rock, Arkansas under my supervision. As his district superintendent, I saw his uncanny ability to provide effective ministry in a wide variety of places. He was effective in working with children and youth. At the same time, he was loved, supported, and appreciated by the older adults in his parish. He could be present with and learn from people of all ages and stations in life.

One of the special gifts I quickly recognized in Rodney was the way he cared for his own soul. He did not carry his piety on his sleeves for all to see. He did not stand before groups and brag about how he worked on a daily and weekly basis to make certain that he was enjoying being in the presence of God. Rather, Rodney demonstrated a quiet spirituality.

I had a practice of regularly asking the pastors under my supervision how they were taking care of themselves in the midst of the constant demands of ministry, especially those serving in remote, rural settings. Rodney would tell me how he would go and sit on the cliffs overlooking the White River and just watch the sunset. It was in those moments his soul rejoiced in the wonder and awe of God. On other occasions, he would ride his bicycle for several miles and enjoy the beauty of God's creation. He also made sure he had time with friends and family to relax and renew himself. His parish recognized the value of these efforts and supported him faithfully as he cared for his own soul. They recognized that as he cared for himself, he was even more effective in helping them in their spiritual journey.

I remember vividly the day that Rodney approached me about his desire to spend a year on Christian pilgrimage. I regret not being more supportive that day. I thought it was a pipe dream. Fortunately, Rodney put together a more detailed plan and brought it back for me to reflect upon a second time. His pilgrimage would end with forty days alone in the Ozark wilderness where he planned to fast and pray. This time I remember being more supportive.

Rodney has the ability to make detailed plans and yet to remain open to spontaneous developments. He is adept at discovering the presence and power of Jesus Christ. These gifts were to transform a trip into a pilgrimage.

One of the many lessons this book provides is helping all of us to look for and discover the presence of God in the ordinary events of life. God does not wait for those extraordinary moments to enter into a relationship with us as God's beloved creatures. God is searching, wooing, calling, hoping to find some way into our too busy, demanding, empty world. The initiative to be in a meaningful, redeeming relationship with God does not begin with us. God takes the initiative, walking beside us in the most unusual places and times.

Rodney opens the doors and enables us to see some of the pathways and people that God has provided him to foster and advance his relationship with the One who is our Creator, Sustainer and Redeemer. I pray that my eyes will always be as open and willing to see what God has prepared for me.

Fortunately for me, my relationship with Rodney did not end when he left upon his spiritual pilgrimage. When he returned to Arkansas, I was able to convince the bishop to appoint Rodney again to a church under my supervision. I was able to hear at least some of these stories first hand and meet a few of the people he had come to know during his pilgrimage.

There have been several lessons I have learned from him, and I will only mention a few:

Encourage people to pursue their dreams. They will come back stronger and more effective.

Be constantly looking for the presence of God. God is not hidden except for the blindness of our own eyes.

Try the new and different. Others have discovered and renewed their souls by practices and activities that may be foreign to us. They may open the door for the glory and honor of God to flow into our lives.

Do not be afraid to be a trailblazer. I know of no other pastor who has dared such a long, involved pilgrimage. If he had been unwilling to be a trailblazer, he would have missed so much that God had in store for him. During Rodney's travels, he was able to learn from other church fathers and mothers who were also pursuing their dreams of walking in a closer relationship with the Almighty God.

Look for God in the ordinary people and events of each day. If there is one message I hope to always treasure and practice, it is to slow down and open myself to the presence of God in the day-to-day experiences of life.

It is my hope each reader will enjoy having the opportunity to share this spiritual pilgrimage that Rodney has so gracious prepared. It has greatly enriched my life.

Bishop D. Max Whitfield
Northwest Texas/New Mexico Area
United Methodist Church

Preface

It is my hope that this book in someway reflects the events, thoughts, and conversations that transpired throughout the course of a recent Christian pilgrimage that I undertook to places near and far around this wonderful planet. To be reflective of this experience, the narrative incorporates a wide range of form and content; it is full of description, narrative, self-reflection and numerous quotes. Moreover, the serious and the humorous as well as the common, the strange, and even the slightly offensive are intertwined.

My travels were full of joy, surprise, excitement, disappointment, exhaustion, and anxiety. But, so it is: the pilgrimage of life is a complexity of events, emotions, and experiences. The spiritual life is lived amidst the details and demands of daily life, and seldom, if ever, are the divine moments far removed from the mundane. As these pages highlight, we discover God through the actual events of our lives. While thoughts, activities, and emotions are often heightened when one's *on the road*, the lessons, goals, and purposes remain the same for us all: we are constantly seeking the Divine, and we do so in the context of often rough and uneven lives.

This book explores how the presence of God is experienced in a diversity of people, places, cultures, and denominations. While recognizing differences that exist among Christians, it is hoped that these pages will stimulate in the reader an appreciation of the vitality of the Christian faith worldwide. Vibrant Christian communities exist around the globe; individual persons committed to the life of Christ can be found in all corners of the world.

The title *Voices in the Wind* expresses two fundamental elements of my pilgrimage experience. The first is the notion of the wind as the Holy Spirit. The Holy Spirit is actively in motion, constantly moving across the plane of our lives. Invisible but ever-present, it is life-giving and sustaining. As Jesus tells Nicodemus by the cover of night, *The wind blows where it chooses, and you hear the sound of it, but you do not know where it comes from or where it goes* (John 3:8). The Holy Spirit is mystery and surprise. Sometimes, its breeze is gentle, fresh, and soothing; at other times, it is more invigorating, fierce, and even violent. For most of my pilgrimage, I felt the wind at my back – the Holy Spirit ever supporting me along the way.

Secondly, the voices are those of my fellow pilgrims. Some of these voices are explicitly quoted throughout the book; however, far more people than those mentioned within these pages have supported this journey – and indeed my life and ministry as a whole.

While aware of the risk of leaving out specific persons who have contributed to the formation of this book, I, nonetheless, want to acknowledge those who have been instrumental in this project. I begin with the United Methodist churches of Spring Creek and Calico Rock and other persons in the Calico Rock, Arkansas community who supported my dreams and sent me off with their love, prayers and blessings.

Throughout the planning stage, several individual persons added valuable suggestions and support, including pastors and laity in the North Arkansas Conference. The North Arkansas Board of Ordained Ministry and my former district superintendent, the Bishop D. Max Whitfield, were both helpful and encouraging in many ways. Moreover, I would like to thank Jane Dennis who gave me the opportunity to communicate with the readers of the *Arkansas United Methodist* during my travels. She has since helped me on a number of other projects.

I cannot adequately thank everyone who assisted me on the journey itself. This list is amazingly long. I received the hospitality of food and shelter from both friends and strangers; over and again, I was fortunate to be befriended by some of the world's most wonderful people. In each instance, their generosity was gratefully received. I do, however, extend a special thank you to Bob and Kay Burton who made my hermitage experience possible and who never failed to leave out food for me! They do indeed live on a creek called Roasting Ear.

Upon completion of my pilgrimage, I received valuable support and encouragement from many people. Foremost, I would like to thank the congregation of Sequoyah United Methodist Church in Fayetteville, Arkansas, including the Rev. Don Hall, who provided numerous opportunities for me to process my pilgrimage experiences.

The creation of this manuscript has taken many shapes and has been developed by the support of many people who have read it in its various stages. Each of them has provided valuable insights, corrections, and encouragement. They include Donna Huie, the Rev. David Fleming, the Rev. Mark Statler, Tracy Radosevik, Diane Lysiak, the Rev. Rebecca McFee, Dr. Thomas O'Loughlin, and the Rev. Daniel McFee. The errors that remain, of course, are creations of my own.

A final and most sincere thank you has been reserved for my parents, Gene and Anna Aist. They were not only involved in countless practical details of my trip – answering mail, balancing bank accounts, and providing airport shuttles – but they have embraced my ministry with an unreserved enthusiasm. Their dedicated support and unwavering love have been most appreciated.

May this book be a tribute to the many voices in my life, my fellow pilgrims who will forever travel with me – if not by foot – then in my heart, mind, and soul:

Rodney Aist

Sweet Corn

I've just finished going around the world, and my only regret is not stopping at the world's largest corn maze in Ankeny, Iowa. I drove right past it on Interstate 35. Advertisements on the radio had announced its coming: *Amazing Corn Maze . . . built inside a cornfield . . . over two miles of pathways . . . great family fun . . . take I-35 to Exit 90 in Ankeny and follow the signs . . . only six dollars per person.*

I came to the exit, noticed the large white banner – *Amazing Maize Maze* – and foolishly, I kept on driving. Certain opportunities only come once in a lifetime.

It was a Sunday in August, and I was driving from Minnesota to Arkansas. After waking up in a tent in southern Minnesota, I caught a worship service at a staid Presbyterian church in a nearby town, fulfilling my Sunday morning obligation. By the time I reached Ankeny, Iowa, I had ten more hours of driving, and it was already well past noon.

Sometimes, you wish you hadn't gone to church.

***

The night before, I had left family camp in northern Minnesota, my annual August tradition, where I work as a counselor. After cleaning out my cabin and saying my good-byes, I took a last look across the serene waters of Lake Hubert; a solitary loon flew overhead, its lonely call cleared the air with a melancholic gloss. I hate good-byes, and nowhere are they more difficult for me than at camp.

I got in my car, turned on the radio, and slowly drove down the camp road, waving good-bye to the few remaining staff persons who were still packing their cars. It was exactly five o'clock on a Saturday afternoon. I was leaving camp with *A Prairie Home Companion.*

There are four great things in life, Garrison Keillor, the radio host, insisted during his monologue, *The News from Lake Woebegon. The first is the joy of knowing God. The second is the love of learning. The third is what you all first thought of . . . and the fourth is sweet corn. It's rare that someone experiences all four, especially someone unfortunate enough to live in a city. Many of you may have experienced two or three of these but not all four. Some of you are perhaps quite content, thinking that you have experienced everything only to realize now that your life is actually quite unfulfilled. You're missing sweet corn.[1]*

It was corn season in Minnesota, and an hour later, I stopped at an old dilapidated gas station where I bought a dozen ears of corn off a wagon in front of the pumps. *Yep, just picked today. They've brought it out four or five times,* the attendant told me, who had apparently sold more corn that day than gas. A few hours later, at a state park just east of Albert Lea, I pitched my tent in the dusk and quickly fell into a deep sleep.

***

I began hearing advertisements for the corn maze about thirty miles north of Ankeny. The Amazing Corn Maze was spearheaded by Paul Chistoffers, a member of the Resurrection Lutheran Church, who first learned about a similar maze in Pennsylvania three years before. *Our church men's group was looking for a unique family-oriented, fund-raising activity, and I was intrigued by the maze concept. It seemed like an ideal project for Iowa.*

The Amazing Corn Maze covered over 280,000 square feet with two and a half miles of paths and could hold up to three thousand people at any one time. The maze, designed by Lori Bergland, an architectural student at Iowa State University, had a tower overlooking the maze to help any visitors who might get stranded. Clues assisted people along the way. The maze closed at dusk to make sure that everyone was out before dark. That just made sense.

But, no, I kept on driving.

***

---

[1] From a repeat broadcast of *A Prairie Home Companion* from   August 17, 1996. I have paraphrased the monologue.

According to C. S. Lewis, the Grand Miracle of the Christian faith, of history itself, is the incarnation. God became man; the divine became human, dwelling within the created form of humanity in the person of Jesus.[2] In the Christian story, God descends to re-ascend. Lewis points out that we will all recognize this familiar pattern: it is the pattern of all vegetable life. Life takes the form of something hard, small and deathlike, falls upon the ground and from hence spawns the new life.

This pattern of death and re-birth is in nature, because it was first there in God. We see in the life, death, and resurrection of Christ what we find patterned elsewhere throughout creation and particularly modeled in the annual death and resurrection of the corn. As Lewis notes, there have been many religions in which the central deity was a personification of the corn, a corn-king who died and rose again each year.

Is not Christ simply another corn-king?[3]

On the contrary, Lewis maintains. Christ resembles the corn-king because the corn-king is a portrait of Christ. The concept of the corn-king is derived from the facts of nature, and the facts of nature are derived from her Creator. Christ is not simply another corn-king. He does not die and come to life each year as a true corn-king should. Rather, he died once – and now he inhabits eternity. Christ's sacrifice was once and for all. He defeated death, and there is no need to repeat what has been accomplished. What he did is not repeated but rather remembered – we remember that Christ, the dying God, held bread, that is, corn, in his hand and said, *This is my body.*[4]

What the dying God does is bring salvation to all humanity.

***

I am on a journey to observe and experience the Grand Miracle, the incarnation of God. God became human, dwelling within the person

---

[2] C. S. Lewis, *Miracles: A Preliminary Study* (New York: The Macmillan Company, 1947), pp. 131-158.
[3] Lewis, p. 137.
[4] Lewis, p. 137.

of Jesus. Now, the resurrected Christ dwells in humanity. In people and places around the globe. In communities and individuals. In every spoken language and in the silence of our hearts. I am interested in the infinite manifestations of God and, moreover, in how we as humans experience the Divine.

I am on a journey to a myriad of landscapes where I will see the God of nature, and occasionally, I hope, where I will witness glimpses of the God that stands behind and beyond all that he has created. He sends the rain; he causes the corn to grow; he regenerates the fallen seed. He is in the rainbow, the volcano, and the mystery of the northern lights.

***

Driving home to Arkansas, wrapping up eight weeks of stateside pilgrimage before embarking around the world, I reflected upon the events of the summer. In June, I had finished up a successful three-year pastorate of two small Methodist churches in Calico Rock in rural northern Arkansas. Now, as clearly as God had called me into the ministry, God was calling me on pilgrimage. Before me lay eight months of international travel to Christian communities and pilgrimage sites. I would finish the year with forty days of solitude and prayer in the Ozark wilderness.

Ten years earlier, while an undergraduate student, I took a class on medieval pilgrimage. I loved the class, but I attributed my interests to a general appreciation for medieval church history. I never thought twice about pilgrimage.

Over the next few years, I studied in Denmark and Germany and served a year as an assistant pastor in Scotland, traveling extensively throughout parts of Europe, exposing myself to more history and culture while developing and maintaining international friendships. I often met people who had circled the globe. I had friends in places I had never been and knew other people whom I wanted to see again.

Although I was interested in such a journey, I was aware that I would never allow myself to take one. I was a church pastor, and I could not justify *taking a year off*. However, in my third year at Calico Rock, I received what I believe was a definitive calling – to be a pilgrim. In short, God gave me permission to pursue that which I was most predisposed to do. *But you're going to do it my way*, to put words in the mouth of the Divine. *It's going to be a pilgrimage.* I can describe some of the background, but the bottom line is – it was calling, and I can't account for that. To explain it is to reduce it.

I immediately began working up sample itineraries. Where would I go? Whom would I visit? Each place had its own story. Some places, like Africa University, Santiago de Compostela, and Iona, were on my initial list. Ironically, Israel was not. Other destinations, like Casa Materna and Taizé, were introduced to me during the six months of planning. The last phase included making contacts in places where my around-the-world airline ticket would take me.

In June, I preached my last sermon and early on a Friday morning, after an evening of tearful good-byes, I slipped out of Calico Rock as quietly as I had arrived three years before. My car packed for the summer, I drove to Garrett-Evangelical Theological Seminary on the shore of Lake Michigan to take a two-week class on John Wesley, the founder of Methodism.

***

(Evanston, Illinois: June 17th – 28th)

Holy! Holy! Holy! With the words of this beautiful hymn, a chapter of my life was closed. After three wonderful years at Calico Rock, we ended our final worship service by singing the hymn, *Holy! Holy! Holy!*

Today I begin a new journey: a journey of faith and discovery, a spiritual and professional pilgrimage, a year of corporate worship and individual retreat, a journey that will take me to Christian communities in countries around the globe. I journey alone, but I journey in covenant with the community of faith. Every prayer, every blessing, every meal extended to me reminds me that I am not my own. The body of Christ is with me wherever I go.

I seek to be a pilgrim – discovering faith, observing faith. More than anything else, this year will be one of connections. There is a thread, which joins our past with our future; there is a Spirit, which connects one Christian community to another.

This morning I experienced the needle of God which pieces our lives, and the sinew which mends our souls with healing, wholeness, and gladness, the hand of God which delights in connecting our past with our present, our former community with our present one. Gathering with new friends in the Garrett chapel, we began worship by singing:

> *Holy! Holy! Holy!*
> *Lord God Almighty!*
> *Early in the morning our song shall rise to thee;*
> *Only thou art holy; there is none beside thee,*
> *Perfect in power, in love, and purity.*[5]

With the same song, a chapter ends and a new one begins. A new community, but the same God. Every time we are pierced with the emotions of life, our souls are opened up to the connective thread of God. So it was today as the hymn was sung. The memories of Calico Rock, the pain of separation filled my eyes with tears. Yet as voices were raised in adoration, I felt the healing of a God who is the totality of my life – and the unifier of all my broken pieces.

***

This morning is gorgeous – sunny, warm, and beautiful. The lakeside is full of bikers, walkers, and roller bladers. Boats and sailboats dot the shore. Nearby, a soccer game is going on, and I can hear whistles, clapping, and encouragement.

I need to spend more time experiencing the grace of God through prayer, Bible study, and journaling. These disciplines are windows to God. In turn, they make me more available to those around me.

***

During chapel, we heard these words from Revelation: *Behold I stand*

---

[5] Taken from two different stanzas of *Holy, Holy, Holy* written by Reginald Heber, 1826.

at the door and knock.[6]

I struggle at times understanding the historical Christ, the beliefs, the doctrines. Yet, I understand faith. Faith is leaning into the future in a state of unknowing, being led by something that I cannot see, cannot put a name on. The spiritual presence is One who remains a mystery yet whose substance is love. I have based my life upon a faith that I cannot see. My faith is a pilgrimage, a walk of trust. I live within the arms of a being that assures me that I am forgiven and loved.

Christ is my example, my understanding of the nature of God. In my struggle to understand, I can only bring myself to the posture of passiveness. I allow a knocking God to come into my life.

***

In the bookstore, I stumbled upon the Russian spiritual classic, *The Way of a Pilgrim.*

By the grace of God, I am a Christian man, by my actions a great sinner, and by calling a homeless wanderer of the humblest birth who roams from place to place. My worldly goods are a knapsack with some dried bread in it on my back, and in my breast pocket a Bible. And that is all.[7]

***

The Edidin's, a Chicago family I know from family camp, picked me up near campus, and we drove downtown, eating pizza before walking along the Navy Pier. On the Ferris wheel, Ira and I talked about spiritual disciplines. At the time, as a discipline, I was not eating meat. Ira reminded me that disciplines teach us that we are not perfect and that there is only One who is.

I got back to the dorm around sunset and ran into Preston, an African-American student from Detroit, in the lobby. We talked for two hours about our class. Preston said, *We have experienced a week that no one*

---

[6] Revelation 3:20.
[7] *The Way of a Pilgrim and The Pilgrim Continues His Way*, trans. R. M. French (London: SPCK, 1963), p. 1.

will ever forget. I was grateful – my pilgrimage was beginning well.

In the morning, I went to church with Preston at the Second Baptist Church of Evanston. I debated whether or not to dress up. I figured that it did not matter. It was summer, and I was a visitor, so I just threw on some khakis and a tie, and much to my regret, I left my jacket in the room.

We arrived at the church as the Rev. Dr. Taylor drove up. Preston knew him, and I was introduced. He shook my hand hard and raised it up toward his chest. We entered the church, where we went upstairs to Rev. Taylor's study, and then sat there for a long time talking. I could hear the choir singing in the sanctuary, and I was eager for Preston to excuse us so that we could get comfortably seated in the sanctuary.

Finally, Rev. Taylor left his study. He hurried down the stairs, walking briskly through several hallways. Preston followed – and I tried to stay close behind. All the while, I kept asking myself: *Why are we wasting so much time? Why aren't we grabbing a seat? We are missing the music.* At last, we entered a room located behind the choir where another half-dozen men were gathering. I caught my breath and stood looking around at everyone, sizing up the situation, waiting for Preston to say something, anything to me. Finally, with horror, it dawned upon me: *My God, I'm sitting with the preachers!*

I was urged forward, walking in line behind the senior pastor and the other men. All the while, Preston never spoke a word. We climbed some stairs, ascending the main chancel area, and there I stood, the only Caucasian in the sanctuary, noticeably visible to several hundred people. For some reason, I grimaced, flushed with embarrassment, while all my feeble mind could think of was: *I can't believe I left my jacket in the room.*

I took a seat, squirming in my khakis, looking out over the congregation, watching them watching me, noticing some pews in the back where I wanted to be sitting. I stood up for the singing, clapping my hands, trying to move my body to a rhythm that I could never quite find. The atmosphere was friendly, though, and eventually, I felt more at ease. The spirited music and the enthused participation of the congregation carried the service – in contrast to a lot of Christian worship that is oriented solely around the sermon. Eventually, Rev. Taylor stood up to deliver a message on the three Cs: Courage, Commitment and Character, and long before I was ready, the service was over.

We returned to campus, and after lunch, I drove down to Custer's Last Stand, a local street festival. I walked around for about four hours, eating carnival food, and listening to blues, getting rather sun burned before returning to campus.

***

This week we are leaving John Wesley behind in favor of nineteenth-century American Methodism. My final presentation will be on Samuel Worchester, an American Mission Society missionary from New England who was sent to Georgia in the 1820s to work with the Cherokee Indians. During this time, Georgia was actively pursuing a policy of Indian removal, and seeing the Christian missions as a hindrance, the state passed a law requiring all whites to get a license to work on Native American land. When Worchester, who operated a mission school at New Echota, refused to acknowledge the Georgian law, reasoning correctly that the law threatened Cherokee sovereignty, he was arrested, brought to trial, and convicted. From prison, Worchester filed suit against the state of Georgia.

In the landmark 1831 Supreme Court case, *Worchester v. Georgia,* the high court ruled in favor of Native American sovereignty, citing that state laws had no jurisdiction over Indian nations. Andrew Jackson, the U.S. president, however, would not enforce the ruling. Had federal troops been sent into Georgia to implement the Supreme Court's ruling on Native American sovereignty, in all likelihood, the Civil War would have started two decades earlier. In the end, Worchester gave up his fight and followed the Cherokee to Oklahoma.

***

Today's worship had something to do with rocks.

***

The morning is beautiful. I'm facing the sun over Lake Michigan as I write. The downtown skyline is crisp and distinct. There is a cool gentle breeze on my neck, and the sky is as clear as I've seen it in two weeks.

***

On Wednesday evening, I went with a group of students to Willow Creek Church, one of America's foremost megachurches. An hour drive with seven people crammed into an old station wagon, we were threatened with carsickness, but we all made it intact about twenty minutes before the service.

At first, I was skeptical, but soon I felt at home. I am trying to live more by the words: *Don't quench the spirit.*[8] There were three thousand people worshipping God on an incredibly gorgeous Wednesday night in June. Something good was going on.

An orchestra began with a prelude medley of Christian songs. Then, four singers came out and sang: *They say there is no God.* After we sang praise music for half an hour, the offering was taken, and a time of silence followed. I was eager to hear the speaker, anxious to observe his use of catchy presentations and contemporary techniques. What I saw amazed me. The speaker simply lectured from the Bible for nearly an hour. I was shocked. Shocked that the place was packed, that in an age in which our attention span is less than five minutes we were given a forty-five minute, gimmick-free talk. It was solid but not necessarily eloquent or charismatic. He simply taught.

Are we thirsting for entertainment or content?

The mission statement of Willow Creek is *Taking the irreligious and transforming them to be followers of Christ.*

***

An hour before dark, I went to study by the lake. The sun was already

---

[8] 1 Thessalonians 5:19.

setting, but the evening light lingered on. As I reviewed books on Samuel Worchester, I listened to distant music coming from the student center. Several times, it was announced that *Field of Dreams* would be shown outside starting at dusk.

I studied until the mosquitoes took over. As I walked by the student center, the movie was starting. I needed to study and to pack, so naturally, I took my books to the room, grabbed a comforter, and returned to the lawn where the movie was being projected against the wall of the multi-storied student center. Vowing to leave after each scene, I continued to stay until I finally settled in for the entire movie.

***

Iowans have a fetish for cutting down corn.

***

In *Field of Dreams*, Ray Kinsella, a young Iowa corn farmer, begins to hear voices: *If you build it, they will come.* Eventually, he sees a vision of a baseball field built in the middle of his cornfield. He plows up his corn, develops a baseball diamond, and, suddenly, old baseball players materialize out of nowhere and begin playing baseball on his field of dreams.

For some reason, Kinsella also feels called to bring others to his field including Terrance Mann, a forgotten writer from Boston, and Archibald Graham, an old small town doctor from Minnesota. Doc Graham played in one major league baseball game but never got to bat. Before the beginning of the next season, Graham was out of baseball, pursuing the life of a small town doctor in Chisholm, Minnesota.

Kinsella and Mann go to Chisholm and find the doctor returning home late one night from his office. Kinsella tells him that he is supposed to take him to his field of dreams, but Graham refuses to go. Baseball was a dream that happened a long time ago. As a doctor, he had lived out a wonderful and generous life, supporting the needy kids of the town and helping people for many years. Kinsella's field of dreams held no interest for him.

Disappointed, Kinsella and Mann return home to Iowa. On their way, they pick up a hitchhiker. It's Archibald Graham, now a young kid, looking for a place to play baseball. Graham is taken to Kinsella's field where he is introduced to an odd assortment of famous baseball players. Graham joins in the scrimmage and soon realizes his dream of hitting against major league pitching.

While they are playing, Kinsella's daughter falls off the bleachers and begins choking on a hot dog. Suddenly, the young Graham senses his calling as a doctor. He walks toward the bleachers, stopping momentarily at the first base line. When he steps across the line, the young Graham turns into the old doctor. He then walks over to the girl, dislodges the hot dog, and saves her life. The scene confirms to the doctor that he made the right decision in life. When he crossed the line, he gave up his dream to play baseball, but the doctor was content – he knew that he had fulfilled his calling.

Field of Dreams is not so much about chasing after dreams but rather about discovering one's personal calling. Even as the events unfold, Mann states to Kinsella, *I know why you are here, and I know why he is here. But why am I here?* Before long, it is revealed to him as well.

As I watched the scene, I felt a divine Presence, and I understood that God has a plan for me – a specific, concrete plan. I, too, will have to cross a line that I can never cross back over. As I step into the future to serve others, I will leave many of my dreams behind, but I will fulfill many more along the way.

Christians believe in salvation, but it's another thing altogether to believe that God has a specific, individual plan for us. God loves us so much that he not only wants to save us, but he has created each of us for a unique purpose.

∗∗∗

Ten hours past Ankeny, I arrived at my grandfather's house, late in the night, tired and ready for bed. In the morning, we had to get up at 6:30 to drive two hours to Little Rock to see my grandmother, who was convalescing in a nursing home. My grandfather, however, was still up, patiently waiting for me, watching over a plate of food that he had prepared for me hours earlier – a can of Mountain Dew, a cold brown-n-serve dinner roll, and a single ear of corn.

The Berry Stick

I had a long but delightful drive from Chicago to Montana, making it only as far as Madison, Wisconsin on the first night where I stayed with a West African friend, Diallo, whom I had met while we were both students in Germany. Diallo invited some of his African friends over to share a traditional meal with me, and then we took a walk around the university. I timidly told them of my plans for the year, proud, though, to tell them that I was going to Kenya and Zimbabwe. Ajume, Diallo's friend from Cameroon, spoke up, interjecting as though he was my pilgrim mentor: *Deciding to go on your pilgrimage is everything. Anything you learn from here on is just extra.*

The next day I drove a thousand miles before pitching a tent in a state park in Wyoming. Driving through South Dakota, Americana culture at its best, I thought all day of my Scottish friend, Andy, an Americana connoisseur. Only he would have enjoyed the Mitchell Corn Palace, Wall Drug, the Badlands, and Mount Rushmore more than I did.

Since 1892, Mitchell, South Dakota has boasted the world's only corn palace. Originally called the Corn Belt Exposition, the present building, a multi-use events arena whose exterior is decorated yearly with murals made from thousands of bushels of corn, grain, and grasses, has been around since 1921. Two of my closest friends in college were from South Dakota, and they bragged extensively about the corn palace, one Christmas even returning with a Mitchell Corn Palace snow tumbler for me. Now, I stood before the Palace of the Plains, realizing yet another dream. I walked around the building, studying the various murals and glancing up at the minarets and turrets crowning the roof of the fabled monument that commemorates the fertility of South Dakota soil. I took a seat inside the arena where I watched a video on life on the prairie. Commercial booths selling Western souvenirs filled the large room. In the lobby, there was an exhibit displaying yearly photos of the Corn Palace's various organic murals. There was something else neat about the Corn Palace, but it escapes me. Outside, I grabbed a cup of lemonade at the barbecue stand on the way to the car.

Hours later, I pulled into Wall Drug, famous for its free ice water and nickel coffee – a kitsch wonderland on the edge of the Badlands. You haven't been to South Dakota, if you haven't been to Wall Drug. Supposedly up to twenty thousand people pass through this drug-store-gone-wild on a summer day, but I found a parking spot around the corner and began my tour of Wall Drug, leaving the car running to avoid the temptation of staying too long. I ran through the pharmacy museum, the art gallery, and the Black Hills jewelry shop, stopping breathlessly at Traveler's Chapel where I prayed for someone – I think myself – and then ducked into the Wall Drug Mall (a re-created Western town) and the Back Yard Mall (with a shooting gallery and a life-size T. Rex!) before emerging into the Back Yard itself, where I had my photo taken next to the giant six-foot jackalope.

T. Rex was the highlight of my six-year-old son's trip, says David of Illinois on the Wall Drug web page. I definitely liked the jackalope better.

I walked back to my idling car with a cup of coffee and a glass of ice water and once again hit the interstate heading west. If a person had a lot of time to spend in South Dakota, Wall Drug could be a lot of fun. But I didn't, and so it wasn't. Still, someday, I'm coming back with Andy.

In the late afternoon, I reached the Badlands, one of the National Parks that I hadn't seen as a kid. The long afternoon shadows stretched out over the intricate relief of eroded rock as I drove over the ribbon of highway locking bumpers with a few slow moving RVs. Like the Black Hills, the Badlands are ancient sacred grounds of the Sioux.

The Badlands provide a sanctuary, a place to hide, to seek visions, and to connect with the spirits of nature. The last ghost dancers found refuge in the Badlands, and still today, the physical and spiritual journeys of the Sioux go through the Badlands. *We are part of the nature around us,* says Lame Deer. *The older we get, the more we come to look like it. In the end, we become part of the landscape with a face like the Badlands.*[9] I was sorry to escape, but heading west, I

---

[9] Lame Deer, *Lame Deer: Seeker of Visions* (New York: Simon and Schuster, 1972), photo caption.

again found the interstate.

I arrived at Mount Rushmore just as the evening program, held in the outdoor amphitheater at the foot of the mountain, began. A ranger gave a short talk, which was followed by a twenty-minute film on the historical importance of Washington, Jefferson, Lincoln, and Roosevelt. The presentation ended with the playing of *The Star-Spangled Banner*. Suddenly, the four presidents were bathed in light, and I sat with the crowd in a prolonged silence, looking up at what William Zinsser describes as the *four pharaohs in the sky*.[10] Perhaps no other American monument so strongly portrays the personality of the nation – confidence, ambition, individualism, and love of size. *This isn't a monument to presidents – it's a monument to America*, said Jim Popovich, chief of interpretation for the National Park Service.[11]

Started in 1927, by Gutzon Borglum, a son of a Danish immigrant, this depression era project cost $982,992.32. Calvin Coolidge launched the project with a speech predicting that future Americans would flock to Mount Rushmore *to declare their continuing allegiance to independence, to self-government, to freedom and to economic justice*.[12]

Although the monument represents the nation's *finest ideas*, nobody seemed to have been particularly concerned at the time that the Black Hills are sacred to the Sioux. Mount Rushmore is a tale of two peoples, a story of two nations. Lame Deer, a Sioux medicine man, tells his nation's side in his classic, *Lame Deer: Seeker of Visions*:[13]

Here we are, sitting on Teddy Roosevelt's head, giving him a headache, maybe. If we get tired of the view from here, we could move over and sit for a while on Washington or Lincoln or Jefferson, but Teddy is by far the best. There is moss growing near the back of his skull, lots of trees, firewood, boulders to lean your back against, a little hollow surrounded by pines, which makes a nice campground. ..

---

[10] William K. Zinsser, *American Places: A Writer's Pilgrimage to Fifteen of this Country's Most Visited and Cherished Sites* (New York: HarperPerennial, 1992), p. 6. For information on Mount Rushmore, see pp. 6-16.
[11] Zinsser, p. 8.
[12] Zinsser, p. 13.
[13] *Lame Deer*, pp. 91-107.

Don't get me wrong – we hold no grudge against Lincoln, Jefferson or Washington. They signed a few good treaties with us, and it wasn't their fault that they weren't kept. What we object to is the white man's arrogance and self-love, his disregard for nature which makes him desecrate one of our holy mountains with these oversized pale faces.

He describes the monument, carved out in their sacred Black Hills, like a hot iron poker stuck into their eyes: *It is the disease of white society to confuse bigness with greatness. . . . What does this Mount Rushmore mean to us Indians? It means that these big white faces are telling us, 'First, we gave you Indians a treaty that you could keep these Black Hills forever, as long as the sun would shine, in exchange for all of the Dakotas, Wyoming, and Montana. . . . Then, we found the gold and took [the] land . . . and when you didn't want to leave, we wiped you out, and those of you who survived we put on reservations. . . . After we did all this we carved up this mountain, the dwelling place of your spirits, and put our four gleaming white faces here. We are the conquerors.'*

One man's shrine is another man's cemetery, he laments.

Lame Deer also tells about Korczak Ziolkowski, a pupil of Gutzon Borglum.

Ziolkowski started working on Thunderhead Mountain, which is about twice as big as Mount Rushmore. *Now, Ziolkowski says he is a friend of the Indian. He says he wants to do something for us. If a white man says that, it's time for us Indians to run. What Ziolkowski wants to do for us is put up a giant statue of Crazy Horse, which will make those four Presidents look like dwarfs.*

The Crazy Horse statue is supposed to be about 650 feet long and 560 feet high. It will have a forty-foot feather sticking out from its head. *Crazy Horse doesn't look very Indian and neither does his pony. Crazy Horse doesn't have braids, and the feather coming out of his hair looks like an air valve sticking out of a tire. The chief's arm is pointing ahead like 'this way to the men's room.' It is said that all the people on our reservation could stand on that arm, or maybe just on his hand. . . .*

Crazy Horse never let a white man take his picture. He didn't want white people to look at him. He died fighting before he would let white soldiers shut him up in a stone guardhouse. He was buried the way he wanted it, with nobody knowing his grave. The whole idea of making a beautiful wild mountain into a statue of him . . . is against the spirit of Crazy Horse.

Half a year after Lame Deer put the chapter together about Mount Rushmore and the Crazy Horse monument, he and his friend John decided on the spur of the moment to drop in on Ziolkowski.

It is probably always a mistake to meet a man after you have criticized him. The fact is that John and I liked Korczak at first sight. Shaggy as a bear, with a big, unkempt beard, he was wearing a sun-bleached Levi jacket with the sleeves ripped off. . . . We told him that we had written some bad things about his monument, and why. He just grinned and put a bottle of very palatable French wine before me and a bottle of good whisky before John. He readily agreed with some of what we had to say. He, too, thought that maybe his mountain would be a better sight if left uncarved. . . . At the same time, he was in no way apologetic. . . . Korczak was a good and entertaining host and we talked 'til late into the night. . . . Driving back to our campsite John and I agreed that we still did not like Korczak's project, but that we like Korczak, the man.

* * *

(Montana: July 3rd – 16th)

I toured Little Bighorn National Battlefield – changed in 1991 by an act of congress from Custer's Last Stand, and back in my car, I drove really fast to Missoula, breaking 100 miles per hour just because I could. At the time, the daylight speed limit was *safe and prudent*. In Montana, speeding is a philosophical question – of interest only to tourists – but somewhere between ninety and ninety-five mph my car began to shake. The local Missoula paper had an article of concern about tourists like me. It was Montana's first summer without a speed limit.[14] In effect, Montana hasn't had a speed limit for years, but now everyone knew that.

---

[14] Since my visit, Montana has reinstated a speed limit.

By late afternoon, I had arrived at the Stahls, family camp friends that I have known for years. Bob, the father, is an anthropologist and a lawyer, working as a legal assistant on the Flathead Indian Reservation. He and Susan have four children, Mandi, Bob, Laura, and Jeff. A perfect evening was spent relaxing outside, eating Italian take-out food on the deck.

***

I sipped morning coffee with Susan and Bob on the front porch while looking at the surrounding mountains. Afterwards, we headed for Flathead Lake to celebrate the Fourth of July, soon passing through the Flathead Indian Reservation itself, which contains the Confederated tribes of the Salish and the Kootenai. Reservation land was allotted according to the Dawes Act, which broke up the communal land holdings and forced individual ownership of land. The surplus land was given or sold to non-Indians, and so, there exists a patchwork of Indian and non-Indian owned land within the reservation.

Soon, we arrived at the cabin – a rustic, A-frame, shingled hut – right on the lake. A deck overlooking the lake gave us a gorgeous north view. Mountains lined the shoreline, and a few islands were scattered about the waters.

The Stahls did not know that I was on a meatless fast, and I decided not to them tell, because it was now time to break it. Over a year before, starting with Lent, I had given up meat. But now, during my pilgrimage, eating meat would be the right thing to do. As a pilgrim, I am obliged to receive whatever hospitality I am given. In certain countries, I would have no choice what to eat.

God is very active in our lives, and sometimes he tells us to do something only to have us do the opposite at a later time. I am reminded of the story of Abraham and Isaac in which Abraham was told to sacrifice his only son Isaac as a burnt offering.[15] Abraham obeyed God only to have God intervene at the last moment, providing Abraham with a sacrificial ram instead. During this fast, I have learned about strength, grace and will power. I have learned about my

---

[15] Genesis 22:1-14.

weaknesses and my mortality. For now, though, letting go of the discipline is the better way. Throughout the coming year, my life will be in the hands of others. I take each day as it comes, and I graciously eat what is provided. That night, we sat on the deck eating burgers and watching fireworks from across the lake.

***

I grabbed some coffee and then went down with Laura and Jeff to the dock. Intending to light fireworks, we spent a long time lighting matches instead. Finally, after burning a couple of small brush piles of scrap paper, we finally got some charcoal snakes lit.

We drove back to Missoula where we spent the afternoon swimming at the country club. Actress and model, Andi McDowell was there. She lived at the time in Missoula with her husband and children. Susan knew her from a project that they had worked on together, and they struck up a lengthy conversation. Rose Anderson, Andi's real name, wore a wide brim hat to keep the sun off her face, and for the most part, she looked no different than the other mothers at the pool.

Eventually, Susan introduced me to Rose. Andi smiled, looking me in the eyes, and asked, *Are you from around here?*

Uh . . . no, I managed.

Oh. She replied.

Not just anyone can look Andi McDowell in the eyes and say *no.* But I did. I simply held my ground . . . and then slid over and started playing with the kids.

***

Sitting on the bleachers in Arlee, Montana with the sun at my back, I am watching my first powwow. The tribal circle is full of men, women, and children dressed in tribal costumes. I have seen the fancy men. Now, the women's jingle is on. The women have a single feather in their headband; their hair is pulled back, braided into a tail. Silver bells line their outfits.

I wonder who they are, what they do for a living. What are their loves, dreams, and fears? I am confronted by their existence, their culture, and by my own presence. I long for an avenue of understanding.

A young girl asks me what I am writing. She and her friends think that I am from a newspaper. I smile and tell them that I am keeping a journal. They seem disappointed.

I have just driven from St. Ignatius United Methodist Church where I have spent the day visiting with Rev. Donna. Donna has recently finished serving six years at the Browning United Methodist parish – a three-church, 150-mile circuit on the Blackfeet Indian Reservation.

I arrived at the quaint, white church as the morning service was starting. As I took my seat, I discovered that it was Donna's first Sunday. Lois, the lay leader and the piano player, led the liturgy: *Celebration of a New Appointment*. As we sang the opening hymn, *This is a Day of New Beginning*, Donna was in tears. I, too, was moved, recalling both the pain of leaving a community and the privilege of being appointed to serve a new one.

Worship is a time of understanding my mortality and letting God's hands mold me.

After the benediction, I learned that I had been sitting next to Harvey, an eighty-eight-year-old man. He has been suffering with diabetes for twenty-five years and is now losing his sight. He reached out his hand. *They say that Christ is coming back*, Harvey began. *When I shake your hand, he's here.*

After the service, I went to the parsonage to visit with Donna about her experiences at Browning. She shared with me stories of the pain and frustrations of working on the reservation – frustrations with an institutional church that often leaves pastors feeling lonely and isolated, pain from the stories of the lives of the Blackfeet. *I never left the reservation without tears in my eyes,* she told me. She had given unconditionally of herself and now admitted her own need for healing. For me, however, her presence was an encounter with the words of Christ: *My grace is sufficient for you, for my power is made*

perfect in weakness.[16] Her strengths were her sincerity, her passion
and her own vulnerability.

***

I found the Browning United Methodist Church with relative ease.
There, youth from Pennsylvania on their summer mission trip were
milling around, finishing up their first day's work. Hoping to plug in
with them for the week, I introduced myself to Ron, the head of the
group. He warmly welcomed me saying, *If the Lord has called you
here, then you're to stay here as our guest.* The group was staying
across the street in the Head Start center. I would sleep in the church
with John, the cook.

At supper, I was introduced to the group who greeted me with smiles
of curiosity, and by the end of the meal, I met Roland, the new pastor.
Roland was welcoming, immediately asking me to help him with a
healing service that was planned later in the week. He then invited me
to go with him to the church in Heart Butte, thirty minutes away, and
we rode in his car, visiting along the way. A Vietnam vet, an asset in
this parish, Roland told me that he was ready to make a new start of
things. *God has been preparing me for this ministry all of my life,* he
emphasized.

The church at Heart Butte sits peacefully alone in a field, slightly
away the village. A youth group from Lacrosse, Wisconsin was
staying there, and with them was Bill from Fayetteville, Arkansas,
who was working in Heart Butte as a two-year missionary. My brief
encounter with Bill would become my small world story of the year.
Ten months later, after being appointed as a pastor to Bill's church in
Fayetteville, Bill and I would become racquetball partners.

Back in Browning, a drunk Indian was hanging out at the church. He
was homeless and apparently a late night regular around the church.
He asked me questions about Baptists, Methodists, and Catholics, and
then he told me of his love for Jesus. He spoke in a soft rage: *I am a
warrior. . . . I can't give up. . . . there is a black cloud over the
reservation, and a preacher will be raised up to tell things as they
are.*

---

[16] 2 Corinthians 12:9.

***

Donna and Roland have two very different approaches to life and ministry. Roland is passionate; Donna is compassionate. Donna is in touch her people; Roland is perhaps more in touch with his own personal spirituality. Roland likes to *proclaim the name of Jesus* and sees the church building as hallow, sacred ground – not a place for children to be running carelessly around. The church is the temple of God and should exist primarily to support worship rather than missions and outreach. But what is the purpose and function of a church? To serve the community? To be effective? To be a witness? When, if ever, should a church be closed? *Lord, for ten righteous would you not save your church?*[17]

What is the youth group's purpose for being here? What are they trying to accomplish? I believe that mission trips should focus as much on cultural and religious exchange – as much on what can be received from others – as on what can be given.

***

A service of healing and anointing was held outside at the village teepee, a small park in the middle of town. A lot of work had been done in preparation – distributing flyers, setting up a sound system. Roland has been preoccupied with this since before my arrival. But the service dragged. The music was dead; the sound system buzzed. The crowd was sparse, and God was slow in arriving.

Suddenly, though, the Spirit poured itself out – not upon the citizens of Browning, the *objects* of the service, but rather upon the youth group. Leading the Blackfeet in a community-wide healing service was perhaps a bit presumptuous, but, ironically, those who received healing were the members of the mission team. Grown men, teenage girls, leaders and youth brought their pain and brokenness forward and were anointed to be better fathers and mothers, sons and daughters, and followers of Christ. The singing vastly improved, and the service finished with a tearful passing of the peace. Healing services are very powerful and should be treated with care. Later in the evening, the group talked about the service and how they had

---

[17] Genesis 18:1-33.

experienced God's presence. For many of the youth, it was one of the most memorable worship services of their life.

***

Roland is devout in his spiritual disciplines, and today before lunch, he invited me to join him in the bell tower to pray the Rosary. I had never imagined that my first experience with the Rosary would be on an Indian reservation with an evangelical Methodist minister.

The Rosary is repetitive and calming. I do not question the presence of God, nor do I doubt that Mary is a part of the cloud of witness, interceding on our behalf. I accept the power and the effect of the prayer, but I am not ready to embrace its theology. I am more comfortable with the simple Jesus Prayer: *Lord Jesus Christ, have mercy on me.*

I sat in a chair next to Roland, my hands on the beads, repeating the words of the prayer. I was uncomfortable. My thoughts were racing. Afterwards, we descended the stairs of the bell tower and joined the lunch line. *I know she's there. I have absolutely no doubt*, Roland said of Mary. He was intense, spiritually confident.

I spent the day outdoors, observing the youth leading the local children at Vacation Bible School. Afterwards, I scraped some paint off a house and then helped with a car wash. I held Cassie, one of the youth, by the legs as she went headfirst into the dumpster looking for rags that had been accidentally thrown away. Today, I have spoken with more Native Americans – often drunken men, never eager to leave, telling their stories in broken, repetitive sentences.

***

What does ministry with the Blackfeet look like? Relationships are possible, though they are slow and difficult to nurture. But there are opportunities for contact: the ongoing ministries of a small but vital church, playing basketball with the teenagers, meeting men at the gym. There is a place for ministry.

But can there be more than a ministry of presence here? Can the

Church affect the big picture in any significant way? The homeless, the drunk, the uneducated and the unemployed? I will leave here without any answers. I am still very much on the outside. I have no idea what is going on around me.

After dinner, we went to the indoor pool at the YMCA. In the sauna, I sat with a stranger. He was Shishone, and he began to tell me stories: *When I was young, I rode my horse many miles looking for a strong Blackfoot Indian to be my wife. I came upon six of them in a field picking berries. I got off my horse and looked them over to see if maybe I had found what I was looking for. One of them came up behind me and clubbed me on the head with her berry stick. I fell to the ground. When I woke up, we were married. I've been with the Blackfeet ever since.*

Kenneth works at the YMCA. He is thirty-three years old, divorced, a father of three, and a recovering drug and alcohol addict. He desperately wants to go to Blackfeet Community College, and, currently, he is thinking about marrying his girlfriend. *Please write me from the Holy Land,* he asked me. *Also, pray for my family, for my choice of a wife, and that I live a life full of truth and honesty.*

A gorgeous sunset crowned an elegant and festive evening at the Indian Days Powwow. A beautiful five-year-old crow girl and her seven-year-old cousin sat next to me while her father was dancing. She asked me if I wanted some sunflower seeds, and opening her small fist, she revealed the tightly held seeds. A little Indian baby boy was in front of us crying. *I wish he'd be quiet. He sounds like a cat,* she said. Soon, the girl's mother came, and they disappeared into the crowd.

Later in the evening, while still at the powwow, I visited with Diane, a layperson in the church. We spoke about Donna. *We loved her. She listened to us, loved us, and cared for us. But at the end, she was burnt out.* The conversation then turned to Roland. Diane said that she had not gotten to know him, but she made a general comment about pastors. *A pastor can't come in here and tell people what to do; he or she has to listen and get to know people first.* Then she mentioned pastors in the past that came in and began throwing things away. *We don't have a lot. We understand that. But what we have is ours.*

Pastors need to understand that we are the church not them – we have been here a long time.

***

John is sixty-eight years old and has a ninth grade education. In his prime, he had a thirty-inch waist and weighed between 180 and 190 pounds. He was in the service for a few years and then made a living as a meat cutter, moonlighting throughout his life as a foundry worker and as a cook. *I have loved every job, and I have approached every one as a challenge.* John raised a family of five children including identical twin boys.

John told me that he participates in missions because according to Matthew 10:37-42: *Do a prophet's job and receive a prophet's reward.* Missions give John the opportunity to relate with other people and communities. *I often feel guilty for some unknown reason upon returning home after missions. I receive all the pats on the back – all the 'atta boy's. But that's not what it's all about for me. I have experienced something that others at home haven't. I am very privileged and honored to be able to serve the Lord.*

I am a big believer in prayer. At my age, most of my prayers are prayers of thanksgiving. I am so blessed. I see so many people complaining about things that are of no importance. Upon returning, John will try to get his folks back home to pray for Browning. *If we do, I know that there will be fruits from our prayers.*

***

I left Browning and drove toward Glacier National Park. High in the park, overlooking a large valley, I stopped to write postcards. The Trail of the Cedars and Avalanche Creek were brilliant, and I could have sat beside the roaring mountain rivers all day. As it was, I was ready to drive back to Flathead Lake where the Stahls were waiting for me.

It was an evening of relaxation, debriefing the week with Bob. There were no new insights – just the acknowledgment of a difficult situation, acknowledgment of problems that we can't solve, and affirmation that in limited and self-understood roles there are ways to help.

I spent a couple more days with the Stahls before returning to the Midwest. On two evenings, I joined their family ritual of evening story time in Bob and Susan's bedroom. Bob was reading *Redwall* to the children.

I am improving my ability to wait – to wait with expectation for new experiences and special moments. When I wait, I hear something, see something, meet someone, and I am blessed. Waiting upon God with a perceptive and expectant heart – that's the way of a pilgrim.

I took the road south out of Missoula through the scenic Bitterroot Mountains, and I arrived the next day in Denver at my brother Kelvin's house just as my alternator went out. I was fortunate to have car problems where I would be staying for a few days. I thought about the vast, remote country that I had driven through. I was often miles and miles away from anything.

I went to the Butterfly Pavilion with my sister-in-law, Ann, and my four nephews, Mitchell, Nathan, Rudy, and Jed. I loved the butterfly room, a tropical arboretum full of large plants and small butterflies. I felt like I was in a different dimension. Colors fluttering all around me, belonging to species of butterflies that I had never seen before, their cocoons having been shipped in from all over the world.

The boys, however, like the bug room more.

Homecoming

Heading east, I caught an episode of *Car Talk* during the long Kansas stretch of I-70. A listener had sent in the following letter, which he had written in the 1960s:

Research Division Volvo Auto Company
Gothenburg, Sweden

Dear Sirs,

I have owned a 1953 Volvo wagon for two years. In the course of which, I have replaced almost every moving part in the drive train, brakes and suspension. If you would be willing to underwrite the expense of replacing the few remaining parts of the car, we will have evidence for solving one of the enduring philosophical problems known as 'The Problem of Ulysses' Ship.' If in the course of his voyage, Ulysses replaces every board in his ship, is it the same ship at the end? In other words, does identity consists of continuity of essence or substance? In the research I propose, if the car remains unreliable after all of its parts have been changed, we will have hard evidence that its identity is unchanged because its essence will be unchanged. It is essentially unreliable.[18]

The letter triggered thoughts of homecoming: I was heading to my childhood church, the First United Methodist Church of Warrensburg, Missouri, returning to worship for the first time in thirteen years. When I was a child, the congregation had nurtured me, providing me with a foundation of faith. During my teenage years, they had helped me discern a calling to the ministry.

Thirteen years later, the church had changed. Youth had grown up; pastors had moved away, and many of the older adults had died. I was hoping that a handful of fellow youth, their parents, and former Sunday school teachers would be there, but I only expected to recognize a few faces that I couldn't name and to remember names of people that I couldn't identify. For the most part, I knew that I would be walking into a sanctuary full of strangers.

---

[18] From a *Cartalk* episode that aired July 20, 1996.

I wanted to thank the congregation for their past faithfulness and steadfast love; yet, I wondered what kind of congregation they were now. I thought of the *Problem of Ulysses' Ship*. If in the course of several years, every member of the church is replaced, is it the same congregation at the end? Does the identity of a church consist of continuity of essence or substance? Does the Church possess a consistent and essential character, which remains unchangeable through time? Or is she merely the collection of individuals whom make up her parts at any given time? Surely, the Holy Spirit has a role in the solution of Ulysses' church. Years before, the church of my childhood had been a faithful congregation – I was confident that it still was.

***

I am sitting alone in the sanctuary of my home church. Here, I grew up in the faith and discovered and accepted God's call to full-time Christian ministry. Now, the sanctuary is mostly empty, and I have time to listen to the quiet and to see in the memory of my soul the many scenes of my life that have transpired here. This is a holy place. This is my church, my home.

Pilgrimage is not always a journey into the unknown; it can be homecoming as well. However, since God is active and creating, homecoming is not a return to the past but rather a new discovery of God in an old, familiar place.

During the service, I sat with the Hudsons, one my best friend's parents. The highlight of the service was hearing the elementary Cherub Choir, led by Sherrilyn, an old high school friend, sing *I am a Promise*. As the kids sang about possibilities and potentiality, I remembered that once upon a time, I had been one of those kids. For Sherrilyn, for myself, and for so many others who had grown up in that church, God's promise was being fulfilled.

***

I cannot identify the moment when I was called into the ministry. I can only identify a year – my sophomore year in high school – when it happened. Once Mr. Willard, my high school art teacher and

Sunday school teacher, asked me if I had ever thought about being a preacher. I thought that it was a peculiar question. Frankly, I had never thought of it. A year later, however, I knew that there was nothing else that I wanted to be.

During high school, Camp Galilee in El Dorado Springs, Missouri had a great influence on my faith. When I began to plan my around-the-world pilgrimage, I had no difficulty committing to return to church camp as an adult counselor. Not only do I want to travel to new places, but I want to return to old ones as well. My pilgrimage is also about reclaiming my roots and rediscovering the foundations of my faith.

***

(Camp Galilee, Missouri: July 21st – 27th)

I'm on the grounds of Camp Galilee. Like all good camps, it seems as though nothing has changed. The sulfur water, however, is not as strong, but there is still a unique smell to the dining hall. The swimming pool and the open-air pavilion, affectionately known as the *Slab*, look exactly the same. The cabins, the small-group huts, and the showers haven't aged. That's both good and bad, but I feel like I belong here.

I'm here with three of my best friends. Aaron and Damon grew up with me. Mark is a friend from seminary. Today is Aaron's birthday. He's used to spending his birthdays here.

***

Besides the friends I made, Camp Galilee was special to me because of its emphases on scripture and worship. At Galilee, the entire day led up to evening worship, and seldom were we disappointed. They didn't bring in big-named preachers. Instead, our counselors – *ordinary* people like Dave and Jeff and Bob – preached. It was a thrill to listen to them. We wanted to know what they had to say.

However, our counselors were often ordained clergy, and their example, perhaps more than anything else in my life, led me into the ministry. That is, I just didn't want to take my faith more seriously; I wanted to be like them.

***

I went to Camp Galilee once as a fourth grader. I don't remember much – just that I went with Stephan, the pastor's kid, and that we did a bunch of stuff together. I can remember, though, singing the *Austrian Song*, which I mistook for several years as the *Ostrich Song*:

> *Once an Austrian went yodeling on a mountain so high.*
> *When along came a cuckoo bird interrupting its cry.*

I always wondered what an ostrich would be doing on top of a mountain.

My counselor was tall and had red hair. One night during vespers, we talked about Jesus being in the room. Our counselor pointed to an empty chair beside one of our beds. *Here's sitting right there*, he told us. It sort of spooked us, and I went to bed feeling sorry for the kid who had to sleep next to Jesus.

***

In ninth grade, I returned with my best friend, Aaron.

In tenth and then eleventh grade, Aaron and I returned with Greg, a weight and chain, a dead bird, various costumes and a Bible. We chained and locked a fifteen-pound weight to the ankles of Bob, our counselor, while he was sleeping. During kangaroo court, we made Dave, our youth director, wear a dead bird around his neck for running into a bird with the church bus on the way to camp. We successfully launched *The Three Dogs Tonight*, a contemporary Christian rock group that sang about our dogs, and we memorized all of John 16.

Camp Galilee is a special place.

***

I was very nervous to preach at Camp Galilee, which I did the second night of camp. Before the service, as is the custom, I sat on the prayer rock while the other counselors laid their hands upon me. When I went back to the *Slab* after the prayer, it was as if I had walked into a warm, comforting light.

The theme for the week is *Run the Good Race*. The topic of the day was *marathon*, which I defined as *anything that we can't see the end of*. I told the story of Duane, the potato sack champion of Peppersauce County. At twenty-five feet, he could not be beaten, always falling right across the finish line. Unfortunately, his championship days were over as soon as they moved the finish line back five more feet. Duane continued to crash and fall at the twenty-five foot mark.

Sometimes we can get away with things – lies, unfaithfulness, drugs, alcohol – at least for a while. But life is a marathon. We deceive ourselves by thinking that the finishing line is closer than it is.

We have to let go of our potato sacks: *Let us throw off everything that hinders us and the sin that so easily entangles, and let us run with perseverance the race marked out for us (Hebrews 12:1).*

***

While typically each evening worship service has an altar call, traditionally, there is a three-part call on Thursday night – for people who want to make a first-time commitment to Christ, for others who want to rededicate themselves, and for those who feel called to explore full-time ministry as a vocation. Seventeen people came forward when the third call was offered.

God is always raising up a new generation of leaders!

***

I love spending time with my family group, *Generosity*. Each of the groups is named for one of the fruits of the Spirit.[19] Our youth are comfortable with each other – laughing, crying, and taking care of one another.

---

[19] Galatians 5:22.

For me, the golden moments include watching youth during Bible quizzing. They are learning scripture. Their faces glow as they follow the words of the quizzer. Their eyes light up with the correct answers.

I spent the last afternoon playing foursquare with my family group. We'd just finished Bible quizzing and volleyball. Winding down, soaking in the love, basking in the grace of God. We were mellow yet empowered, subdued yet blessed.

***

Dennis gave Friday night's sermon: *We're here to finish. We're here to take care of any unfinished business.* We ended with communion. A circle of youth sitting in the dark. Candles on the floor. Singing songs and sharing hugs.

***

Camp is over. We said our good-byes and began our journeys home. However, during the week, our lives were stirred. Like a pile of leaves blown by the wind, we will never be the same.

And the Band Played On

(Chautauqua, New York: July 27th – August 5th)

I had a great view of Niagara Falls as I flew into Buffalo. I was on my way to the Chautauqua Institute, an intellectual and cultural retreat center in western New York.

A couple of years ago while driving through southern Missouri, I stumbled upon *The Radio Reader* on public radio. Syndicated from Michigan State University, *The Radio Reader* has a fairly simple format – a man reads a book, one chapter at a time, over the air. That particular night, the book was *American Places* by William Zinsser, and within a couple of weeks, I had my very own copy. Subtitled *A Writer's Pilgrimage to Fifteen of this Country's Most Visited and Cherished Sites*, *American Places* describes many of the places that I had visited with my family as a child – Mount Rushmore, Yellowstone Park, Hannibal, and Niagara Falls. I was surprised with a couple of the author's choices. I was even more shocked that I had never even heard of one of these most *cherished* places – Chautauqua – but now I was on my way there. [20]

In 1874, Lewis Miller, an Akron businessman, and John Heyl Vincent, a Methodist minister, organized a two-week training course for Sunday school teachers on the shores of Lake Chautauqua. The event was an overwhelming success. Teachers came from twenty-five states to listen to the lecturers and to attend classes, and the Chautauqua movement was born. A hotel, a 6,000-seat amphitheater, and numerous Victorian houses were built; the summer program continued to expand. Chautauqua became one the most prestigious platforms in the country for sharing political and intellectual ideas. When the summer music program with a residential symphony orchestra, opera and theatre companies were added in 1929, the four pillars of Chautauqua – religion, education, music and recreation – were complete. Theodore Roosevelt, one of the many presidents who visited Chautauqua, called it the *most American place in America*, because it embodied the values of self-improvement, self-help, and adult education.

---

[20] For information on Chautauqua, see Zinsser, pp. 139-149.

The most influential venture of Chautauqua has been the Chautauqua Literary and Scientific Circle, the CLSC, which Vincent launched in 1878. Knowing that more people wanted to take courses at Chautauqua than could possibly attend them, Vincent created America's first book club and its first correspondence course. The CLSC would send books to its members who attended small discussion groups in their hometown, and those who completed the four-year course would come to Chautauqua for a summer graduation ceremony, a tradition that is still in place. By 1914, the program had enlisted half a million members, most of whom lived in towns of 3,500 people or less.

The Chautauqua model was soon copied, and *chautauqua* became part of our national vocabulary. Tent chautauquas – local programs of lectures and concerts – sprang up in small frontier towns across the country bringing culture and education to unlikely places. Summer chautauquas flourished until the mid 1930s when the arrival of the radio, the movie house, and the automobile changed the way Americans got their information and spent their spare time.

Today, the 750-acre Chautauqua Institute welcomes more than 18,000 people during its nine-week summer season. Over 2,000 students enroll annually in the Chautauqua summer school program of fine and performing arts.

A month into my pilgrimage planning, Denise, a seminary friend and a United Church of Christ minister, invited me to join her and her parents for a week at Chautauqua where she would be serving as the United Church of Christ chaplain.

***

Denise picked me up at the airport in Buffalo, and we arrived at the main gate of Chautauqua around ten o'clock. Inside the Victorian village, a jazz band, filling the night air with music, was playing on the plaza. Crowds of people, having been dismissed from an evening performance, filled the square.

On Sunday, our first morning there, Denise preached in the quaint UCC chapel. Her sermon was on the parable, *The Wheat and the*

Weeds:

Jesus told them another parable: 'The Kingdom of heaven is like a man who sowed good seed in his field. But while everyone was sleeping, his enemy came and sowed weeds among the wheat and went away. When the wheat sprouted and formed heads, then the weeds also appeared.

The owner's servants came to him and said, 'Sir, didn't you sow good seed in your field? Where then did the weeds come from?'

'An enemy did this,' he replied.

The servants asked him, 'Do you want us to go and pull them up?'

'No,' he answered, 'because while you are pulling the weeds, you may root up the wheat with them. Let both grow together until the harvest. At that time I will tell the harvesters: First, collect the weeds and tie them in bundles to be burned; then, gather the wheat and bring it into my barn.'

– Matthew 13:24-30

Denise spoke about her Grandma's garden, mentioned some recent events around the world, and cautioned us not to judge.

***

While each mainline Protestant denomination has their own house – with their own weekly chaplain – there is also a guest preacher of the week who gives a sermon each morning in the large amphitheater. This week's preacher is John T. Galloway, Jr., a Presbyterian pastor from Philadelphia, who is delivering a series on *Critiques against Christianity and Organized Religion*. His Sunday sermon was on violence – Christians are to suffer with the oppressed rather than to use violence against the violent. Galloway spoke about the anger of the righteous – many righteous people are not of the right spirit. He gave an example of a KKK rally in Ann Arbor where an African-American woman dove on top of a white supremacist to protect him from being kicked to death by an angry, righteous crowd.

I spent the afternoon walking around the grounds, looking over the lake, and learning the pathways through the village. I was tired from yesterday's travels, and I spent a Sunday Sabbath resting. In times past, the gates were locked on Sundays, keeping its guests safely away from outside perils. Today, I had no desire to go anywhere.

I am staying in the Mayflower House with about twenty-five other people. Bathrooms are shared; there is a common kitchen in the basement. Denise is staying in the United Church of Christ headquarters with the chaplain and his wife. It is a stately brick building directly across from the amphitheater, the heartbeat of the institute. From the porch of the UCC building, one can sit in a rocking chair and listen to the program going on in the amphitheater. After supper, we did just that, listening to the traditional Sunday night sacred hymn service featuring songs from Scandinavian countries.

***

The theme for morning lectures this week is evolving (or tenuous) democracies, focusing on Russia and Mexico. Frederick Starr, an expert on Russian affairs, gave the opening lecture. *Yes, it's working* was his premise. He talked about U.S. phantom fears and then mentioned real *unsexy* problems. The main problem in Russia is their inability to collect taxes. Ethical and economic problems exist. The infrastructure is bad, and industry and agriculture are poor. But things are moving along.

Other speakers this week include: Jack F. Matlock, Jr., former ambassador to the Soviet Union; Ilana Kass, professor of military strategy at the National War College; Adolfo Aguilar Zinser, a member of the Mexican Congress; and Sergio Aguayo, a representative of the Mexican Academy of Human Rights.

Chautauqua is serious about being an intellectual retreat center.

***

It was pouring as Denise and I left to go to the performance of the Louisiana Jazz and Reparatory Ensemble. The nine-piece band included morning lecturer Frederick Starr on the clarinet. Under the cover of the amphitheater, we were warm and dry, enjoying the celebratory music. Outside, a deluge of rain, lightning, and thunder was adding heavy percussion to the performance. Suddenly, in the middle of a song, the lights went out . . .

. . . but the band played on. We sat in the darkness listening to the jazz, lit up only occasionally by the lightening. When the lights came back on a minute or two later, the band was still together in rhythm and in song, and they finished their number while the place erupted.

By the end of the concert, the rain still hadn't let up. *Let me make a proposal*, Starr suggested. *One more song and the concert is over, but for those of you without umbrellas, the band will play on!* They played on for another thirty minutes. People stood, dancing and clapping. It was one of my all-time favorite storms.

***

The Department of Religion is sponsoring an afternoon lecture series by Marcus J. Borg, professor of religion and culture at Oregon State University. Chautauqua gave me my first introduction to Borg, one of America's more popular theologians.

In a sound bite prepared for the secular audience of NBC's *Today's Show,* Borg once presented this brief sketch of the historical Jesus:

Jesus was a peasant – which tells us about his social class.

Clearly, he was brilliant. His use of language was remarkable and poetic, filled with images and stories. He had a metaphoric mind.

He was not an ascetic but world affirming, with a zest for life.

There was a socio-political passion to him; like a Gandhi or a Martin Luther King, Jr.; he challenged the dominant system of his day.

He was a religious ecstatic – a Jewish mystic, if you will – for whom God was an experiential reality. As such, he was also a healer. And there seems to have been a spiritual presence around him, like that reported of Saint Francis or the Dalai Lama.

And I suggest that as a figure of history, he was an ambiguous figure – you could experience him and conclude that he was insane, as his family did, or that he was simply eccentric, or that he was a dangerous threat – or you could conclude that he was filled with the Spirit of God.[21]

Borg is also one of the leaders of the Jesus Seminar, which since 1985 has met for the sake of voting on the historical accuracy of the sayings of Jesus. To many people, this seems bizarre; for others, it is blasphemous. The scholars that make up the Jesus Seminar, however, are quite diverse – liberal and conservative, Jewish and Christian. Their purpose is to measure the degree of scholarly consensus on how much of the Gospel material goes back to Jesus himself.

Borg differentiates between what he describes as a pre-Easter and a post-Easter Jesus. Who was Jesus before the resurrection – what did he say and think? Who was Jesus after the resurrection – how did the Christian community experience him?

Reaction to Borg is generally polarized between liberals and conservatives – conservatives aren't afraid to use the word *heresy* in their descriptions of him; liberals often love him. What I found in Borg, however, defied the simple label of *liberal*. Borg's *persona* was gentle and transparent. I liked him immediately.

I guess I'm an extreme moderate, which means that I usually react against both extremes; however, that doesn't mean that my theology is reactive. I'm more interested in disciplines than doctrines, revelations than rules. I'm interested in journey and transformation while still valuing morals and ethics.

Moderates don't live in a world of unbelief; often, we live with the tension of believing too much. We don't lack convictions; it's just that our convictions lead us to realize the complexity of situations and to struggle understanding apparent contradictions. For example, how do you ever reconcile justice and compassion, truth and grace, mercy and judgement? Somehow it all needs to be held together. Moreover, God is all of the above.

---

[21] Marcus J. Borg, *The God We Never Knew* (San Francisco: HarperSanFrancisco, 1997), p. 90.

During a question and answer period after one of Borg's lectures, a middle-aged woman from a mainline Protestant denomination asked a question concerning the growth of fundamentalism in America. She thought she knew the answer herself:

Don't you think that fundamentalist churches are growing because they tell their members exactly what to believe – and this fulfills the need of many people to have a very black-and-white faith rather than to think for themselves?

No, rebuked Borg. *I think that fundamentalist churches are growing, because they have a very strong understanding and experience of the Divine, while frankly over the last generation, mainstream churches have come to doubt God's very existence.*

This is really the focus of my spiritual pilgrimage: How does one experience the presence of the Divine? What is our access to such a being? Where do we go to find God's revelation? How do we respond?

The presence of the Divine is not found exclusively within communities that would identity themselves as liberal nor those who would identify themselves as conservative. My pilgrimage is taking me through a variety of Christian expressions – conservative, liberal, Protestant, Catholic, parochial, and international. I want to know how people experience the Divine. I want to experience the Divine myself.

And that's how I listened to Borg.

Borg's distinctions between a pre-Easter and a post-Easter Jesus are problematic for some and insightful for others. His academic pursuits, though, are sustained by a personal journey of faith – a journey of honesty and integrity – a journey stressing relationship and transformation. In the end, Borg's faith is a simple, three-fold conviction:

God is real.

The Christian life is about entering into a relationship with God as known in Jesus Christ.

That relationship can – and will – change your life.[22]

***

Denise held an open forum on the church as tenuous democracy. At first, I thought that it was an abstract topic, but it soon became apparent that many people were there because they needed to talk about their frustrated and hurtful experiences with church governance.

After dinner, we went to a lecture on the evening concert. The Chautauqua Symphony Orchestra was playing Beethoven's *Seventh Symphony*, Wagner's *Tannhauser Overture*, and *A Night on Bald Mountain* by Mussorgsky. The lecture was fascinating; however, when the concert came, I was swept away, failing to recall most of the lecturer's points.

***

I sat on the porch with a paper and a cup of coffee, listening to Galloway's morning sermon on religion as a crutch. *Sometimes Jesus says 'walk.' Sometimes we fall, and we can't get up.* I was surprised to hear a resident of the Mayflower House say that he thought Galloway had fallen flat on his face. There is such a wide divergence of opinions around here. It is odd to walk the streets at night and overhear people (who you wouldn't expect) engaged in intellectual and serious conversations. I am often surprised at myself.

While encouraging an open forum, Chautauqua has always been grounded in liberal Protestantism. However, the liberal left can be as oppressive and judgmental as the religious right. Galloway in his sermon on censorship said, *Say the wrong thing at any politically correct university and see how quickly you will be thrown off.*

***

Bill McKibben, author of *The End of Nature*, gave an afternoon talk on his new book, *Hope, Human and Wild: True Stories of Living Lightly on the Earth*. His talk immediately sent me to the Chautauqua bookstore to look over his other works.

---

[22] Borg. p. 51.

***

May 3, 1990 lasted nearly one thousand hours for Bill McKibben. I don't even remember it, although I would have been in Germany at the time. I'm sure that I did not watch any television that day, but McKibben did. For twenty-four hours, he had all ninety-three channels of the enormous Fairfax, Virginia cable system, the largest in the world at the time, videotaped, and over the next several weeks, he spent eight-hour days watching the tapes:

'If you have a cold, you do not need to worry about reinfecting yourself with your lip balm.' That's Beverly, who leads Christian calisthenics on Channel 116, Family Net. 'If you use someone else's lip balm, I could see that. But not your own.'

On Good Morning, America, Joel, the movie critic says, 'For sore throats, the actors of Shakespeare's time used to take a live frog and lower the frog by its foot into their mouths. They figured that would keep the juices going. That's where the expression "a frog in your throat" comes from.'

On the Fox affiliate, a cartoon Mr. Wilson is sure that's Dennis (the Menace) in the gorilla suit, so he uses a pair of pliers on the snout; entertainingly, however, it's an actual gorilla escaped from the zoo.

In Czechoslovakia, Ambassador Rita Klimova tells C-SPAN, the newly emerging democracy has spawned dozens of political parties, including one for beer drinkers.

Only eleven percent of Americans feel the penny should be banned.

Research from the University of Wisconsin indicates that hamburger may contain certain substances that inhibit skin cancer.[23]

That was all before eight in the morning.

McKibben then spent a day outside, alone in the Adirondack Mountains.

---

[23] Bill McKibben, *The Age of Missing Information* (New York: Random House, 1993), pp. 3-7.

In his fascinating book, *The Age of Missing Information*, McKibben compares the two days.

We believe that we live in the 'age of information,' that there has been an information 'explosion,' an information 'revolution.' While in a certain narrow sense this is the case, in many important ways, just the opposite is true. We also live at a moment of deep ignorance, when vital knowledge that humans have always possessed about who we are and where we live seems beyond our reach. An Unenlightenment. An age of missing information.[24]

And that's his point. Not that television is all bad, although it is often full of violence and questionable values. His point is that in spite of all the information that television gives us – the constant dribble of trivia, the continuous bombardment of commercial persuasion, even the enlightened science and learning channels – there is a lot that television doesn't and can't tell us about the world. Television chops away perspective; television limits our senses; television distorts our sense of time. The list is long.

For McKibben, nature, symbolized by an Adirondack mountaintop, gives us different information about God. Television, even sound religious programming, lacks a sense of the experience of the Divine. On the mountain, *information* about the Divine makes perfect sense.

McKibben concludes: *All the information offered by the natural world suggests that somewhere between the meaninglessness of life lived in destitute struggle and the emptiness of life lived in swaddled affluence, there is a daily, ordinary life filled with meaning.* McKibben quotes Erazim Kohak, a philosopher at Boston University: *A life wholly absorbed in need and its satisfaction, be in on the level of conspicuous consumption or of marginal survival, falls short of realizing the inner-most human possibility of cherishing beauty, knowing the truth, doing the good, worshipping the holy.*[25]

I don't always have a lot to say around celebrities. But I think that I would like to meet McKibben sometime. Anyway, I like what he did – he experienced something unique and wrote about it.

---

[24] McKibben, p. 9.
[25] McKibben, p. 245.

***

I have been going to the Episcopal chapel for early morning communion. It is wonderful to wake up to the gift of a new day and then to walk expectantly to the house of God where God's Presence waits. In the chapel, I feel the embrace of God. There, time and place are sacred.

I kneel at the altar. I feel the body of Christ pressed into my hands, and I drink the wine as the common cup is placed to my lips. It is a tangy, sweet substance of both earth and God. One day's frustration and anxiety becomes eclipsed by the excitement of a new day.

***

I grabbed a newspaper and a cup of coffee and sat on the United Church of Christ porch for morning worship. I was postured to overhear, not to participate. I wanted to listen, to pick and choose, to critique and correct. Ironically, the message was: *Come and see! It is true? Come and see!*

Worship unifies and transforms us. Compassion is created out of our apathy, and our hatred turns into understanding. In worship, we encounter the risen Christ.

Much of this year I'm worshipping – and reflecting upon worship. Worship creates the community, changes individuals. Worship is the starting point for understanding. It is the bridge between people, a place where time, opinions, hatreds, and selfishness are suspended. Worship is a place where sacred time and place merge, where sins are confessed, where the Spirit is evoked and where the Word is proclaimed. In worship, God is the recipient of our praise, and we are opened to the divine probing of the lives, opened to see the failures of our God-imitating behaviors and attitudes.

***

The Friday night concert was Peter, Paul, and Mary. They sang *Puff the Magic Dragon* and *If I had a Hammer*. My Chautauqua experience was complete.

***

On Saturday evening, in Lucille Ball's hometown of Jamestown, New York, Denise and I watched a minor league baseball game between the Jamestown Jammers and the Williamsport Cubs. A couple of dysfunctional families were sitting near us providing non-stop diversions. The game was also fun, won 3-1 by the Cubs.

It was *Balloon Sky Jam Festival* weekend in Jamestown, and after the game, seventeen hot air balloons were set up on the field for a balloon glow. The stadium lights were turned off, and the balloons glowed each time the burners were lit; music accompanied the display. The crowd stood in awe, appreciative of the historical event that they were witnessing: a new world record for the number of balloons in a balloon glow in an outdoor stadium had just been set. Jamestown was once again on the map

***

We drove to the decrepit-looking First Christian Church in Dunkirk for morning worship. Every popular portrait of Jesus hung prominently in the sanctuary – Jesus knocking on the door, Jesus kneeling in Gethsemane, the famous portrait. A big patch of plaster was torn off the wall in the choir. A few windows were broken.

An old lady in a walker, who recently had hip replacement surgery, greeted us. She told us that we could sit anywhere we wanted as long as it was on the right side. The left side was used by the Baptists, and they had different hymnals. A very old, hunched-back lady played the organ; the songs were pitched a little too high for the dozen present to sing.

The minister wore an orange polyester sport coat that blended in well with the décor of the church. During the sermon, he came forward carrying a microphone in one hand and holding two slips of scrap paper with diagonally scribbled sermon notes in the other.

The scripture was the Gerasene Demoniac.

When Jesus got out of the boat, a man with an evil spirit came from

the tomb to meet him. This man lived in the tombs, and no one could bind him any more, not even with chains. For he had often been chained hand and foot, but he tore the chains apart and broke the irons on his feet. No one was strong enough to subdue him. Night and day among the tombs and in the hills he would cry out and cut himself with stones.

When he saw Jesus from a distance, he ran and fell on his knees in front of him, He shouted at the top of his voice, 'What do you want with me, Jesus, Son of the Most High?'

A large herd of pigs was feeding on the nearby hillside. The demons begged Jesus, 'Send us among the pigs; allow us to go into them.' He gave them permission, and the evil spirits came out and went into the pigs. The herd, about two thousand in number, rushed down the steep bank into the lake and were drowned.

– Mark 5:1-13

The sermon was on God's healing – we see the effects, but we don't understand the method.

Afterwards, I went up and spoke to the organist. I noticed that one of the men who had been singing had an artificial voice box. Only one child was present – and just one other young adult. I was reminded of God's words: *My grace is sufficient for you. My power is made perfect in your weakness.*[26] The church of Dunkirk reflected the impoverished state of the city; however, their faith reflected the kingdom of God.

***

An hour ago, I waved good-bye to Denise as she drove away from the airport terminal. Life is sad, but wonderful, happy experiences make it so.

This is a year of the extraordinary in which I find God revealed in the ordinary. Eventually, I will return to the ordinary where I will again

---

[26] 2 Corinthians 12:9.

experience God in the extraordinary.

Aurora Borealis

(Camp Lake Hubert, Minnesota: August 9th – 17th)

I can't talk about family camp without talking about Cathy. Eleven months earlier, after she had lost a miraculous ten-year bout with cancer, I eulogized my sixty-one-year-old friend at her funeral in Cleveland:

It was an August night in 1985. The campers were all safely in bed, and with another staff person staying in the cabin, I was free to leave camp.

I went down to the waterfront, pulled a canoe off the rack, grabbed a paddle and a life jacket, and started across the lake to the girls' camp.

For the past month, a fellow counselor had been telling me about family camp, which was now being held across the lake. In particular, he kept telling me about a certain lady, who also lived in Dallas, that I had to meet.

So it was the typical scene: boy gets in canoe, paddles to girls' camp in the middle of the night, and meets female. I anxiously paddled the moonlit mile, docked the canoe and eagerly went in search for her.

I stumbled around camp for several minutes until I found the cabin; inside, a party going on. I eased my way in and found over a half-dozen people sitting in a circle dressed in outfits and costumes alien to camp. I had stumbled unto the beginnings of a murder mystery party – as well as the beginnings of one of the most celebrated friendships of my life. Over in the corner, decked out in necklaces, a dress, and all the contraband appropriate to her part was the character of Mrs. Elizabeth Livingston, who was being played that night by Mrs. Catherine Lowe.

I could only speak to her for a second; she basically ignored me, insisting that she stay in character. She was too busy figuring out 'whodunnit.'

It was back in Dallas that fall that I discovered Cathy's 'true' character, and soon the 'whodunnit' turned to 'wedunnit.'

Cathy and I along with our families and friends began to build memories.

In Dallas, it was microwave s'mores; shrimp, rice and peas; playing cards and Rummicube; hot tubbing while eating orange sherbet; dressing up in overcoats, pretending that we were playing the player piano while chewing gum cigarettes. There was the Texas State Fair, the Mesquite Rodeo, Fourth of July fireworks, and two well-spent Thanksgivings.

Our memories continued here in Cleveland with three more Thanksgivings. We would begin Thanksgiving with worship in an old restored log cabin. There was a Thanksgiving dinner in a homeless shelter where Cathy introduced me to her friends from the streets [She worked for an agency that helped homeless people]. *And there were more cards, more Rummicube, and more microwave s'mores.*

But the foundation of our relationship and the source of so much of our strength was family camp at Camp Lake Hubert, where the s'mores aren't microwaved. And together, we'd listen to loons and watch the stars and the northern lights; where we'd go midnight sailing and horseback riding. We'd square dance on square dance night, do skits on skit night, and on kids' make-your-own-pizza night, we'd leave camp altogether!

During camp, we'd sit around the campfire, singing sad songs and then we'd tie friendship bracelets to last throughout the year. We hated saying 'good-bye' at camp, and so we'd sneak in a couple of extra days after camp on the North Shore of Lake Superior.

Just a month ago, though she was weak and frail, we shared a truly golden and magical moment, together with our friend, John, eating dinner on the shore of Lake Superior at the Angry Trout Cafe. We were happy – and we knew it.

All this began with a moonlit canoe ride across a lake – the most magical ride I've ever taken. I wished that more of my friendships would begin this way. I think Cathy would say that they all should.

***

I'm in my cabin, writing next to a warmly burning fire. Family camp begins tomorrow. Another year in the circle of life. Yet this year will be very different. Cathy is not here, and I miss her. Cathy always made camp special.

I love camp: old friends, new people, the loons, the stars and the lake. I love being in community, sharing common feelings and experiences with friends and families.

***

The opening campfire was great. Songs, skits, stories, and family introductions. We had s'mores around the campfire.

***

This morning was absolutely gorgeous. I walked down to Bass Beach where I heard two raccoons fighting inside a trash barrel. I pushed the barrel over, but instead of the raccoons darting out, they remained inside huddling silently. Afterwards, seven loons flew overhead, their calls echoing in the early morning quiet. I took a refreshing dip in Lake Hubert. The sauna was warm and rewarding.

Chapel was held in the Little Chief Chapel. Again, more stories, poems, and songs.

Camp is a reminder that life is cyclical, a revolving circle. We do the same things over and over, and there is not necessarily any room or reason to change. Tradition and familiarity.

I'm sitting in the shade on the sailing dock watching the boats out on the lake. Water is gently lapping on the shore around me. A sailboat, a couple hundred yards away, has tipped over.

***

It was a beautiful morning for sunrise paintings. A few of us sat on the dock, painting the silence of the early morning light. The lake was calm. A few clouds were overhead. The scene was full of yellows, oranges, reds, blues, and greens.

***

This morning, I went canoeing at sunrise. The early morning breeze was somewhat stiff. A few loons flew overhead. Circling the lake, they landed right in front of us.

One cabin of families was cooking breakfast on Bass Beach. The smell of coffee was in the air. I joined the families around the warm campfire, eating omelets, and talking about camp. It was an unexpected and delightful gift.

After lunch, several families went into Nisswa for the turtle races.

Once again, the family camp skit night was great – making fun of camp, but mostly just having fun:

> *Chicken today! Chicken salad tomorrow!*
> *Hot dogs today! Hot dog salad tomorrow!*

***

John remarked that Cathy was wonderful at taking the unimportant things in life seriously and not being serious about the really important things. Six months before her death, she was in Antarctica playing with penguins.

Life is about relationships, community, and family. Sometimes, around the campfire, the children best articulate this:

Chelsea: *What I love about Family Camp is that if you do it wrong or if you don't finish it . . . it is okay.*

Neil: *I want to say that I love my family, and they love me.*

Bailey: *Daddy, I love you because I love you.*

It is amazing that kids can arise from their sandcastles and articulate such profound messages. They remind us why we are here.

The final campfire was traditional – stories, songs, reflections on the week, and, of course, s'mores. Afterwards, several of us lay on the dock, watching a meteor shower until two o'clock in the morning.

***

We have just said goodbye to the families. Staff must stay on for another day to break down camp. It's a hard day of work, a difficult emotional transition.

A community is built around its shared experiences, common lingo, intelligible inside jokes, and shorthand communication. The week is over, people part ways and that particular community is gone forever. No longer is there a group of people who will laugh every time you say the right words.

I am spending a year participating in the repeated act of humans struggling to say good-bye. I am sharing the tears of departure, the wonderful human expression, which says, *I want you to be near me, and I will grieve over our separation.* This is a year of hugs and handshakes, smiles and sadness, laughter and tears.

***

The Dance: Cathy's Committal Service

We knew what she had said. *I'll send you a sign when I get there.* We never disbelieved her. We knew Cathy. Now Cathy was gone; she died last September. Ten years with cancer. A medical miracle for most of that time.

She was cremated, her ashes waiting to be released into Lake Hubert where each year she'd come and listen to the loons, sit on the dock and watch the stars and the northern lights.

Betsy, her daughter, packaged Cathy in a box and sent her in the mail to camp. We told Marty, the warehouse manager, to be on alert.

There's a special package coming. It's Cathy. She arrived, spending a couple of days with John and me in our cabin – in a box on top of a dresser.

Now, it was Friday night. Camp was over; the families had left.

Bill, Jeff, John, and I gathered at the dock around dusk. With wildflowers in hand, we grabbed life jackets and headed towards the pontoon boat. I fought a rare headache. An echo bounced in my head telling me what I had come to believe: something was about to happen. All week long, I had gone to the dock and looked up at the stars. *Wait until Friday.* Now that it was Friday, I was physically and emotionally exhausted.

Jeff drove us out to the middle of the lake. He cut the motor, and we sat in the quiet stillness of the dying day. The fresh evening stars were rich and brilliant, and the last traces of the sun were being absorbed by the darkness of the night.

We talked about Cathy, her life and her struggle. We shared stories; it was calm, peaceful. Time was suspended with meaning. I was content, eager to avoid the inevitable. But then an awkward silence suggested that I should begin the service. A prayer, the ashes, and some flowers.

I sat with my back to the north, looking at the three figures in the dark, and I opened my mouth. . . . I saw John's body go erect. Then, his eyes lit up in the darkness; his face was alive with joy. I looked over my shoulder. The black night had given birth to a pulsating fire of light. The northern sky was alive.

She began to dance. A year ago, she was a shadow, a crippled body refusing to die. A year later, she was dancing with proud laughter. Giving us her sign, reminding us of our limited understandings, our inability to perceive, filling ourselves with overwhelming joy, leaving us speechless, tearful and with an anxious peace.

The northern lights lasted for only a few minutes. We stood for ages, though, arm in arm, tears running down our cheeks. Cathy was doing just fine. She was safe in God's eternal presence.

Back under the night's veil, we slipped her physical remains into the water. I prayed; each of us took a turn with the ashes, and flowers were tossed upon the dark water. However, none of this mattered any more: Cathy was alive.

We gently motored back to camp, and as we looked to the north, the sky was black as coal. The brevity of the sign only seemed to authenticate itself, and the present darkness felt appropriate. We were recipients of a message, people of the promise, the children of God. And we knew it.

Foundations

Several hours after driving past the *Amazing Maize Maze* in Iowa, I arrived at my grandfather's house in Arkansas. The next morning, I took him to Little Rock, where my parents lived and where my grandmother, who had suffered a stroke in May, was convalescing in a nursing home.

I saw Ma-Maw for a few minutes. She called me by name, although that was about all she could manage. Pa-Paw looked unsettled when I left him, but I drove over to my parents' house to spend the day figuring out what I needed to do before I left for Costa Rica.

In the evening, worried that it wouldn't work, we took Ma-Maw out to eat. She ended up having a wonderful time, eating ravenously, even stealing food off other people's plates, smiling all the while. We were all greatly pleased.

The next morning, I took Pa-Paw back to the nursing home. Ma-Maw was almost completely despondent, and we could barely elicit a response. I said good-bye to them and walked away, turning around to wave a final time. It would be the last time that I would see Ma-Maw.

Before I left for Costa Rica, I managed a visit with Granny, my other grandmother. She asked a lot of questions about my trip. Somehow, we started laughing about falling down. The first thing you do, she said, even as an eighty-five-year-old woman, is to look around to see if anyone saw you. She spoke of the pain of recently losing a friend. She often repeated, *You can only do the best you know how.* We spoke about homesickness and loneliness. *These feelings come over you like a wave without ever washing out your mouth*, she said.

***

(Costa Rica: August 22nd – September 2nd)

Bishop Fernando Palomo, the Methodist bishop of Costa Rica, looked at me and began speaking in English:

Do you know the song, 'The wise man built his house upon a rock?'...The question for us is: Where do we build the church? The church needs good foundations – people who are devoted and dedicated in their walk with God, people who are well grounded in the scriptures. People want the Holy Spirit to do something special without opening themselves up to the Word.

Take John Wesley. He was rooted in the Word. Long before his dramatic experience at Aldersgate, he was open and ready for the Spirit. The same was true for Paul. The church needs to lay good solid foundations in order to support its structures. The temptation is to build the structure before the foundation is laid, but I can see the whole church structure completely collapsing. Like the roads in Costa Rica, they keep building them on mud, and they keep washing away. You have to build them on rock.

I was sitting in the bishop's office with Ray and Steve, two professors at the Methodist seminary near San José. Ray, a close friend of mine from college, was teaching classes, facilitating volunteer work teams from the United States, and serving as an assistant to the bishop. Ray and his wife, Lidia, were serving as my hosts for a ten-day stay in Costa Rica.

***

We began the ascent up Vulcan Irazu in Ray's 1976 Chevy Blazer. It was a narrow, steep road, and along the way, we met dairy farmers attending their cows and saw people selling vegetables from roadside shacks. We stopped at a house of two small girls, Maria and Marcella, whom Lidia and Ray had befriended on previous trips up the volcano. The two girls were outside playing. Their small house had a metal roof and a wood stove; the walls were lined with newspapers.

At the top, Lidia stayed in the truck while Ray and I walked to the crater. The weather had set in, and the area was covered in fog. A cold, brisk wind swept across the barren landscape of dark volcanic sand. I peered into the crater where a pea green pond appeared lifelessly below. The fog kept us from having a clear vista to points beyond, and when the wind blew, it rattled through my head. After walking along the length of the crater, the pelting rain and wind drove us hurriedly back to the truck. I was short of breath, running in the eleven-thousand-foot altitude. We grabbed some hot chocolate at a portable coffee stand and then went back into the truck to warm up.

In Cartago, still under the watchful eye of Irazu, we drove by the ruins of the old Cathedral, *La Basilica de Nuestra Senora de Los Angeles*, destroyed by an earthquake, now a city plaza.

On August 2, 1635, the Virgin appeared as a doll made of stone to a poor girl named Juana Pereira. The girl took the doll home to play with, but the doll disappeared only to reappear where the girl had first found it. On that spot, a church was built, and still, each August, thousands of pilgrims make the journey to Cartago.

The new Cathedral of Angels is a white multi-dome structure standing at the back of another open plaza. The interior was dark, yet illuminated, decorated by elaborate stencils and precision geometric patterns. At the entrance, some devout pilgrims fell to the ground, crawling on their knees the entire length of the nave.

We left Cartago and hurriedly traveled through the beautiful Orosi Valley to Turriabla. Coffee, potatoes, onions, sugar cane, ferns and bananas covered the steep banks.

We met Eli, a local pastor, at the park across from the Catholic church. A good-looking and well-dressed man, Eli climbed into our truck, and we drove around Turriabla, passing a coffee field that was being broken up and sold as lots. The Methodist Church of Costa Rica was in the process of trying to buy some land for a new church and parsonage. Although four or five Methodist groups meet in the area, they were without a church building.

We drove down a narrow neighborhood street and stopped in front of the house that was hosting an evening worship service. Most of the children playing outside joined us for the service.

Inside, the congregation was gathering. One long, single room served as kitchen, dining room, and living room. The room's decor included a couple of sinks, a television set, a stereo, diplomas and baptism records, a sofa, chairs, and a table. The ceiling was corrugated sheet metal, and the room opened up directly onto the driveway.

Drinking some local coffee, we sat at the table and ate tamales wrapped in banana leaves picked from Eli's father's farm. Over 150 tamales had been prepared during the day and sold in order to cancel a debt incurred from a recent Mother's Day activity.

Forty people were now gathered; twenty of them were children. We began singing to tapes played on the stereo. Afterwards, the children were excused to children's church, exiting through the curtain leading to the back bedroom.

The children went to learn a scripture for the day, and Eli began his sermon about worship and its benefits for the family. Eli preached until his voice finally gave way, and, sweating, he closed worship with prayer. Shortly beforehand, I began smelling heated grease coming from the back of the room where some women were preparing quesadillas. The children then returned and recited their scripture. The adults did the same: *As for me and my house, we will serve the Lord.*[27]

One of the worship leaders was Rosa, who had miraculously survived breast cancer eight years ago. She has since dedicated herself to full-time Christian work. She spoke with Lidia about getting a replacement for her silicon external implant. Now in pieces, she keeps the implant together inside a sock.

Before we left Turriabla, we stopped by Eli's house. Earlier in the day, a snake had been found in a basket in the living room, and the contents of the basket were still scattered about the room. We said our good-byes and began driving back to San José after first stopping for some Fanta.

***

On Sunday morning, we worshipped with the congregation that meets at the Methodist high school. The modern facility was a dramatic contrast to the service in Turriabla. While there were still thirty or forty people, it felt almost empty – especially compared with the

---

[27] Joshua 24:14-15.

same amount of people crammed into a single room the night before. Afterwards, I met some of the congregation. Many of them were Cubans, including Carlos who was a professor of physics and astronomy in Cuba. Now in Costa Rica, he kills roaches for a living.

***

Ray and I drove north along the National Highway until we got to San Ramon where we began to cut across the mountains to Fortuna. The climb was steep and mountainous, bumpy and beautiful. We finally hit some flat ranch land and off in the distance, we were able to see Vulcan Arenal, one of the most perfectly shaped volcanoes in the world.

In Fortuna, we met Lender, the pastor, who was in the parsonage, emptying water out of his house that had come in with the morning rains. We then walked next door to the Fortuna Methodist Church, where inside, the sanctuary was absent of pews. Worship attendance was so great that they had already shifted the pews to the new construction sight. They only used the sanctuary for their weekday services.

The congregation was currently between two and three hundred people, necessitating the building of a new church. We drove out of town to the construction sight. So far, the church was just an unfinished cinder-block frame. The main sanctuary had not been started yet. However, there was a slanting roof over one of the wings, and there we found the missing pews.

Afterwards, Ray and I headed to the waterfall, *La Catarata de la Fortuna*. Scattered trees formed a beautiful foreground for the ever-present volcano. From the car park, we could immediately see the murky waters of the long ribbon-like cascade falling down the far side of the forested canyon.

We descended the steep, stair-stepped trail down to the base of the falls. The muddy falls poured into a churning, chocolate pool, which roared with violent intensity. Finding a large boulder, we sat and had our lunch. We were wet and muddy but also refreshed and alive. I was in the heart of the rain forest, and I felt both its density and power.

We spent rest of the afternoon at the hot baths. A mountain river, heated by the volcano, empties into a series of cascading, stonewalled pools, one pouring into the next. As the afternoon turned to dusk, a light mist fell from the sky through the rain forest canopy above us.

That night, Ray and I sat on the hood of his Chevy truck, which we had parked off to the side of the road. A few miles away, Volcan Arenal was on fire. Molten lava streamed continuously down its side; burning rocks shot high into the air. Occasionally, lingering fog covered the cone, hiding the peak but not the glow. Lightning flashed in the background. Above us, the moon shone through the clouds, providing relief and outline to the surrounding landscape. We lay there for over an hour in silence, and I wondered what it must have been like millions of years ago with dozens and dozens of volcanoes erupting, creating earth, molding and shaping our planet?

Now, I wondered why there was only one volcano here.

***

We left Fortuna and headed for the Pacific side of Costa Rica where we spent a few hours at Flamingo Beach before driving through the rain towards Nicoya to attend an evening worship service. On the way, we drove through flooded back streets to the construction site of a church in the town of Santa Cruz. Nearby, serving as their temporary sanctuary was a large tent protecting enough pews for one to two hundred people. Like the churches of Fortuna and Nicoya, the church in Santa Cruz depended upon work crews from the United States.

We arrived at the Nicoya church and met Jorge, the pastor. The congregation was only four years old and consisted of about one hundred members. Besides Sunday morning, there was Tuesday and Thursday night worship. Mondays, Wednesdays and Fridays began with five o'clock morning prayer. The newly built church, which could comfortably hold up to three hundred people, had been recently dedicated. Behind the altar was a painting of a person held in God's hand with the words: *God gives us eternal life, and he will not let anyone take us out of his hands!*

For the next full hour, we were engaged in unbroken praise and singing. Altar prayer was mixed in between the songs. The offering was taken while the singing continued, and during the peace, we were kissed by women and hugged by men.

Jorge then presented a meditation: *Where is Jesus? He has been resurrected!* We closed with a testimony and a final song. For the next thirty minutes, we visited with the congregation, and I soon began trying to communicate with the kids – Juan, Andreas, Sophia, Jennifer and Rachel. They counted to ten in English, asked me my age, and told me that they had English tests at school in the morning that they hadn't studied for! Jennifer, age eleven, wished that I could stay longer so that she could teach me Spanish. *We'd be professors for each other.* She was clever for her age, making me laugh when she said of herself and her friends:

> *In Spanish, Juan; in English, John.*
> *In Spanish, Andres; in English, Andrew.*
> *In Spanish, Jennifer; in English, Jennifer!*

***

Ray and I were talking about our days in college when all of a sudden we heard a sound like a rock bouncing around in the engine and then as if a rod was being dragged along the ground. We were stranded in Costa Rica on a long, narrow stretch of highway, two to three hours from San José. Within five minutes, a man driving a small Mazda stopped in front of us. He happened to be a mechanic! He quickly surveyed the problem; he listened to the truck as Ray drove it a few yards, located the problem and said that a bolt had fallen out of a rod.

The man began to look for a bolt or something to secure the rod. Ray suggested to me that the bolt could be on the road, and so I took a walk back down the highway in the direction from which we had come. It would have been nice to find the bolt, but I wasn't very expectant. Actually, I just walked away so they could attend to the truck.

I thought of the book, *Lame Deer*, in which Lame Deer describes how women who were having their periods were excluded from religious ceremonies.[28] It wasn't necessarily done to discriminate against them. Rather, they thought that menstruating women had special powers that would negate the forces of the ceremony.

I looked back over the years and saw how my presence had often hindered basic mechanical functions and how if I just left the scene, my father or brother could easily fix whatever was broken. That was why I was walking away from the truck. I have learned to leave anytime something breaks. When I returned, the truck was temporarily fixed. We thanked the man and headed on down the highway.

After we got back on the National Highway, the noise started back up again, and we stopped at a small garage. Ray talked with the mechanic, and I began to play with Francilla, his five-year-old daughter. She was scrubbing down her Barbie with an old, dirty toothbrush, putting some mechanics' soap on the doll and cleaning it over a filthy sink. We played in the open-air garage while Ray and the mechanic took a ride in the truck. Francilla got out her toy cash register and began selling me plastic meats. You don't have to know a lot of Spanish to be able to play house and store with a five-year-old.

Beyond the garage in the backyard were a couple of jungle gyms. Underneath them were scraps of sharp, rusty sheet metal. Francilla's mother was cleaning a couple of chickens; she chopped off their feet and gave them to the cats. ·

Ray returned with the mechanic, who had fixed the truck, and after settling up with him, Ray and I returned to San José where we learned that an earthquake of 5.0 had been felt that day in all of Costa Rica except in the region where we had broken down.

***

We drove to the Caribbean for the weekend, climbing the central mountain range out of San José, dropping down into the rain forest, and later passing several banana plantations. On the way, our muffler

---

[28] *Lame Deer*, pp. 148 -149.

became disengaged, and the noise was deafening.

We came to Puerto Limon where civil disorder had followed the government's announcement to privatize the port. There had been a workers strike in Limon during the week. Looting and rioting had left one person dead.

Blockades were still in the streets. At one barricade, two kids charged us two dollars for the right of passage. We paid, and they moved the logs out of the way. Armed police were scattered throughout the streets.

We finally rumbled out of town and down the beautiful, palm-lined coastal road, occasionally passing poor shanties. We were heading, if not to the end of the earth, certainly to the end of Costa Rica.

We arrived in Cahuita and walked to the national park, a peninsula jutting out into the Caribbean. The water was enticing. We took off our shoes and waded and then watched a marvelous pink sunset. Crabs were playing on the beach. One lone woman was swimming.

The main street of Cahuita, a simple dirt road, was lined with hotels, restaurants, and reggae boutiques. People were out walking in the streets; others were sitting on porches and against storefronts.

Cahuita had only one phone line. It's a weird, frightening, but fascinating village – a black Creole culture of the Caribbean settled by Jamaicans a couple of centuries ago and cut off from San José and the rest of Costa Rica until the last century.

We stopped to eat at Restaurant Edith's, advertised in one of Lidia's travel books for its authentic Creole food. Run by a Creole family, it was an unassuming open-air structure tucked off a street corner near our cabins. We expected slow service, and we weren't disappointed. We ordered, and then a few minutes later our waitress returned to tell us that they didn't have anything that we had requested. I settled for tomato fish and water.

Five minutes later, we saw our waitress, a teenage girl, strolling down the dirt road into the night. We thought that it was a bit strange – our waitress had just left the building. Her younger brother took over the service, bringing Ray and Lidia their Pepsis. I was tempted several times to ask him about my water, which she apparently hadn't told him that I had ordered, but I didn't say anything.

Several minutes later, Ray and Lidia spotted our waitress ambling lazily back down the road. In her left hand, illuminated in the darkness by a streetlight, was my bottle of water. The waitress went back into the kitchen, brought out a glass, and set the water in front of me without saying a word. When our food finally came, I ate hungrily, and halfway through the meal, I ordered some more water.

The moon was out, and after the meal, we walked down to the beach. It was a beautiful night, and we soaked up the sights and the sounds of the evening – ocean waves, reggae music, and the constant offer of drugs. From the beach, we looked back into the town – a veiled mystery of darkness lifted slightly by the lights of the tiny, provincial village. The remote, undeveloped area now hosts tourists from around the world. Here and there, mixed in with the black Creole locals were Europeans and North Americans enjoying a cheap and random destination.

***

I am sitting under a palm tree, listening to the constant crash of waves. The early morning sunlight is upon my face. The palm trees are brilliant – reflecting the golden sun. I look out to sea. The Caribbean is beautiful.

We woke up at a quarter before five and walked down to a rocky, coral point. The night's darkness had already been broken, and the faintest light of golden rays could be seen behind Cahuita Point. The moon hung overhead. We have been here now for over half an hour, taking photos of the sky, sea and shore.

Back at the cabins, we had coffee and cinnamon rolls under a grass-roofed patio, and then we took a boat ride out to the reefs. The palm-lined beach, the mountains in the background, and the village were all timeless and picturesque. The water was clear and calm; the sky bright and blue.

We stopped inside the bay, a hundred yards or so off the point and began snorkeling around the coral reef. An old Spanish ship had sunk in these waters. We could see a few canons and a broken anchor. Their forms were clearly visible, though grown over with coral. Scores of colorful fish darted in and out of the reef.

We got back into the boat and motored slowly inside the breakers. Our guides dropped us off on the beach, and we spent the next four hours swimming. Around a dozen other tourists, in pairs and singles, dotted the shore.

In the afternoon, we walked the streets one last time. Back at our cabins, we showered and dressed for the ride back. It was very hot, and we went from sandy and sweaty to just sweaty. We piled into the truck and rumbled out of town.

The drive down the beach towards Limon was still beautiful. We passed dilapidated shanties scattered along the road and saw several ruined bridges that had been destroyed in the 1991 earthquake. Locals were swimming in the rivers.

In Limon, the streets were busier than Friday. We drove through the obstacle course of barriers without incident. The residents seemed more relaxed and went about their business. We turned onto the main Limon-San José highway and only had the long drive ahead of us. We passed the banana plantations, ascended the rain forest in the misty twilight, and at last, we approached the lights of the Central Valley.

***

After church, I had an opportunity to speak with Samuel, the pastor, and his wife, Norma. Ray and I told him what we had seen in Limon. Samuel responded, *We Cubans do not like revolutions. We know what they mean.*

Ray, Lidia, and I ate lunch at the Lone Star Grill, a Tex-Mex restaurant owned by a woman from San Antonio. While we ate, Ray told me a random tale of a German tourist. He was shot to death in a bar. He had his passport on him, but no one bothered to look for it. He was taken to the morgue and then moved to the university medical center where he was kept. A couple of months later, his family came from Germany in search of him. They finally found him, and after complaints from the family and the German government, the Costa Rican government replied that it's just a courtesy that they would inform another embassy about a citizen's death. It wasn't protocol.

In the afternoon, I went for a walk, finally coming to a neighborhood park where a soccer game was going on. Several people lined the sidelines – girlfriends, brothers, parents and friends of the players. The green team, scoring five goals in a very short time, was killing the team in yellow.

Across the street was a large, modern church – a metal building with a high, steep slanted roof. Several well-dressed families were walking down the streets. Many of them were carrying Bibles.

I walked on, passing the modern building until I came to a Catholic church, and I went inside to pray. The interior was elaborately decorated, beautiful and peaceful. I sat in prayer, praying for family, Ray and Lidia, and others whom I had encountered so far on my travels.

A man lit some candles on the altar and put on some beautiful, inspiring music. I felt at home, at peace, centered on God and happy. With God's guidance, I was ready to move on. Yet, momentarily, I did not want to leave the confines of the sanctuary. Other people began to gather, perhaps for Mass. Reluctantly, I left, and outside, I was rewarded with the last colors of a pink sunset.

***

We have just recently taken off. Soon, we will be flying over Nicaragua. I see volcanic cones, remote towns, mountain ranges, deep canyons, and scattered farms. But you can't see the poverty from the air.

***

(Mexico: September 2nd – 9th)

I took a taxi from the Mexico City airport to Lisa's office, my hostess for the week. A Fulbright scholar from Minnesota, she was living in Germany when I met her. At home, she prepared dinner while I unpacked the jars of peanut butter – a common request of ex-patriots – that I had brought her from the States.

***

Sitting in Mexico City's famous cathedral, I am surrounded by scaffolding. The building, which is slowly sinking into the soft ground, is permanently supported by a complex series of heavy bars. In between every archway, up and down the nave, and throughout the aisles, there are metal beams bracing the walls, the columns, and the ceiling. Every side chapel is a discovery – a small, sacred enclave in what otherwise feels like an old abandoned fort. A safety net extends the length of the ceiling assuring me that nothing will fall on my head as I pray.

Choral music is coming from a chapel behind me. A few minutes ago, the candelabras were lit, illuminating the central altar. A few people are gathering in expectation of something.

All around the cathedral are signs in Spanish and broken English telling everyone to keep out until the Mass is over:

Attention: Don't visit the Cathedral in hours of Holly Mass or others celebrations. Thanks.

It seems a bit offensive and exclusive. I understand that tourists can be distracting, even obnoxious. Still, the message is: *Stay out while we worship our God.* Well, I wish them a very *holly* Mass indeed.

I have been overhearing choir practice for the last half hour. Now, several priests and choirboys have made their way to the main chancel. Behind me, a dozen boys are singing beautiful and ethereal music. The Mass is starting . . .

It's now forty-five minutes later. The candles have just been extinguished. The worshippers left quickly. Already the tourists have been ushered in.

When I first sat down, I was struck by the eerie, dilapidated condition of the building. But once the people of God gathered, the candles were lit, and gifts of bread and wine were offered, the cathedral was transcended by the radiance of God. We entered into sacred space and sacred time.

***

On December 9, 1531, a poor Indian peasant named Juan Diego saw a vision of a beautiful lady in a rich blue mantle trimmed in gold. He reported to the local priest that he had seen the Virgin Mary, but the priest didn't believe him. Juan returned to the hill, saw the vision again, and an image of the lady was miraculously emblazoned on the poor boy's ragged cloak. The priest believed, and he ordered a church to be built on the spot where Diego had seen the vision. Our Lady of Guadalupe has become the patron saint of Mexico.

I walked down the two-block promenade towards the impressive sixteenth-century original basilica. Soon the modern Basilica de Guadalupe, built in 1976 by Pedro Ramirez Vasquez, appeared on the left – huge, impressive, looking like a giant cave. Inside, the roof slopes up to a central point above the choir. On the right of the choir was a massive pipe organ. On the left wall were flags of various nations. The backdrop is a wooden patch-blocked façade rising nearly 150 feet, and well above the choir is the portrait of Our Lady. Assorted gold blocks and rectangles surrounded her. The same materials formed a tall three-dimensional thin cross rising half way up the façade.

I found a place in the crowded sanctuary as Mass was beginning. Sitting in awe of the beauty and magnificence of the building, I reflected upon my recent experiences.

Just as the elements were being prepared, the electricity went out. The organ went silent, and a dark, silent shadow was cast upon the Mass. A few minutes later, the lights were restored.

During communion, the congregation sang in Spanish a song that was a favorite of my church in Calico Rock. Immediately, I felt the connective touch of God through the emotional and familiar medium of music. Intense and overwhelming yet tangible and real. Calico Rock and the Basilica de Guadalupe share the Divine. In the form of a song, our common faith is expressed. There is one God – all-present, all-loving, all-knowing, and all-powerful. His spirit permeates our lives and our communities. In Arkansas or in Mexico, I can't escape him. We are all connected.

***

C. S. Lewis writes that brightness more than bigness was revered by the ancient people.[29]

***

It was a quiet night in Lisa's apartment. I made a fire and read an English newspaper. There was an article about a bus wreck:

A passenger bus crashed into two trucks on a highway south of Mexico City on Monday killing twenty-three people and injuring fifteen others. The bus first hit a three-ton truck and then veered into another truck. The dead included men, women, and children. 'It is terrible. I have seen a lot of tragedies in my life but this is one of the worst. There is a girl with her schoolbooks. It is really terrible,' a Radio Red reporter said.

Death is all around us. Horrible death. In a city of twenty-three million, perhaps a lot goes unnoticed. But there are friends, families, and individuals whose worlds are forever changed.

***

The day was spent in the village of Tepotzlan about two hours south of Mexico City. The town is beautifully located at the base of high, impressive craggy cliffs. High above, an ancient pyramid overlooks the village.

---

[29] Lewis, p. 65.

Lisa and I walked the markets, looking over the crafts, baskets, figurines, and kitchen supplies. The village is colorful, and the many shops and restaurants cater to a steady tourist trade. Lisa and I had lunch at Sandria Azul, the Blue Watermelon. We were engaged in a good conversation after a lot of easy silence on the trip. A man began playing the guitar. Nice music, great food, and a good friend.

People in Tepotzlan were getting ready for a festival that night. After dark, people would walk up to the ancient pyramid overlooking the town. There would be fireworks and music. Already little girls were dressed in white. People were making fancy murals out of beans. Streamers lined the streets and covered the churches.

The afternoon ride home, however, was as uncomfortable as the ride there had been pleasant. The bus was hot and stuffy, and the roads were hilly. Worse yet, a really disturbing movie was being shown. It was about a demented couple who lived in a large house; they were keeping a couple of children as slaves and killing all adult intruders.

***

Lisa and I spent Sunday afternoon at the pyramids of Teotihuacan. The grounds were vast; the distance between the pyramids was deceptively long. The day was beautiful, sunny, and windy. Clouds raced across the sky. Tourists were exploring the grounds; vendors were selling their wares. In the breeze, distant music could be heard.

It was a long, long ride home. The bus took the back roads, stopping often along the way – letting some people buy wine and others use the bathroom. If you wanted something, you just had to ask the bus driver.

***

Mexico is a treasury of sights, sounds, and smells. *Sounds*: guitar music, honking horns, and church organs. Sounds of the zoo, the market, street venders, and pyramid peddlers. *Smells:* corn tortillas, dirty streets, open sewers, and burning wood. *Common sights*: green taxis, organ grinders, Mexican flags, the military presence, bars on windows, newspaper stands, and street beggars.

Each day was one of fighting traffic, taking public transportation, struggling with language barriers, and worrying about possessions. But through the clouds of constant hassle broke the sun of golden moments. Each day had its hard-earned respites of relaxation, revelation, and relief. In these moments, I was content, peaceful, and extremely appreciative.

What does it mean that I am on a spiritual journey? Am I supposed to be experiencing spiritual growth in some qualitative way? Am I not also learning about my own vulnerabilities, fears, and discomforts? I need to have patience, to foster a sense of outward and inward joy, and to stop taking myself so seriously.

After dinner, Lisa went to sleep early, and I sat watching the fire, listening to the Gypsy Kings, and feeling extremely content and miles and miles away from the rest of my life.

All Will Be Well

I just took off on a puddle jumper out of Little Rock, the first leg of my actual around-the-world trip. Below on my right, I see the Arkansas River winding its way towards the Mississippi. Below is a power plant and a lock and dam. There are three passengers and two crewmembers on the plane. Everybody and their luggage could have fit into a car. When I boarded the plane, the co-pilot said, *Welcome aboard. You can choose any seat you want. It's less noisy in the back.*

***

Though we travel the world over to find the beautiful, we must carry it with us or we find it not.

— Emerson

***

(Scotland: September 12th – October 3rd)

My first full-time job was serving as the assistant minister to Cadder Parish Church (Church of Scotland) in Bishopbriggs (Glasgow), Scotland. I spent my afternoons visiting widows, drinking tea, and listening to stories of Scottish life. It was a precious year of culture and community, one of purpose and pleasure. I preached; I held funerals, and I worked with the youth. And so, when I spent my Saturdays driving through the Scottish landscape in my Ford Orion, exploring castles and fish and chip shops, it was done with a sense of both joy and fulfillment.

The people of Cadder remain one of the closer communities in my life, and it was natural that my first European destination would be *back home* to Glasgow where over a three-week period, I would speak at a wedding and attend a weeklong retreat on the island of Iona. Before I would leave Scotland, however, I would be profoundly amazed at the timing of my visit.

***

Today was Graeme and Wendy's wedding. I shared a few words during the service, reassuming for a day my role as assistant pastor. The wedding was beautiful, and afterwards, I stood around the churchyard visiting with old friends while bag pipers played in the background. It was a magical day that slipped away much too quickly.

***

I went to the Museum of Religious Art near the Glasgow Cathedral and bought a couple of posters of Dali's *Christ of St. John of the Cross*. I had fallen in love with the painting when I first saw the original hanging in the Glasgow Art Gallery. While I was the pastor in Calico Rock, we placed a framed copy of the painting in the choir of the church. Now, this was the first time that I had seen the painting in the new museum. Years ago, soon after Glasgow acquired it, *Christ of St. John of the Cross* was vandalized. In the glare, I could see where the ripped painting had been patched up, but nonetheless, the imposing image of Christ, now towering above me, was more impressive and meaningful than ever before.

***

Andy's father, Joe, was in the hospital, and I went with Andy and his mother, Elizabeth, to visit him throughout the week. Joe was a quiet man, adored by his children and grandchildren. I knew Joe fairly well – he is the only one with whom I have ever watched *Baywatch*.

Later in the week, Andy and I went sailing on the Firth of Forth at Queensferry with Dane, the pastor of Cadder Parish. We grabbed lunch at a cold, drafty pub, and then headed up the Forth for a couple of hours before turning around. The view of the Forth Railroad Bridge was fantastic. The wind and waves were strong, and we were soaking by the time we returned.

Andy called his mother from the marina: *Hurry home, Son.*

***

I was awakened by a call from Andy telling me that his father had passed away in his sleep. I spent the whole day with Andy and his family, helping to make arrangements and just being there.

In the living room of Elizabeth's house, Joanna, her eight-year-old granddaughter, interjected during a break in the adult conversation: *D'you know when yer dead they can use yer bits to make other people well?*

***

Today, I traveled to Iona, a seven-hour trip from Glasgow. Two buses and two ferries. It was a beautiful trip, full of both excitement and anxiety. Throughout the journey, I kept an eye out for other Iona pilgrims.

The ferry docked at Iona after the short crossing from Fionnphort. I walked alone with the crowd towards the abbey. I found my room and then attended a short orientation for the abbey guests. The hostess described Iona as a pilgrimage site: *We are all seekers – including our staff and volunteers. This is a place where people come and go. There is a lot of movement.* Afterwards, we stayed in the refractory for our first meal together.

Evening worship was in the abbey. I sat beside Marion, a regular Iona pilgrim from England. *Whenever I'm here*, she said. *I feel like I'm home. There is something so indescribable about this place. I look at the walls and imagine that they have been impregnated by worship for so many hundreds of years. I always feel close to God when I'm on the island.*

When the service was over, I didn't want to move. Iona had already laid a claim upon me. I was centered, and I remained in prayer for a while thinking about Andy and his father, Ma-Maw, and others.

I left the contemplation of worship and entered the excitement of new acquaintances. As I walked into the refractory for tea, I saw an auburn-haired young woman. When she saw me, her face lit up. We had traveled together all the way from Glasgow without speaking a word. Now, after a day of traveling as strangers, we were immediately consumed in conversation. After a long visit, I walked her – Julia, a university student from Germany – back to the Macleod Centre where she was staying.

I wandered back across the sheep field looking at the massive stone structure before me. The abbey was neither a museum nor simply a place for worship. For a week, it was my home.

***

I helped with the morning communion service, taking the offering and serving the bread. After lunch, I wanted to spend the afternoon with Julia, but I couldn't find her. One goes so quickly from enjoying someone's company to becoming discontent when not in that person's presence.

On this blustery Sunday afternoon, I have climbed the highest hill on the island to read and journal, seeking contentment in the sacredness of the moment. On top of the hill, it is windy. In the fields, the sheep and cattle are grazing. People – couples, small groups and singles – are scattered all over the island, dots along the beach, climbing the hill, walking through the fields. Below, the waves are crashing; the spray is splashing up upon the rocks. Oddly, as I look across the island and towards the sea, I have a strange sensation of the stillness of the scene, the silence of creation. Before me is a still life.

All around me is quiet. I feel the solitude. The spiritual and the temporal are hand in hand.

***

Iona is a sacred place – fifteen hundred years of Christian history and spirituality. Since 563 when St. Columba arrived from Ireland, Iona has been a center of Christianity. From their base on Iona, Columba's monks spread Christianity throughout Scotland and northern England.

In the depression years of the 1930s, Church of Scotland minister George Macleod brought unemployed craftsmen from his parish in industrial Glasgow where, against a background of unemployment, war and the breakdown of urban life, the ancient abbey and cloister were restored, and the Iona Community was born. Now, it is a community with its own program, purpose, and mission.

Today, there are approximately two hundred members of the Iona Community living mostly throughout Great Britain. They commit themselves to prayer and Bible study, to accountability in the use of time and money, and to peace and justice work. Each member participates in a regional home group, which meets periodically, and the members return to the island for a week during the year. The real work of the Iona Community, therefore, does not take place on the island but rather in the home communities of its members. Friends and associate members also support the work of the community.

Housed in both the abbey and the adjacent Macleod Center, the Iona Programme offers weeklong retreats on the island. Several people work on the island as volunteers and resident staff. The abbey itself is an historic monument, open to visitors throughout the day. The small village of Iona contains a couple of bed-and-breakfasts, gift shops and restaurants. The ferry to Mull leaves about every hour.

***

Work and worship are integrated at Iona. Together, they form the ethos of the community. At the end of morning worship, there is no formal benediction. Worship continues throughout the morning in the form of communal work. From worship, we leave to do our chores.

Rita, Achim, and I had the task of chopping vegetables – often onions – for each day's meals. Nadia, a cook from England, commented one morning: *You look like you cook lasagna.*
What?

You're an intelligent, romantic-looking American man.

Ah, but looks can be deceiving.

***

Angela Knowles, a clown and storyteller, is leading the week's program entitled, *A Festival of Fools*. During the mornings, we are exploring the role of the fool and the dictator in our lives, listening to stories and meeting in small groups.

***

Helen, a woman from North Yorkshire, does not find the worship services in the abbey to be very Scottish. She went to the Church of Scotland service on Sunday saying that she felt more at home there. *Lots of traditional hymns. That's what makes worship for me.*

Helen talks about faith and tragedy – how she lost her husband at an early age. But she said that she wouldn't be living her faith if she was bitter or kept asking, *Why?*

If I can't leave it to God, then I am not really living my faith. God knows better than I do.

***

It is both wonderful and weary to be an individual pilgrim. As an individual pilgrim, I enter communities quickly and completely. I don't have the possibility of hiding in the familiar. I am alone, exposed. It is to my benefit to engage. There is a great loneliness, too. The real sadness is not in arriving alone. The sadness is in leaving people behind.

I returned to Glasgow for Joe's funeral right after lunch, feeling turned up and unsettled. I took the ferry across to Fionnport where several buses were idling, waiting to take passengers back across the island of Mull. I got on one and settled in for the hour's ride. We started down the single-lane road as the driver began a running commentary of the island, jokes about its people, and facts about its economy.

I handed him my ticket when I got off the bus, and he began yelling at me, telling me that I was on the wrong bus. *This is a tourist bus. That's no ticket – you should be paying me.* I just wanted to attend a funeral. I was furious, but I got off without opening my mouth.

***

Bill and Pat Marwick, who more than took care of me when I lived in Glasgow, were my hosts when I returned. Walking in the dark rain to the Marwicks' house seemed odd, because everything was so familiar and natural. I was coming *home* late at night. It is nice when our journeys take us home – especially when our reasons for being there aren't exactly welcomed.

***

During the funeral, I sat behind Andy and the family, reflecting upon past memorial services that I had held in the chapel.

Once again, we sang *The Lord's My Shepherd* and *How Great Thou Art*, and I experienced the emotion of a Scottish crematorium. Dane shared beautiful words about the life of Joe, his love for family. The words of committal were given, and soon the service was over.

We gathered at the Eagle Lodge for a reception. Sausage rolls and Iron Bru.[30] I talked with Andy, the family, members of Cadder. The room was full of relief, gratitude, and occasional laughter. I said good-bye to Andy and Elizabeth, and Pat and Bill drove me down to the bus station for my return trip to Iona.

In the past, the ride through the beautiful Highlands was the purpose of the trip. Today, there were other things on my mind, and the journey was simply the means back to Iona. The only purpose, perhaps, was the time it gave me to reflect upon the events of the week.

On the ferry, while sitting below the deck contently reading *In Search of a Way* by Gerard Hughes, I fell upon a quote by Julian of Norwich that gave comfort and perspective to the day: *All will be well, all will be well, all manner of things will be well.*[31]

I put the book away and went outside to the deck. The ferry was in open water approaching the isle of Mull. To the east was the mainland; tiny islands dotted the seascape. The wind was gusty but not too cold. Large isolated rain clouds competed with the sun for

---

[30] Iron Bru is Scotland's leading soft drink.

[31] Hughes, *In Search of a Way* (London: Darton, Longman, and Todd, 1994), p. 39.

control of the sky.

In their struggle, they merged, and I saw in the east the beginnings of a rainbow. Bright, intense hews arching from the sea to the sky and back to the sea. And beside it, concentric to the first, was a second complete rainbow – only with softer colors. A bright, yellow light strangely filled the sky, radiating from the double rainbows. I squinted in the glare, my eyes blinking in the golden light.

I took a deep breath and held the moment. She was right. *All will be well, all will be well, all manner of things will be well.* I thought of Joe, Cathy, friends lost to death, and I watched the rainbows slowly fade away. When we reached Mull, I could see a little color still lingering in the sky.

Everything was going to be all right.

An hour later, I was on the ferry to Iona, thinking about all that I had missed over last thirty-six hours – the relationships, worship, group chores, and the walking pilgrimage around the island. As the abbey came into full view, I was grateful to be returning to a community that was eagerly expecting my return.

***

Evening worship followed the week's theme: *Fools for Christ.* There was singing, dancing, and finger painting. I was tired, however, and the energy and the movement of the service left me behind. Quietly, I painted a rainbow on the mural with my fingers and waited for the service to be over.

Before I went to bed, I checked my mailbox. There was a single hand-written note:

Dear Rodney,

> *Christ be within you, Christ be with you.*
> *Christ behind you, Christ before you.*
> *Christ beside you, Christ to win you.*
> *Christ to comfort you and restore you.*
> *Christ beneath you, Christ above you.*

Christ in quiet, Christ in danger.
Christ in all the hearts that love you.
Christ in the mouth of a friend and stranger.[32]
God bless you.

It was good to be back home.

***

Rodney and Jillian met each other at Iona a couple of years ago. At the time, Rodney was at the end of his marriage. Jillian was divorced. Experiences like Iona are double-edged swords. They are places of healing, but they are also places where we discover our brokenness, and they can easily become places of great struggle and pain. *On a vacation, you go to get away. On a pilgrimage, you face your life. There is nothing to hide. At Iona, I came face to face with the problems of my life and marriage,* said Rodney.

Iona, however, became a place of new birth in the midst of their broken lives. *I was able to receive spiritual healing and self-affirmation. I discovered gifts and qualities about myself that I liked. I met people who affirmed who I was,* Rodney reflected. *I discovered a new, enjoyable side to myself,* added Jillian. After a couple of years of courting, they were married at Iona. This past week, they renewed their vows in the abbey. *'What God has brought together let no one pull asunder' – We wanted to omit this phrase from our vows, but our pastor advised against it. We are now glad that we listened to her.*

***

Evening worship was a service of commitment. We made boats out of paper and then placed them into a small pool of water. I felt a real sense of release as I dropped my boat. It fell a couple of inches until the water rippled with excitement as it received the load. That is faith – falling into the hands of God.

***

Remember, said Angela, *you are nobody.*

---

[32] From *Patrick's Breastplate,* Irish blessing.

***

Rob, Julia and I stood in the kitchen of the Macleod Centre until three in the morning, drinking tea and watching the final phases of a lunar eclipse cast a dark and eerie shadow over the ancient and holy island. We had heard reports that a lunar eclipse was going to take place; however, none of us knew when it would start. We stayed up for a few hours, questioning whether or not the reports were true. Finally, we decided to go to sleep. On my way to the abbey, I detected the first signs of the eclipse, and I went back and found Rob and Julia still talking in the hallway.

We put the kettle back on and stayed up for another hour, staring through the windows at the darkening moon. Clouds lightly covered the sky; however, they were thin enough that they amplified rather than blocked the moonlight.

As I walked through the sheep field back to my room in the restored thirteenth-century abbey, I was again reminded of the Celtic understanding that natural landscape is both a concrete reality and a doorway into another spiritual world. The late Dr. George Macleod, founder of the modern Iona Community, spoke of the Isle of Iona as a *thin place*, tissue thin, where the membrane between the material and spiritual world is very permeable.

***

I have just been to the beach with Julia. We climbed some rocks, took some photos, and sat in the blustery wind. When we got ready to leave, we saw that the large rock that we were on was now surrounded by the rising tide. We had no choice but to get wet up to our knees. The rain came on strong as we walked back; the wind was whipping our faces. We were fairly soaking by the time we reached the abbey.

My spiritual journey has been like a roller coaster this week. I am exhausted and frustrated, sensing loneliness and isolation. For several months, I have walked a path of peace and contentment. Now, I feel unsettled. However, since this year is a calling and *not just a year off*, I have given myself permission not to enjoy everything.

So much has escaped me. Like sand slipping through my fingers, I am letting a lot slip away. The essence is all around me, but I can't seem to access it all.

Death, travel and emotions have replaced the themes of community, landscape, and history.

***

May you be an isle in the sea.
May you be a hill on the shore.
May you be a star in the darkness.
May you be a staff to the weak.

***

We gathered around a long banquet table in the nave of the abbey for communion. We prayed and then sang: *Behold, behold. I make all things new beginning with you.* The service was intimate. Sitting around the candle-lit table, we could see our brothers and sisters around us.

Rick, a pilgrim from Boston, gave a meditation:

Watching the dawn break over Mull, in the east where things begin – and watching the sunset over the sea in the west where things end – it seems to me that the boundary between light and darkness is thin indeed. Thin, like the tissue between heaven and earth on Iona (as the saints have told us), through which we see both the light and the darkness of God, the darkness and light of ourselves.

This is the place. This island, this table, where opposites meet. . . . the shared [is] just out ahead of us, in the pillar of cloud, the pillar of moonlight, the pillar of song, leading us on, teaching us to believe in our journeys, teaching us slowly to trust our journeys. By the unusual light of this place, we see the most astonishing thing: that home and pilgrimage are not opposites after all; they are the same things. Beginning and end are not opposites; they embrace at the table where the last supper became the first feast, where death became life, where an act of outrageous violence became the harbinger of the deep peace of the Prince of peace.[33]

We passed the bread and cup – the gifts of God – to one another. It was truly a banquet table, and we were community, family. The meditation, the music, the silence all manifested God's healing presence.

The closing hymn was *Through the Love of God our Savior:*

> *Through the love of God our Savior, all will be well.*
> *Free and changeless is his favor, all, all is well.*
>
> *Precious is the blood that healed us.*
> *Perfect is the grace that sealed us.*
> *Strong the hand stretched forth to shield us.*
> *All must be well.*[34]

Julian of Norwich was right again: *All will be well, all will be well, all manner of things will be well.*

As I sang the final song through unchecked tears, I experienced my own healing for the week. The pilgrim does not possess anything; rather, at the end of the day, it is God who possesses us. I could now let go of the sand because an even greater hand was holding me.

***

We woke up to a final morning of Iona porridge, and soon we were leaving the island. The departure from Iona is a strange good-bye. Since almost everyone took the ferry together, the island seemed to leave us before we left each other. Together, we stood crowded on the exposed deck, waving in silence to a place and an experience that was already starting to diminish before our eyes.

The community broke up slowly and unevenly, and it was difficult to know when and where to say good-bye. I gave Julia a formal good-bye on the second ferry, and at Oban, the diaspora was complete,

---

[33] Rev. Rick Spalding is an Episcopal priest in the Boston area.
[34] M. Peters, *Through the Love of God our Savior*, copyright held by Church of Scotland (St. Andrews Press, 1998), used by permission.

accelerated by the driving rain that greeted us. People went into shops, caught buses and trains, and drove away in cars.

I was with Angela on the bus ride home to Glasgow. We sat drying off, sharing stories and talking about the week as we rode through the Highlands on a rain-saturated Saturday, leaving Iona farther and farther behind.

Cows Don't Eat Hot Dogs

(Rainhill, England: October 4th – 7th)

I arrived wet and in tatters to the Loyola House, a Jesuit retreat center, near Rainhill, England, exhausted from carrying my heavy suitcase in the rain. I received a friendly welcome and was soon taken to my room. There, I stayed for a few minutes, cooling off and drying out. I then walked down to the Blake Room, where the weekend seminar, Psychological Issues in Spiritual Direction, was already in session. I opened the door, and once again, I entered into a new world, a new community.

One minute, I am a traveler, a stranger on a train. The next, I am a participant in a Christian community.

Eucharist preceded dinner. I didn't want to miss worship; yet, I was uncertain whether or not I would be allowed to commune. Confident that God's peace would be present even if his gifts were denied, I went to the chapel.

It was St. Francis' Day.

> *Lord, make me an instrument of thy peace;*
> *Where there is hatred, let me sow love;*
> *Where there is injury, pardon;*
> *Where there is doubt, faith;*
> *Where there is despair, hope;*
> *Where there is darkness, light;*
> *And where there is sadness, joy.*
> *O Divine Master,*
> *Grant that I may not so much seek*
> *To be consoled as to console;*
> *To be understood, as to understand;*
> *To be loved, as to love;*
> *For it is in giving that we receive,*
> *It is in pardoning that we are pardoned,*
> *And it is in dying that we are born to eternal life.*[35]

---

[35] Prayer of St. Francis of Assisi, thirteenth century.

When time came for communion, I went forward, and the priest did not hesitate to give me the bread of life. Grace is more appreciated when, after waiting anxiously, unsure if we will receive it, the gift is given. Receiving the Eucharistic as a Protestant in a Catholic community can be rich in spiritual meaning.

We closed by singing words from Isaiah 43:

> *Do not be afraid,*
> *For I have redeemed you.*
> *I have called you by your name.*
> *You are mine.*[36]

***

During dinner, I sat with John, a retired mechanic from Manchester, who has led Christian meditation groups for twenty years. *I'm glad that you went up for communion,* he told me. *I know that some traditional people would have looked down on it. But I encourage you.*

Communion is very important to me, I told him. *It is God's gift not the Church's. I feel a strong sense of anxiety when I don't know until the end if the gift is for me.*

John: *All the priests know the official ruling. But no one is going to refuse anybody. That's where the priests are right now. We've got to change. Would you refuse anybody? Well, neither could they.*

The Church has got to be more that just a place of adoration. The Church must address people's needs. However, I believe that the Church is being pruned now, and new growth is going to follow.

This week is a good example of the growth. People are talking openly about real issues – abuse, sexuality, emotions. These are real stories, real people. This stuff is important.

In the past, we Catholics have shot ourselves in the foot. Now we are talking with people from other traditions. We need unity with all the

---

[36] Isaiah 43:1-4.

people of God . . . whether Hindu, Buddha or Methodist, we are all interconnected . . . humanity to humanity.

Spirituality is going to eventually dissolve religion. Religion will go away and what will remain will be spirituality. I wasn't exactly sure what he meant.

***

I am sharing the weekend with priests, monks, nuns, and various spiritual directors of the Catholic and Anglican traditions. People have come from as far away as Malta and the Philippine Islands. Everyone has a deep love and compassion for each other. They are devoted to the Church but are open to change.

***

Everyone needs spiritual direction. . . . Salvation is community living with limitations. . . . Pain is an opportunity for growth. . . . Spiritual and psychological maturity is the ability to live with the tensions.
– Retreat leader, Paul Lyons

***

Ma-Maw is ill, and everyone here is aware of it. The sisters are concerned about me. I will never forget their gentle sweetness. To be loved by a nun is a beautiful thing.

During lunch, I received a phone call from Andy. My father had been in touch with him.

I'm sorry, mate. I've got bad news for you. Yer grans passed away. I spoke with Andy for a little while, and then I called Pa-Paw.

Pa-Paw, I've heard the bad news. . . .

Yeah, he said. *When I woke up this morning, she wasn't breathing . . . but now she is breathing a lot better.*

What? I asked.

Ma-Maw was still alive.

***

Ma-Maw was the woman who refused to die.

The previous May, I told the members of my Spring Creek Church that Ma-Maw had died. That's what I had thought when I answered the phone at five that morning. It was a crazy, embarrassing misunderstanding. Someone had died. But it wasn't Ma-Maw.

It wasn't until later in the morning that I realized my mistake.

Ma-Maw had had a terrible stroke a few weeks earlier and so when the phone woke me up, I naturally thought about her. When the voice said, *This is Beverly. Momma passed away in the middle of the night*, I just knew that it was my Aunt Jane, confused (her daughter is Beverly), confirming the inevitable.

Oh, . . . okay, was all I said, and I hung up the phone. I carried on with my Sunday morning plans, not realizing that it was odd that Mom and Dad hadn't called.

When I drove into my driveway before the Calico Rock service (the second church service of the morning), Dwight, one of my parishioners, came up to the car. *I guess you know that Elva has passed away.*

What? Elva is gone? I realized my mistake. Ma-Maw was still alive.

It was Beverly, Elva's daughter, who had called to tell me that her mother had died. *Oh, . . . okay*, was all I had said, and I had hung up on her.

I called Willene, a member of Spring Creek, and told her that my grandmother was not dead after all. *Could you . . . uh . . . spread the word?*

Ma-Maw hung on throughout the summer. I saw her for the last time in August, and I left on my pilgrimage certain that I'd never see her again – and doubtful that I would be at her funeral.

Then, here in England, I received the call from Andy: *I have bad news for you. Yer gran's passed away.* That's when I called Pa-Paw. *Yeah,* he said. *This morning when I woke her she wasn't breathing . . . but now she is breathing.*

Kelvin, Ann and the kids were already on their way to Arkansas from Colorado. Now what? Do we pray for death?

***

Ma-Maw passed away today. The funeral will be on Wednesday.

Kelvin arrived at the house fifteen minutes before Ma-Maw passed away. Mom was at her bedside talking to her sister, Jane, on the phone. Ma-Maw took her last breath and died in peace.

***

(Arkansas: October 8th – 13th)

A sound but broken sleep quickly brought the dawn. I got up, put on a suit that I hadn't worn for several months, and soon left with Mom, Dad and Pa-Paw for the funeral home to view the body. I didn't really want to go, but I knew that I had no choice. Once there, I recognized the funeral director. A couple of years ago I did the infamous *Cows Don't Eat Hotdogs* funeral with him.

***

I was walking around the lobby of the funeral home when a slightly disheveled man with bulging eyes sitting behind a desk seized upon me:

D'ya ever see anything gross?

Well, yeah . . . I guess I have, I replied, missing my chance to flee. *No, I mean something really gross – human beings. They have to be the grossest things on earth,* he began in a unpolished Jack Nicholson accent, referring to his work as an undertaker. *Take what they eat. Hotdogs. Cheese. Beer. That stuff just rots inside people's stomachs. It's a mess to clean up. Have you ever smelled hotdogs and cheese after they've been in someone's stomach for a couple of days? I'm telling you. It's not very pretty.*

But you take cows, for instance. Cows, they don't eat hotdogs. They eat grass. No, grass doesn't rot – not like hotdogs and cheese, anyway. It's far less smelly, trust me. I'd rather embalm a cow than a human any day.

***

Now, he sat in the parlor with the four of us. Ma-Maw was just a few feet away in the coffin.

Did ya know that I'm a part of an international group of undertakers chosen to investigate the Lockerby crash? Well, we've spent hours studying the speed and the angle that those bodies hit the ground. 'Course a lot of the bodies just burned up. I don't think anybody realizes how much fuel was on board that plane. They were just like flaming arrows. . . . There was hardly anything left of a lot of them when they hit the ground. . . . That plane made some hole in the ground.

Fortunately, Pa-Paw couldn't hear; Mom wasn't listening.

Did ya know how easy it is to kill somebody in Arkansas? Anybody could get away with murder here. Well, Dewell, you could have knocked Lillie off, and no one would have ever known.

We drove back to Bethesda. The front yard was full of cars; the house was crowded.

During the funeral, we were ushered down the aisle in pairs. Pa-Paw sat between my aunt and my mother. My little nephew, Nathan, sat beside me, putting his hands on his ears when the choir sang. The service was beautiful and soothing. The pastor said some nice words about Ma-Maw. As a kid, he used to call upon my grandparents' small general store.

The graveside service was brief. Afterwards, I visited with other relatives before driving Mom, Aunt Jane, and Pa-Paw back to the church for dinner. Slowly, people began to leave, gathering outside for a while before going on to their cars. Some of the kids were playing on the old cemetery bridge; others were in the creek playing with a large dead snake.

We spent the afternoon riding around in the back of Pa-Paw's pick-up truck. It was an October hayride, and we went through fields, dirt roads, and ghost towns. We stopped at the old catfish pond, and three generations of kids got out and started skipping stones across the water. As the afternoon passed, cousins began to share stories about their grandparents.

Beverly: *I can remember Pa-Paw helping me with my bug collection. My whole bug collection came from this field. The grass was about waist high, and Pa-Paw drove around the farm while I stood in the back of the pick-up with a net. I got tons of bugs!*

Rodney: *I remember once when we were kids, Pa-Paw had baled this field with small bales of hay, and it had rained an awful lot. Pa-Paw hired Kelvin and me at three cents a bale to run around and push the bales over on their sides so they could dry out. When we were halfway through, Kelvin asked me how many I had pushed over. I told him how many, and he lied, saying that he had pushed over more than I had. Kelvin then began running like crazy, pushing over bales as fast as he could to make sure that his little brother didn't beat him.*

Kimberly: *Daddy, didn't you once spend the night in this old house?*

Uncle Jim: *Yes, I did. I built a fire in the old fireplace. Boy, I froze that night. We were going to fix up the old house at one time.*

Dad: *I was here a couple of months ago to take some lumber away that had been drying in the old house. I noticed a small brown paper bag stuck in the lumber, and it wasn't until I was finished loading the wood that I looked inside and noticed that it was marijuana. I guess the local kids didn't think anyone would find it.*

There were stories about deer hunting. Uncle Jim: *I used to flush the deer out and everybody else got to shoot them.*

And about fishing. The grandchildren: *It would sure be nice to be able to fish here. Too bad Pa-Paw killed all of his fish.* Pa-Paw had once poisoned his fish, because he thought too many people were fishing out of his ponds. It had become a bit of a joke.

Dad: *You wouldn't believe it, but there used to be a couple hundred people living here. Both train and ferry were here then.*

We got out at the cabin. There, the kids threw monkey brains down an old uncapped cistern and fed some horses. The weather was perfect, warm, and life-giving. Cousins and in-laws talked and played, comparing memories and making new ones. And God was there – gently touching each of our lives. Sometimes the best visits are those that are unplanned.

Back at the house, we took family photos out under the large oak tree, and the kids played a game of tag in the yard. I gave each of my nephews quarters, and they began showing me their magic tricks. Both Nathan and Mitchell want to be magicians when they grow up.

I said good-bye to Pa-Paw with a feeling that we would have some good times together when I returned to the States, but I was wrong – he never recovered from Ma-Maw's death.

***

We buried Ma-Maw at Campground Cemetery. Appropriately, the service was held at her church, *Pilgrim's Rest*. It is a name that I have known for years; yet, only now do I notice it. The pilgrim has found her resting place, her *place of resurrection*.[37]

Pilgrim's Rest reminds me that pilgrimage is all around us. We pay tribute to it in thought, song and scripture. Still, pilgrimage is an experience that we are not entirely conscious of. We are all on pilgrimage whether we know it or not. We are travelers along the journey of life, witnesses to the unfolding of God's love, objects of

---

[37] Philip Sheldrake, *Living Between Worlds: Place and Journey in Celtic Spirituality* (London: Darton, Longman and Todd, 1995), p. 55.

connected, though not necessarily sequential, events.

Ma-Maw's pilgrimage of faith was drastically different from my own. A woman of little formal education, raised without a mother, she knew hard work and sacrifice. Our lives and lifestyles were miles apart. She was, though, a woman of faith. Her fundamental orientation in life was toward God, family and the church.

In spite of her education, Ma-Maw was the recipient of a precious gift – she could play the piano. For over sixty years, she played the piano at church. The January before her death, Ma-Maw took me into the living room and played some of her favorite hymns for me. Her aged and withering hands were mysteriously directed to the keys. The notes blended together in perfect four-part harmony. Her health was failing, but her gift was alive and well. I can understand playing melody by ear but not four-part arrangements. *How do you know what to play with your left hand?*

I just do, she said. She didn't understand either.

***

Mom drove me to the airport, giving us some final time alone. We spoke easily and openly about family. Mom was particularly articulate about her faith and about her appreciation of everything that had happened. Although she didn't need to, she thanked me again for coming home.

***

On the flight back to London, I once again saw the movie *Twister*.

Sometimes life is a never-ending, repeating pattern. We walk the same streets, relive the old memories, and if we cross the Atlantic twice within a month – even on two different airlines – we will see the same movie. The same good guys and bad guys, the same terrible romance, and the same cow flying across the screen. I only watched the opening scene in which the little girl loses her father to the tornado, and it reminded me that twice in the past year, people had made a point of saying that their family members had *died* rather than were *lost*. Being lost can be a terrible thing.

We Would Like to See Jesus

My brother and I against my cousin.
My cousin and I against the stranger.
— Palestinian proverb[38]

(Israel: October 29th – November 8th)

I am in the international departure lobby in Athens waiting for my flight to Tel Aviv. The three-hour flight from London was smooth. Once we were over the Alps, the clouds broke, and I could see the majestic, snow-capped peaks below.

During the approach into Athens, I could see some lovely islands, and the sea was beautiful. Mountains were everywhere. I saw the entire city of Athens on my left – the port, thickly packed flats, and the Pantheon. I remembered Mark Twain's account in *The Innocents Abroad* where he slipped one night into Athens from a quarantined ship to see the sights.[39]

Today, I have been surrounded by a warm sense of peace and security, even of excitement and expectation.

So far, my pilgrimage has had less to do with preparation and more to do with opening a new door and simply letting things happen along the way. Along the pilgrimage, everything is constantly moving and changing. One is always encountering something new and different for the first time, and there is very little time to reflect upon expectations of coming events.

The now takes over, and there is less and less regard for the future until that future becomes the now. The sudden surprise of the present moment is sustaining and life-giving. The prior journey itself is the preparation for the next step.

---

[38] Janine di Giovanni, *Against the Stranger: Lives in Occupied Territory* (London: Viking, 1993), p. xiii.
[39] Mark Twain, *The Innocents Abroad, or The New Pilgrims' Progress* (New York: The New American Library, 1966), pp. 244-253.

This is the biggest of all Christian pilgrimages – the Holy Land of Israel – however, I have not prepared myself in any special way. There is a danger in not being adequately prepared for a unique experience; however, the pilgrim trusts in the Holy Spirit to guide, to teach, and to lead along the way. My preparation is learning to see better, learning to ask appropriate questions.

The pilgrim believes that there is a possible spiritual encounter in everything that happens – even if the events seem regretful in and of themselves. Pilgrimage is the practice of learning to be aware of God's presence.

God is both God of the journey and God of the reflection upon the journey. We encounter God first of all through the actual events, but, furthermore, God is present as we meditate on the experience. Revelations and epiphanies are possible at all times, because God is with us in both our outward and our inner journeys.

***

Now there were some Greeks among those who went up to worship at the Feast in Jerusalem. They came to Philip, who was from Bethsaida in Galilee, with a request, 'Sir,' they said, 'we would like to see Jesus.'
                                                                    – John 12:20-21

***

I came with the Greeks to Jerusalem, flying by myself on Olympia Flight 43 from Athens into Tel Aviv. I grabbed a taxi van with nine other people, and squished, we started off for Jerusalem. The man next to me was from Crete. This was his fourth trip to Jerusalem to visit friends. Back home, he and his brother were florists.

I realized that I was flying in to see Jesus. I imagined Jesus and his disciples wandering through the modern city of Jerusalem, stopping at cafés and fighting the traffic. The driver dropped me off near my hostel, and soon, I was settled in for the night.

***

On the first day, I walked aimlessly around the Old City – down steps and through alleys. I passed nice shops, excavations, and memorials. At the outer wall, I sat looking out towards Mount Zion and over the surrounding valleys. Further down the wall, I came to the Dung Gate, where I could see the Dome of the Rock up ahead of me. First, I went to the Wailing Wall and stood watching people for a while, before going to the wall myself to pray. One tourist was covering his head with a Kansas City Chiefs baseball cap.

Later, I sat alone in an isolated corner of the Temple Mount plaza, soaking up the views and reading *A Walk to Jerusalem,* by Gerard Hughes. A security man came over and asked me what I was reading.

***

There is no surer recipe for violence than to keep people in close physical proximity while ensuring that they have little or no communication with each other.[40]

***

I walked over to the entrance of the Dome of the Rock, took off my shoes and went inside. The dome was absolutely beautiful. Simple lines with intricate details. A nice blend of colors and a really big rock in the middle.

Sometimes, this all seems like a big cartoon, like Sunday school comics – Old Jerusalem, the Wailing Wall, the Dome of the Rock. I definitely felt that I was on holy ground as I prayed at the Wailing Wall and walked the Temple Mount. Yet, as the day progressed, I got tired and things began to feel less and less profound. The pilgrimage is as much about the hardships and hard work as it is about the epiphanies and the encounters with God. I still have to find banks and grocery stores and take care of my daily needs.

***

We drove hurriedly in the dark – a van of strangers – arriving to the base of the ancient fortress of Masada shortly before five in the

---

[40] Hughes. *Walk to Jerusalem* (London: Darton. Longman. and Todd. 1991). p. 212.

morning. The moon and stars illuminated the imposing mountain as we began the arduous ascent, but by the time we reached the top, Orion had completely disappeared. Sweating, I was quickly cooled by the wind. I sat upon the edge looking down into the valley. It was light, but the sun was still below the Jordanian hills on the other side.

Separated by two deep gorges, Masada is a natural fortress. During the Jewish Revolt of A.D. 66, Masada was captured by a small group of Zealot Jews, who, along with their families, held out until A.D. 72 when Roman General Silva besieged Masada with an army of ten to fifteen thousand soldiers. When it eventually became clear that the Romans were about to take the fortress, the Jews, led by Elazar ben Yair, took their own lives rather than submit to becoming Romans slaves. Today, Masada is a Jewish symbol of freedom and independence. Recruits to the Israel Defense Forces Armored Unit are sworn in on top of its summit to the cries of *Masada will never fall again.*

As I explored Masada's outer walls, the sun dramatically rose above the hills, and the scenery was breathtaking. I had some French people take my photo. Many of the people became familiar and even friendly as the day wore on.

We drove to the Ein Gedi spa for a dip in the Dead Sea. The water kept me afloat, but the wind and the waves were surprisingly rough, and it was hard to keep the salt water out of my eyes. The Dead Sea was fascinating, but it was certainly more of a dip than a day trip. I cut my foot on a sharp rock on my way out of the water. The next stop was the Ein Gedi nature reserve, an oasis of water, plants and reeds, and gazelles and birds – a delightful walk through unusual scenery leading to a beautiful waterfall.

***

In the evening at Zion Square, as I was watching some Jewish street dancing, I heard a voice behind me, *Sprechen Sie Deutsch?* I turned around and saw a short, middle-aged Israeli man.

Ja, I replied. I speak German. I asked him his name. *Israel,* he replied.

Well, of course, it is, I said. *What else would it be?*

He asked me why I was in Jerusalem. *I would like to see Jesus,* I said. *Hmm,* he nodded, like he'd met my kind before. We went for dessert instead, using our limited knowledge of German to converse about religion, culture, and the world's problems.

***

At the Jaffa Gate, I climbed up the tower and slowly made my way along the old city wall. From the wall, I saw spectacular views of the city and signs of ordinary, every day life – kids at school, boys playing basketball. Stopping above the Damascus Gate, I sat in some shade and ate lunch. It was quiet and relaxing. Below was the busyness of the market. Nearby were a couple of soldiers. I felt like I was in a museum – safe and insulated from the exhibits below.

***

It was Friday afternoon, and I gathered in the courtyard for the weekly Franciscan Stations of the Cross through the streets of Jerusalem. Kids were hawking brochures. I bought one, and I am glad that I did, as I was soon lost in the crowd.

The priests, speaking in four different languages, carried an amplified microphone with them. After the first station in the courtyard, hundreds of pilgrims filed out into the narrow street like cattle down a chute. Stuck towards the end, I reached most of the stations long after the priests had left them.

I had a strange feeling like I was waiting in the hot dog line at the Super Bowl. Something really significant and meaningful was happening, but I was missing the action. It's like I had come to see Jesus, but all I got was a hot dog.

The crowd pressed on in spite of losing contact with the priests. The distant tail of the procession, however, trailed far behind, dangerously close to disconnecting itself. A man lit up a cigarette. Somebody burped. Others were laughing. I reminded myself that Jesus had died for the end of the line. We passed shops and restaurants, tempting the pilgrims with alluring sights and exotic smells. Many would-be followers dropped out.

It's overcrowded, some of the shrines commemorate things that didn't happen in the scriptures, and the Jerusalem of Jesus' day is buried fifteen feet under ground. Hundreds and thousands make this journey every week, but no one was there for Jesus except Simon and the women. Nonetheless, it is Friday in Jerusalem, and we are walking the *Via Delorosa* with the Franciscans. This is sacred stuff.

For many, though, it's a familiar journey, and deep in prayer, they are walking with Christ. They have traveled hundreds of miles at great sacrifice, and now, they are tracing the footsteps not only of Jesus but also of the millions of pilgrims who have preceded them. They are not concerned where in the procession they are; it's a journey best expressed in silence anyway.

Finally, we enter the Church of the Holy Sepulchre for the final stations. Prayers give way to photos.

At the altar . . . Jesus is nailed to the cross (click, click, snap).
Three steps to the left . . . Here he died (click, click, click).
One step back to the right . . . He is taken down from the cross
(snap, snap, click, click).

The last station was the tomb, a small, intimate stone chapel in the middle of the nave. There's a Coptic monk in Jerusalem who can say, *Okay, six more*, in almost a hundred languages. His job is to guard the tomb and make sure that nobody cuts in line. He waved me in. The *X* marks the spot where they laid Jesus' body.

According to tradition, this church sits on the most sacred ground of the Christian faith. Here more than anywhere else Christians have come to see Jesus. Nonetheless, our spiritual journeys do not need to be validated here by a supernatural encounter with Christ as if we need to pass some sort of *Emperor's New Clothes* litmus test.

John tells us that some Greeks at the Passover wanted to see Jesus. The Greeks told this to Philip who told Andrew who told Jesus. But John never tells us if the Greeks ever saw him. Maybe they heard him preach; maybe they witnessed part of the trial. Maybe they were there for the crucifixion. Maybe they never saw him. But that's not necessarily unusual. Strangers go to Jerusalem all the time and never see Jesus. Today is no different.

People here are all trying to see Jesus, and if I'm lucky, maybe I'll actually catch of glimpse of him. But there's a good chance that I won't. I am a stranger to Jerusalem, an outsider to the story. But the power of the resurrection story is what takes place behind the scenes. What we can't see with our eyes, what we can't imagine in our minds, what we can't understand in our hearts is the love of God and the purpose that he has accomplished by sending his Son.

While the Church of the Holy Sepulchre is reportedly the place of his resurrection, it is also the scene of the empty tomb. Jesus' resurrection is confirmed both by presence and absence. It is not in the garden (now the Church of the Holy Sepulchre) but rather on the roads, in houses, by the lakeshore where most people encountered the risen Christ. Likewise for me, the streets, the hills, and the seas speak more of God's presence than the guarded tomb. *Okay, six more.*

Unfortunately, the Church of the Holy Sepulchre, now a multi-level maze of heavy walls, odd chapels, and long, stone hallways, is a poor commentary on the universal Church itself. Initially built in the fourth century, the church has been built, destroyed, rebuilt, added on to, and neglected to achieve its present style – an early twenty-first-century example of a disunified church. Its now dilapidated and decaying walls are a manifestation of the church's factions and divisions that maintain it. Each group (Catholic, Coptic, Armenian, Orthodox – the Evangelical Protestants have opted for a garden outside the city walls) zealously controls their own area while the larger structure is declining due to a strange mixture of apathy, fear and respect. While the Holy Sepulchre is the highlight of many pilgrims' trip to Jerusalem, for me the Holy Sepulchre was a stark reminder of how well the Church models its brokenness to an unbelieving world.

Friday is an important day in Jerusalem – the day Christians remember the crucifixion, the evening Jews begin their Sabbath. In the evening, I went to the Wailing Wall and observed the Jewish families gathering, dressed in black and white, praying at the Wall, beginning their Sabbath.

***

I met Israel for the free city tour of the Old City. This week the tour explored the Jewish Quarter, which was essentially destroyed during the 1948 war. Since then, everything has been rebuilt. One resulting irony is that important archeological finds have been discovered because of the destruction.

Afterwards, Israel invited me for lunch, and we found a restaurant in the Muslim Quarter right across from one of the Stations of the Cross on the *Via Delorosa*. Afterwards, we walked around the outside of the walls to the Jaffa Gate where we had a Turkish coffee in a nearby café before being run out to make room for an incoming group.

Jerusalem has the quality of becoming quickly familiar. It feels like I have been here for a long time. The pictures and images are deeply etched on my mind.

We walked by rows of shops, passed the Holy Sepulchre and ascended the tower of the Lutheran church. After several steps and a couple of rests, we were on top of Jerusalem. We could see in all four directions, and down below, several cats were walking on the rooftops. Back outside, we began walking on the roofs. It was strange knowing that the shops were under my feet. One minute, I'm sitting peacefully in a church. The next, I'm passing through the bustle of the market. Now, I'm walking on the rooftops. Jerusalem is a multi-dimensional maze.

Jerusalem really doesn't have quarters but rather hundreds of self-contained, isolated worlds, each beside the next. I understand what Hughes is referring to when he says that conflict happens when people living in proximity with each other don't communicate.

I had lost control of the day. I didn't know how long I would be with Israel or where we would go next. Moreover, who is Israel? Why is he doing all this for me? Why am I following him so blindly?

It was now dark, but the tour continued, and he began showing me parts of the New City – the massive YMCA, where we had a cup of tea, and the King David Hotel, a luxury hotel where heads of state stay. The Sabbath was now over, and shops were opening up. We then went inside a supermarket, where he grabbed two yogurts, ordered two croissants, and we sat on the bakery barstools eating once again.

***

I attended the English-speaking congregation of Our Redeemer Lutheran Church in the Old City. Today is All Saints Sunday, and as we sang *For All the Saints*, I remembered Cathy, Ma-Maw, and Joe.

> *For all the saints, who from their labors rest,*
> *Who thee by faith before the world confessed,*
> *Thy name, O Jesus, be forever best.*
> *Alleluia, Alleluia!*[41]

All Saints Day is an appropriate time to be in Israel. The pilgrimage to Jerusalem, after all, is not just about *Jesus and me*. Rather, I am placing myself in a holy tradition that includes people of faith from places and languages covering the entire world. Throughout the history of Christendom, pilgrims have sacrificed, struggling to enter these gates.

After church, while walking through St. Stephen's Gate and down a long ramp full of parked cars toward the Mount of Olives, I passed an Arab man who whispered to me without stopping: *Be careful. Some people have had their money stolen.* Where? By whom? The man put me into a panic. Who was he? Friend or foe? Angel or other? I pass a couple of youth hiding behind some cars. Unnerved, I walked on quickly to the Garden of Gethsemane to pray.

I am sitting in a chair with my feet resting on a wall underneath an olive tree on a beautiful, sunny afternoon, writing post cards and journaling. I am on the grounds of a Russian monastery on the Mount of Olives. Before me is the city of Jerusalem.

***

---

[41] William W. How, 1864.

I left the garden and headed up a long walkway in the direction of Mount Zion. There, I found King David's tomb. Five or six Jews were inside wailing, apparently not over his death yet. Nearby, I found an abbey, and I spent a few minutes sitting in its sanctuary. It was warm and comfortable. I have noticed that churches with active congregations have felt alive and holy while the shrine churches have been cold, lifeless, and unpleasant.

In the evening, I attended evensong in St. George's Anglican Church with nine other people and the priest. *Each moment of life is an ultimate act*, the priest told us.

On the way home, I saw two tanks being hauled down the road. They stopped at the traffic light on Jaffa Road in front of the Old City, and then noisily headed out of sight. I realized that there was a world here that I had yet to see. But what occupied me even more were the traffic lights. The green traffic man in Jerusalem is not synchronized with both lanes of traffic. I could only cross half of the road at a time, and I pretended that I was with Jesus and the disciples stranded on the medium.

***

I signed up for an official two-day Israeli tour of Galilee and the Golan Heights. Partly, I wanted some companionship, and I shared the day with my new friends: Abbey (New York), Sharon (Canada) and two attractive young cousins from Virginia and Columbia.

The landscape was spectacular. Outside of Jerusalem, we entered the desert, passing scattered Bedouin communities. As we hit the outskirts of Jericho, we headed north up the Jordan Valley where we saw several kibbutzim lining the valley, including a crocodile farm and olive, banana, and date palm plantations.

We passed Elijah's hometown, the outskirts of the Armageddon Valley, Mount Tabor (the traditional site of the transfiguration) and drove up a winding, nauseating road to Nazareth. On the way, Beni, our tour guide repeatedly stressed two things – the Bedouins are modern people and there is no Jordan River. *You see; they have plastic tents, and see those TV antennas sticking out . . . and over there are some tractors. No, they are well treated and live in the modern world like all of us. . . . We are now entering into the Jordan Valley. You see over there where that line of trees is? You think there's a river there? No, there should be. But there's no water there. There's no Jordan River. It's all a myth.* Water rights are one of the major issues in Middle Eastern relations.

Can anything good come out of Nazareth?[42] Only a few families lived in the Roman-built village in Jesus' time. Now, there are over 100,000 people, and it's impossible to imagine Jesus living here. We visited the main church. A modern sanctuary is built on top of an older one. A cave-like structure, supposedly the first family's house, is the focal point. Mosaics cover the walls.

Leaving Nazareth, we passed Cana of Galilee, the site of Jesus' first miracle, and eventually came to Tiberias. We drove quickly through the city, passing old walls, markets, and shops. Soon, I could see the Sea of Galilee, a peaceful, compelling body of water.

We stopped for lunch at a fish house, billed as a place to get St. Peter's fish. We were ushered in, and, keeping with the group, I ordered the full menu without hesitation – humus, salad, bread, fish and chips, dates and Turkish coffee. It was a scam that we all decided not to participate in again.

In the afternoon, we drove up the seashore, past Magdala (home of Mary of Magdala), and, eventually, stopped in Capernaum to visit the remains of the old synagogue, which beautifully sat on the edge of the water. Here, we can definitively locate the presence of Jesus. He walked these grounds and taught in the former synagogue.

Next to the synagogue is a futuristic-looking church constructed over the supposed sight of Peter's (mother-in-law's) house. Beni polled us to see if anybody liked the church. He claims never to have met a Christian who did.

Apparently, the joke about Jesus telling Peter on the cross that he could see his house is not true unless Peter also had a flat in Jerusalem. One year while I was in high school, a tasteless joke about

---

[42] John 1:46.

Jesus was the rage at church camp:

> Jesus (on the cross): *Peter, Peter, come here.*
> Peter: *What is it, Lord?*
> [repeat with growing intensity]
> Jesus: *Peter, I can see your house from here.*

Sacrilegious but impressionable, it is thoughts, images, and memories like these that naturally seem to surface in our minds when we encounter the sacred. Do we ever experience the Divine with pure hearts? Serving as juxtapositions, the sacrilegious can sometimes help us to put the meaningful into proper perspective.

A mile down the road was the Church of Multiplication, famous for its mosaics of fish and loaves. Passing the Church of the Beatitudes without stopping, we drove on to Safed (Zafet). We had a quick look in a synagogue and then took a stroll through the artists' quarter. While the town was unappealing, the beauty of the surrounding hills was remarkable. I watched the sun drop behind the mountains and turn into a beautiful sunset. We then drove to our hotel just a couple of miles south of the Lebanese border.

***

In the morning, I quickly read through the first half of Luke, aware more than ever of the place names in the Gospel.

Our tour took us to Banias, an old temple of the god Pan and traditionally the place of Peter's confession of Christ. There, Jesus asked his disciples, *Who do you say that I am?* Peter answered. *You are the Messiah, the Son of God.*[43]

We then ascended into the Golan Heights, through former Syrian territory, where we could see bunkers, debris, and damage left from the 1967 war. Beni told us another one of his stories, this time about the eucalyptus trees: *An Israeli spy was in so deep in Syria that he was due to become their prime minister. He told the army that it was important to be protected from the heat, and so they planted non-native, fast growing eucalyptus trees. The trees indicated the Syrian*

---

[43] Matthew 16:13-20, Mark 8:27-29, Luke 9:18-20.

military positions, and the Israelis easily bombed them. This man then committed some sort of suicide that no one can explain. On a regular radio transmission back to Israel, which was generally considered safe under sixty seconds, the man continued to talk for nine minutes – until he was captured. He was never heard from again.

The drive through the Golan Heights was full of stories, images, and scenery – mostly political and military in nature. Along the border with Syria, we saw war monuments, land mine warnings, and oil lines. We stopped on the roadside where a giant map in the shape of a key located Israeli villages and the water sources of the Jordan. Water is the key of life, and the struggle over the Golan Heights is largely one of water.

Below in the valley was a UN base. Just beyond the base was a Syrian village. Behind us on top of a mountain was the Israeli intelligence. Dozens of radar monitor Syria all the way to Damascus and beyond. The Golan Heights are largely a buffer zone, occupied to ensure the security of other parts of Israel – to keep shelling away from the Galilee area.

***

We stopped for a boat ride on the Sea of Galilee. The boat trip was serene and wonderful. Unexpectedly, it became a time of conversation rather than one of meditation. Bud and his wife, both from California, sat near me. They knew that I was a pastor. Bud leaned over, *So what happened here? Tell us some of the stories of Jesus.*

Well, Jesus walked along these shores. He was a preacher, teacher, and healer. Large crowds used to follow him. We know that he often went up into the hills alone to pray. The disciples, the followers of Jesus, were mostly fishermen, who made their living from the sea.

Once Jesus told the disciples to get into their boat and go ahead of him to the other side, while he dismissed the crowd. Afterwards, Jesus went up on the mountainside to pray. When evening came, the boat was a ways from the shore, unable to get back to land because of the wind.

During the night, Jesus went out to them, walking on the water. The disciples were terrified and thought it was a ghost. Jesus told them not to be afraid. And Peter asked if he, too, could walk out of the water. Jesus told him to come. Peter got out of the boat and walked on the water a few steps before becoming afraid because of the wind, and then he began to sink. Jesus reached his hand out to catch him, and they both got into the boat.[44]

Wow! That's fascinating. Bud and his wife said, listening enthusiastically. *There's another similar story.* I continued, telling them the story of Jesus' calming of the storm. Bud and his wife smiled with a look of gratitude and serenity. We talked more about Jesus, relaxing upon the sunny waters and casting our eyes towards the gentle hillside rising in the distance.

The boat dropped us off for lunch. Sharon, from Canada, and I grabbed a falafel, and we sat eating by the lake. She told me about her ex-husband – a divorce lawyer who fell in love with a client and left her – and about her thirty-two-year-old daughter who is divorced and was presently being escorted by a sixty-five-year-old man.

Back in the van, I visited with Jennifer and her cousin. They are both eighteen. One lives in Virginia, the other in Bogotá, Columbia. The subject turned to religion. Jennifer asked, *When you are not brought up with a religious background, how do you know what is what? Where do you get started?*

Peter, Walter and his wife had walked down the street for lunch, and they were twenty-five minutes late returning to the van. Bud was furious. Beni was put out. For the longest time, you could cut the tension with a knife. Beni drove like a madman while reciting a rhetorical monologue of insulting remarks. Walter's wife, falling victim to the attack, was left crippled with guilt for the remainder of the trip.

***

Douglas Dicks, who works for the Middle East Council of Churches, has a rooftop office in East Jerusalem.

---

[44] Matthew 14:22-31.

There are better ways than others to visit the Holy Land, Douglas said. *Often people come to Jerusalem with their own agendas and forget the words of Jesus. They are interested in the 'what' and the 'where' of the Christian holy sights, and they do not want anything to stain the experience. They do not want to know about the poor, the dirty, and the oppressed.*

Our primary focus is to be in solidarity with Palestinian Christians. These indigenous Christians feel forgotten and ignored by Western Christians who come on their tours and leave without making any contact with fellow Christians. We promote what we call 'responsible' or 'alternative' tourism. We seek to make visiting Christians aware of the presence of Palestinian Christians in the area by setting up home stays, cultural exchanges, and educational programs between groups.

There are now more Jerusalem-born Christians living in Sydney than in Jerusalem. Israeli policies are increasingly anti-Christian, and native Christian communities are being squeezed out. Soon, it is feared, there will no longer be a Christian presence in much of the Holy Land.[45]

My conversation with Douglas brought more clarity to the purpose of a pilgrimage to Jerusalem. This week has been one of gathering information, listening to voices, and seeing Israel from different perspectives.

I spent the afternoon in Bethlehem, now a Palestinian village. It is amazing that the birthplace of the king of the Jews is absent of Jews. I walked through the Arab streets and markets to the church where two large sanctuaries stand side by side. Below are caves and grottos, a maze with several side chapels. An *X* marks the spot of Jesus' birth. I had lunch outside, sitting in front of the church, glad that I had chosen to *come and see.*

***

I found my way to Pastor John's house for the mid-week Lutheran

---

[45] See William Dalrymple, *From the Holy Mountain: A Journey Among the Christians of the Middle East* (New York: Henry Holt, 1997), pp. 279-372.

Bible study. A Palestinian lawyer and director of a human rights organization led our discussion. A resident of Bethlehem, she had to sneak through the West Bank checkpoint in order to attend.

We live in a situation of daily human rights violations by the Israeli government. Our primary focus is to document human rights violations in the occupied areas. However, as a human rights worker, I cannot tolerate any human rights violation, no matter who commits it.

Most of our work is with our own Palestinian people. We have two major ongoing projects. First of all, we hold educational training courses for Palestinians. We educate through the media, the Internet, radio and television. We also hold human rights training courses for the Palestinian military.

Secondly, we are working with the Palestinian authorities to build legislation. The Palestinian Authority was established as a military group to oppose Israel. They are not trained in how to govern their own people. We are working to establish a legal code that is based on international standards.

Israel started as an illegal state and legitimized itself through the killings and murders of Arab people. It was established as a religious state. Now Islamic states are increasingly becoming religious states . . . As a Christian woman, I am very afraid of Palestinian legislation, which is clearly based on Islamic code.

I was on scene after the recent shootings at Ramullah. I saw the injured and the massacred. Two hundred and eighty people were treated in two hours. . . . Many of the injured soldiers were children. The children are not afraid of anything; they have nothing to lose.

The Christian community in Palestine is getting smaller and smaller. We must encourage Christians to stay. Christian churches throughout the world should not·encourage the movement of Christians out of Palestine or else Palestine won't have any Christian presence at all. Before 1948, my village was Christian. Now, it is almost all Muslim.

***

The Yad VaShem Holocaust Museum chronicles the history of the holocaust, giving special attention to the residents of the Warsaw and Lodz ghettos. A forty-year-old man stood weeping in the Warsaw Ghetto Sewer Pipe; others were visibly moved by the Children's Memorial, a long, dark hallway of mirrors and lights – each light representing the life of a child killed in the Holocaust. I stopped by the Hall of Remembrance and then walked over to the Valley of the Communities, a maze commemorating every Jewish community in Europe. The library of the Hall of Names has data sheets of over two million recorded deaths.

***

Appropriately, I finished my trip to Jerusalem with a visit to the Garden Tomb. The Garden Tomb, one of two places in Jerusalem that Christians believe to be Calvary, is owned and operated by a London group. It is a beautiful and peaceful setting.

From the tomb, the disciples went out into the world proclaiming a message of hope and resurrection. From the tomb, I also would depart Jerusalem reminded of Jesus' ministry of peace and healing.

The empty tomb destroys an unhealthy view of sacred place. Certain places are perhaps holier than others – yet no place can contain God. God's presence is everywhere yet also always somewhere else. He is always appearing and reappearing, constantly making new places holy.

As the sun set, I could hear singing coming from three different groups in the garden. In the distance, loud speakers were broadcasting Islamic prayers. Throughout the week, I had heard the cries of the Jews, the Christians, and the Muslims. Fear, hope, and grief. Death, ignorance, and mistrust. Religious fervor and abuse. And the words and deeds of Jesus.

I joined a group of Americans from the Missionary Church who was having a communion service in the garden. The pastor told them that this – communion in the garden – would be their finest hour in Israel. A man leading the group in a prayer of confession began weeping. For the second time that day, I had heard a grown man cry.

The old pastor, assisted by a cane, made disparaging remarks against the Muslims, whose prayers we heard in the distance. *They pray the same rote prayer five times a day, but their prayers are ineffective. Their lives are not changed. They do not know Christ who intercedes for us. God hears our prayers, and through Christ, we are saved.*

After the service, I met the president of the denomination, a very likeable guy, who happened to be on the tour. After I told him that I was a Methodist pastor, he began introducing me to everyone, including the old preacher who asked me:

Are you a believer? Are you born again?

Uh, yes, I mumbled unprepared for the assault.

Great, I know you Methodists are trying to get the light back. Well, I've have known of Methodist pastors who were more worried about what robe they were going to wear than they were about preaching Christ.

The president of the denomination stood beside us. I wondered if he realized how offensive his pastor was. Then the old man patted me on the shoulder: *This will change your ministry. Keep preaching the Word.*

The pastor hobbled along with his wife down the dark alley leading out of the garden toward the tour bus, content that once again he had seen Jesus. His many pilgrimages to Jerusalem had only served to confirm his deeply held views. Pilgrimage does not necessarily enlarge one's world. People react differently to the same experiences.

***

God calls us through the facts in which we find ourselves. Every situation is an invitation to arise out of our imprisoning tomb and to walk into freedom. Our problem is our love of the tomb, our preference for the familiar, our fear of freedom and terror at change.[46]

---

[46] Hughes, *Walk to Jerusalem*, p. 119.

***

In the lobby of the hostel, I met Sarah, a black Catholic Jew from Cleveland. She had worked for twenty years as a hospital technician. Her husband was dead; she had a few kids. She told me her story, a story about hearing a call to quit work and to move to Israel: *I wouldn't listen to the voice telling me to come here. Every time I would try to work, I would get hives so bad that I would have to quit. When the hives went away, I would start a new job, and again the hives would return. Finally, I quit working altogether. I arrived a couple of days ago, but I'm not for sure why I'm here.*

Sara spoke about *miracles* and *perfect timing*. She got the shivers as she spoke. Her face was full of rapture. Jerusalem attracts a lot of strangers. Their stories are unique though not uncommon. They all seem to be looking for Jesus.

***

Just before four in the morning, as I was leaving the hostel, I heard noises coming from one of the large trees in the inner courtyard. As I stood on the landing, I saw around three dozen rat-like creatures scurrying down the trunk of the tree and out of sight into the pre-dawn darkness.

I was ready to leave Jerusalem.

At the airport, I waited for my turn to be interrogated. Soon, a young, pimply-face kid waved me forward, and I walked over to a small table and placed my only bag on it. Looking through my eyes to the base of my skull, the young man began rattling off a number of questions: *Name? Purpose of visit? When did you buy your ticket? Where did you stay? What did you do? Did you meet anyone? Did you go into anyone's home? Did anyone give you a package?*

So, let me get this straight, Mr. Aist. You bought your ticket over seven months ago. You say that you are a Christian pilgrim, and yet, you didn't know anybody here, and so you stayed in a hostel by yourself. Mr. Aist, I am aware that there are a number of Christian churches and organizations here in Israel. Are you telling me that during the last seven months you weren't able to make a single Christian contact before your visit, even though you just told me that you came here as a Christian pilgrim? I find that odd, Mr. Aist.

I grinned and nodded, dutifully answering every question. *Yeah,* I kinda admitted. *I know you would have thought. . . .* But before I could finish, the robotic voice cut back in.

Mr. Aist, I am Jewish. I'm sure that within seven months, I could have found a Christian place to stay. He continued, reading his script off the back recesses of my skull. *Thank you, Mr. Aist, for your patience. But are you aware that unknowingly someone may have handed you a bomb and that maybe you're too much of a dimwit to have noticed, and so, I'm asking you these questions for your own protection? . . . Thank you for your understanding, Mr. Aist. Now, if you would stay here for a couple of minutes, one of my colleagues will come over to ask you a few more questions.*

And he left, never once touching my bag, and after standing there scratching myself for a few minutes, a young, fat, pimply-faced girl stood in front of me. Looking through my eyes to the base of my skull, the young woman began rattling off a number of questions: *Name? Purpose of visit? When did you buy your ticket? Where did you stay? What did you do? Did you meet anyone? Did you go into anyone's home? Did anyone give you a package?*

So, let me get this straight, Mr. Aist. You bought your ticket over seven months ago. You say that you are a Christian pilgrim, and yet, you didn't know anybody here, and so you stayed in a hostel by yourself. I find that odd, Mr. Aist.

Yes, I interrupted. *I know you would have thought. . . .* But before I could finish, the robotic voice cut back in.

Mr. Aist, I am Jewish.

Yes, I'm perfectly aware that the whole lot of you are Jewish, I said, beginning to wonder who was listening to whom.

I'm sure that within seven months I could have found a Christian place to stay. She said, never taking a breath.

I grabbed one of her arms, whirled her around, and applied a half nelson, a wrestling move that I learned in boy scouts. I reached my free hand across her face to her far ear, and I began to dig for the mask. I knew that it was the first pimply-face kid dressed up as a pimply-face fat girl. I dug my nails deep into her temple, but the mask was on too tight. The Scooby Doo ending would have to wait.

I stood her back up, and she continued on script, *Thank you, Mr. Aist, for your patience. But are you aware that unknowingly someone may have handed you a bomb and that maybe you're too much of a dimwit to have noticed, and so, I'm asking you these questions for your own protection? Thank you for your understanding, Mr. Aist. Now, you may proceed to check-in.* And, she, too, walked off without ever looking at my luggage.

Listen, Yentil, I screamed, *if you're so worried about a bomb, why don't you check my backpack.* But she was already over in the corner, chewing gum with her buddies.

Oh, the things you think to say once it's too late.

I checked-in, bought some candy with my left-over change, and boarded the plane to Athens.

***

Israel has changed me. I have learned and loved, struggled and worried, prayed and doubted. I felt the hopes and fears of Jerusalem, Nazareth, and Bethlehem.

O little town of Bethlehem how still we wished thee were. . . .

Jerusalem is now a part of me, and I must handle the experience with care. I thought about the tourists that Douglas Dicks described as rushing in and out of Israel thinking about nothing else but their own souls. Perhaps, this is a difference between a pilgrim and a tourist. Tourists miss the world around them – or try to change it to suit their interests. They come with their own agendas, and the pain and fear, the land and its people don't influence them. Rather, the local conditions are only frustrating obstacles to the fulfillment of personal goals.

But who am I to talk? I wasn't in a single Israeli home – nor did I personally meet any Palestinian Christians. Moreover, I know little about the Muslim world. In Jerusalem, I remained fearful of certain areas of the city and cautious in my conversations. My motives for coming to the Holy Land were mixed, but I have experienced Jerusalem slowly and on my own terms, and she is wonderful.

I have prayed alongside God-fearing Christians – people who don't recognize Christ in other Christians let alone Christ in the non-believer. I survived an official Israeli tour and gained a new perspective in doing so. As I leave Israel, I realize that visiting Jerusalem is similar to Loch Ness – a lot of people are going to ask me what I saw.

I now see England out of the airplane window. It feels like home.

Having been up for nearly twenty-two hours, I was tired when I reached the flat where I was staying. I mindlessly flipped on the tube and watched parts of *The Outlaw Josey Wales* before falling asleep.

Always Again for the First Time

(Bossey, Switzerland: November 11th – 18th)

From the train station, I had a thirty-minute walk through serene countryside before entering a long, forested, country lane leading up to the chateau. I walked with eager spirits, enjoying the cool beauty of the wet autumn day, anxious to discover what lay ahead.

Arriving at lunch, I left my backpack with the receptionist, and self-consciously, I entered the dining room, finding an empty chair at a table full of French-speaking Africans, and silently, I ate a hearty meal of sausage and potatoes. I looked around at the room of students, proportionally representing the world's population. Surprised by the number of students of color, I was reminded that Europeans are only a small minority.

***

Reconciliation is not an event; it's a journey. It occurs in steps – sometimes a step forward, sometimes a couple of steps backwards.

Professor Hizkias Assefa, a guest lecturer from the Nairobi (Kenya) Peace Initiative, shared these thoughts with student attending the Ecumenical Institute of the World Council of Churches at Bossey near Geneva, Switzerland. Forty-eight students representing thirty-five different nationalities and several Christian traditions were participating in the four-month seminar, *On Being Agents of God's Peace.*

Are Christians obligated to forgive someone even before the other asks for forgiveness? After several students smugly answered, *yes,* Tanya of the former Yugoslavia spoke up.

Perhaps it's easy to forgive someone when they ask for forgiveness and are truly sorry. But what about those who hurt you and would hurt you again? She asked. *There is a prayer that goes, 'Father, don't forgive them for they know exactly what they do.' During the war, everyone in my family except my father left our house. One night, our house was bombed. Every room was destroyed except one – where my father was. Thank God, he was not hurt. When I heard about it, I cried for many days. I thought, 'I could kill the people who did this,'* she said breaking down into tears. *It's not always easy to forgive someone.*

***

Each time I see Fiji it appears changed
And I feel I view it ever for the first time
How shall I describe Fiji to those who haven't seen it?
It is never seen twice alike
And I know no one way of describing the site
                                                      – Suzuki

***

Life is an ongoing process, Assefa continued. *Nothing is permanent; everything is in change. Therefore, every time we see something, we see it differently. It is new. That is what reconciliation is all about – learning to see one another always again for the first time.*

      ,   ***

Founded in 1946, the Ecumenical Institute is housed in an eighteenth-century mansion approximately fifteen miles from Geneva. The former winepress and tower have been renovated into a prayer chapel, and in the 1960s, a new lecture hall and library facilities were built. From the library, Lake Geneva and the distant Alps are clearly visible. The small campus is situated in the middle of local vineyards and cornfields. It is a quiet, peaceful setting for study and international Christian fellowship. During the day, the students attend lectures and small-group seminars, which are taught in both English and French. They share three meals together and have common prayer in the mornings and evenings.

As part of their course work, students were writing semester papers on issues of peace and violence. Their topics included nuclear testing in the Pacific, militarism in Korea, and domestic violence in the United States. Several students were writing from first-hand experience with war and political oppression.

***

I was assigned a room in Petite Bossey, a large converted farmhouse 200 meters down the road from the main chateau. Rimon, a student from the Gilbert Islands of the South Pacific, lived across the hall.

A small-group seminar was discussing the difficult words of *an eye for an eye* and Jesus' command to love our enemies. A female German Lutheran pastor was the professor. I introduced myself to the students: Ashley (USA), Elvis (Trinidad), Diana (Bulgaria), Battu (Sierra Leone), Dinis (Mozambique), Simphiwe (South Africa), and Osamu (Japan).

An evening prayer service followed in the chapel. We sang, praising God in various languages, and then listened to a short meditation given by a student from the Ivory Coast. At dinner, I sat with people from China, Burma, Indonesia, and South Africa.

***

This week is on conflict resolution: negotiation and mediation. We did an exercise called *The Case of the Last Fifteen Cows*. My debate partner was Simphiwe. In the exercise, it was imperative that we each got ten of the fifteen cows. It was only later that we discovered that one of us was a butcher, and the other one was a tanner. There were more than enough cows for both persons.

***

Osamu . . . jokingly claims that he'll be both the next pope and the next emperor of Japan. He wants to live on an American Indian reservation and sleep with sheep. I told him not to tell too many people. He believes that he is the only Japanese person involved in ecumenical work.

Tanya . . . I walked with her and Stephanie to the shopping center one afternoon. She is very passionate and wants to celebrate life. She is one of many persons here from a war-torn country where peace, justice, and war are personal experiences. Tanya is bright and articulate; she is willing to engage in conversation.

Ashley . . . What do you like best about Bossey? I asked her. *The people – definitely the people. There is such diversity here. And the common prayer – I love singing and worshipping together. But mostly, I like what is going on inside of me.*

Ju-Jin . . . a quiet, sensitive Korean woman. She is very intelligent and is interested in economic and military issues.

Stephanie . . . a German-American from Kansas. She is exact and complete in her work and her studies. She is concerned and always ready to extend a hand of friendship.

Nora . . . a German-Hungarian who hates the food!

Wayne . . . an African-American from Oakland. He is frank and cynical. *Don't stay longer than two weeks,* he told me. *The place loses its charm.* Later, he exclaimed, *I'm tired of looking at the same o' [faces] everyday.* He shared with the class the tension between blacks and Jews in America.

Personalities define communities. Bossey is only what it is now. While the format and structure may remain the same, the community here is short-lived, fluid, and non-permanent. Paths cross, and friendships are made. Some are sustained, but the community itself dissolves. Forty-eight people will soon be departing for thirty-five countries around the globe. When they do, this particular Bossey will be no more.

Life is a journey of permanent change. We are easily deceived, lulled into a lifestyle that fails to recognize this, fails to see the movement, the process, the change. Occasionally, events wake us up, shaking our lives. Perhaps, we can never be adequately prepared for the giant transitions. Yet by deceiving ourselves that life is stable, we neglect our own growth during the stagnant times in our lives.

Growth is change and change hurts. New relationships bring new dreams, new possibilities, and new expectations. Seeds sprout with new growth. But change also shuts doors, and sometimes change causes us to lose hope. Some seeds sprout only to be stomped out. A voice tells us: *This relationship will not be permanent. Your body will not stay healthy. Peace is just an illusion.*

***

I was a bit lost after lunch – everyone just scattered. These are times of temptation – will I choose to relax and center myself through journaling, prayer, or reading, or will I be lonely, discontent, and unsettled? This time, I have chosen the former – sitting outside in the back garden, looking out over the surrounding landscape, drinking coffee, and writing.

In the evening, I watched *Four Weddings and a Funeral* with Ashley and Majirike, two Americans. We sat on a couch, eating Oreo cookies and discussing my relationship with Andi McDowell.

***

Culture shapes the human ears and tongues that hear and answer the voice of Christ. . . . We should look back upon our lives and see how God was present even before we received the Gospel. . . . Gospel is the encounter between the Gospel story and our story. . . . Gospel, the Good News, is what is actually experienced.

– A lecture on Culture and Religion

***

Friends and relationships – a never-ending roller coaster of emotions, fears, and adjustments. The greatest difficulty of my year is the emotion of constantly leaving communities. Both in and out of community, however, I know that God is with me. In my laughter and in my sadness, in times of strength and in times of weaknesses, God is there.

Ashley and Osamu led the evening's prayer service. The thoughts of the past, the emotion of the present, and the hopes and anxieties of the future crowded me. It was meaningful to hear Tanya tell me, *We are going to miss you.*

***

I dreamt that semi-trucks were running the Indianapolis 500.

***

A group of us went into Geneva to attend the English-speaking Lutheran church. After taking communion, I sat back down in the pew, and as we sang, I began to let go of my anxieties. Once more I heard the words: *All is well, all is well, indeed, all manner of things will be well.* I felt the gentleness of God. After church, we had a picnic lunch on Rosseau Island before returning to Bossey. Enveloped by the warmth of a cold winter's rain, I walked alone with everyone. There was no one to return the laugh that was on my mind, so I smiled to myself as the rain fell at my feet.

***

On Monday morning, I worshipped for the last time in the chapel. I was asked to read 1 Peter 2:8-10: *But you are a chosen people, a royal priesthood, a holy nation, a people belonging to God, that you may declare the praises of him who called you out of darkness into his wonderful light. Once you were not a people, but now you are the people of God; once you had not received mercy, but now you have received mercy.*

And then I left. Melancholic but not depressed, I left Bossey and soon arrived in Geneva, where I walked around the city, waiting for my next train. The sky was now full of thick, fluffy white flakes, and I was sad not to be back at Bossey where many of the students were seeing snow for the first time in their lives.

I felt like a bundle of emotions being held by a ball of prayer, held by angels, by life itself. I felt empowered, though saddened by the events – the necessity of the broken connections. I was confident, though, that my sadness wasn't diminishing the meaning of the moment. On the contrary, it was simply another lens through which to understand and to experience the journey.

The constant change of life always creates an opportunity for revelation – if only we had eyes, souls, and hearts to grasp the fleeting yet eternal glimpses of truth that constantly appear in the scattered fragments of life. If we can only absorb the experiences, we can later digest its essence in slower, deliberate increments.

There are changes of season . . . autumn corn mowed down in a field . . . a big snow. And now I am sad, sad to have left my African brothers and sisters, sad not to see their faces, their laughter, and their dancing. It is snowing, and there is a party going on at Bossey.

I went through customs and boarded the train – seat 61, facing towards the back. As we pulled out of the station, I looked at the white flakes, fun and festive, filling the sky. Geneva soon slipped away, and we entered France. I sat reflecting, feeling the week past. A few minutes later, I stood up, turned around, and claimed the opposing seat. My back was now on Bossey, and I sat facing what lay ahead.

Bells of Silence

(Taizé, France: November 18th – 25th)

The Taizé bells rang with expectancy as I arrived on a cold, snowy November night just in time for the evening prayer service. As I entered the dark, candlelit church, my lungs felt the sweet sting of incense; peace and warmth engulfed me.

Another doorway, another world.

The brothers were already present, dressed in white robes and kneeling in prayer. I found a seat on the floor just as the bells stopped, sending a resounding, softening echo through the short, sharp silence that followed.

I took a deep breath and the singing began.

***

Silence. There are ten minutes of silence during each of the three daily prayer services. *It is a rare, precious gift to be with others in silence,* shared Brother Jean-Marie of New York. *In Taizé prayer, we are both with others and alone with God.*

Music. Simple and repetitive – allowing the words to penetrate, little by little, into the depths of one's body and soul.

Music and silence are the fundamental elements of Taizé worship, which attracts thousands of people every year to spend a week in prayer and community life.

In worship, it's important that people are free to receive God. I believe that the strength of Taizé worship is that it allows a person to join in and out of the songs and prayers, as one is comfortable. Moreover, Taizé is neither a style nor a technique. Rather, Taizé prayer is an intention. It is our attempt to pray together with one another.

***

Yesterday, I got off the train, disappointed to discover that the next bus to Taizé didn't leave for another five hours. It was raining heavily, keeping me from venturing away from the station. I had a decision to make – relax, read, and make the most of the next few hours or worry, walk around, and wear myself out.

In normal life, an enforced wait of [five] hours with nothing to do would have so irritated me that I should have wasted the hours in internal grumbling instead of welcoming them as an opportunity to do something different from what I had intended.[47]

I read for the next several hours. Trains came and went. Blowing by without stopping. Shaking the windows and walls of the station. Little boys screamed as the trains raced by.

Another young man caught the bus with me, but I sat by myself, comforted in the warm bus by my thoughts and emotions – anxious and excited for the destination, yet content to be suspended as long as possible in the night ride through rural, wet France.

We eventually came to the village of Taizé, and when the bus stopped, the stranger stepped off with me. We spoke, asking each other where we were to go, and eventually we found the reception. It was warm and cozy inside. A few young men were sitting, talking around a fire.

The stranger on the bus was Paul. A twenty-nine-year-old science teacher from Melbourne, Australia, Paul was on his own around-the-world trip. We were assigned bunks together in the same barrack – assigned to be friends for the week, which we readily accepted. Same bus, same day, same destination. We already had a lot in common.

***

During the war years of the 1940s, Brother Roger, a Swiss Protestant, left his native home and founded a small community of brothers in the sleepy village of Taizé, France. Gradually, other brothers joined

---

[47] Hughes, *Walk to Jerusalem*, p. 119.

him, and now, half a century later, Taizé is synonymous with peace and reconciliation.

Pope John II said of his pilgrimage to Taizé in 1986: *One passes through Taizé as one passes close to a spring of water.* Catholics and Protestants alike share freely in the daily Eucharist. Taizé has become a *parable of communion* and a visible sign of church unity.

                                        ***

Draped, orange banners symbolize the Holy Spirit. Candles, icons, and greenery represent the presence of God.

Incense fills my lungs. I can smell God.

The candles flicker, casting occasional shadows. Jesus said, *I am the light of the world.*[48]

The light shines in the darkness, but the darkness has not overcome it.[49]

The heat of incense and candles rise. I am a prayer to God.

Icons are windows through which we see God. They are passageways, paths for the soul. Jesus said, *I am the way, the truth, and the life.*[50]

I wait in silence. I am a poem waiting to be created. God forms me in the silence of my heart.

The word of God is read. There are Bible studies and discussions, but often one encounters God in silent, non-audible moments.

Here, the Holy Spirit is entrusted to teach, to comfort, and to guide. No one has the last word but God.

People come searching for God. Connections are made with one's

---

[48] John 8:12.
[49] John 1:5.
[50] John 14:6.

self, with others, with God.

Pilgrimage is a journey to community. In the end, we become members of the body of Christ.

***

A brother from India led the Bible study and discussion on the wedding at Cana.[51] The class was made up of people from Spain, Italy, Portugal, Germany, Holland, Belgium, Australia, the USA, Colombia, and Switzerland.

Our common area is Barrack 10, where we take our meals, have Bible study, and keep out of the cold. Optional song practice is also held there everyday after lunch. The majority of the visitors to Taizé are young adults – between eighteen and thirty. Young adults perform chores for the rest of the afternoon. Adults over thirty have the option of using the time for prayer and retreat.

***

Today is awfully cold. Wind, rain, and sleet are taking turns. The day is unrelenting, dark and gray, opening up very little possibility to explore, to relax. I feel tight, shivering, and cautious.

***

My friends and acquaintances include Paul (Australia), Ursula and Simone (Switzerland), Jane (Houston), Emily (Ohio), Hellena (Sweden), John and Petra (Holland), Sabina and Gertrude (Germany), Maria (Portugal), and Karine (France)

***

Today's Bible Study and discussion were on forgiveness: The Prodigal Son.[52]

***

---

[51] John 2:1-11.
[52] Luke 15.

I walked down to the lake in the afternoon. It is in an area of silence reserved for adults over thirty. There is a small, orthodox chapel, but mostly it is the surrounding nature that speaks of God. The moon is up, looking big and round. It is almost full. The sun is going down. Soon, I will go back up the hill.

I thought about my transition from Bossey to Taizé. Leaving Bossey, there was a resigned sadness coupled with the understanding that something else lay ahead. Once the transition was made, the sadness soon left. I was now in a different world, focused on entirely new relationships and experiences.

***

The bells ring in expectation. But even then the bells are silent, waiting for the presence of the Divine, the Awaited One.

The songs repeat, growing stronger and then weaker, harmonies merge and blend, a female voice ascends to the top, rising above the melody. Brothers in white robes, icons of Christ, the scent of incense and candles, and people in need of peace.

We are the brothers' guests, and we watch as the brothers lead us to God through their witness, their lives, and their prayers. We watch as if looking into a fish bowl. We want to swim in the waters of life; we want the freedom of movement, the school of community. The current looks exciting. The water is always moving, never the same. Yet, it is also constant and predictable. Inside, we meet a God who is both familiar and new.

***

The showers or the hot cocoa we are served for breakfast? We are unsure which is colder. There are mice in our room.

***

Back home. Down in Africa. Down Under. In Japan.
Words we use to refer to home.

***

We woke up this morning to a beautiful covering of snow; the sky was clear, blue and sunny. The wind was still; it felt warm. After morning prayers, I walked through the village, taking photos of snow-covered buildings and landscapes before going to breakfast.

Today's Bible lesson was on Christ's suffering and being with people in their suffering. John, a thirty-two-year-old Dutch doctor who works in a nursing home, has come to Taizé several times. He talked about *going to the cross* with his patients' names after they die. We asked each other, *What is resurrection? What does it look like?*

John: *I come to Taizé because I need time for reflection and inspiration. It's a place for renewal. For me, the church is a meeting place for people to talk about their faith. From other people, I gain wisdom, and my faith is strengthened. I see and feel the connections. Sometimes, the fruits of these experiences take a while to grow – now is always just the beginning. The fruits come later. I am still learning from a year I spent eight years ago in a leprosy colony in India.*

***

It is wonderful to watch people deep in prayer. All around me people are seeking God.

Emily, a Catholic from Ohio, is engaged, but she was at Taizé by herself. *Taizé has grounded me in God. I am at a time of transitions… getting married, a new job, having to move. I ask myself, 'Is this the person for me?' 'What do I want to do with my life?' and a hundred other questions. Often, I think too much. But I am reminded that God is in control. I won't leave Taizé with many answers, but I feel that I have the faith resources to face whatever the future brings.*

***

While Taizé has become a pilgrimage place for Christians, Taizé also attracts a number of non-professing, first-time seekers. Taco, from Holland, comes from a secular background. *For me, Taizé is a place where I can find peace and discover God for myself.* Taco was beginning a week in silence, further exploring his new faith in God.

***

Follow the way. Seek the light. Don't listen to the darkness. Our greatest darkness is like day to God. Do not be afraid. The Lord is near.

Smiles to the French. Love and laughter. Leprosy and spirituality.

***

How do I pray? With what do I fill myself? What thoughts and prayers should be in my head? Do I formulate words or simply feel a presence? I seek peace for myself, but how do I pray for others? Am I available to receive messages and gifts from God? Am I any more self-giving, more loving as a result of prayer?

***

The Bible study this morning was on the life of love – taking Taizé with us. People aren't afraid of leaving Taizé, because they take the songs, the silence, and their new selves with them. They leave with God.

In the life of community, one does not notice time slipping away. But there is precious, little time left. Soon, the week will be over.

***

A large snow – big and fluffy – fell in the early afternoon. It was the perfect kind for making snowballs, and almost immediately, an international snowball fight broke out.

Everyone was gathered at the café in the late afternoon, drinking coffee and taking photos. Then, six of us slipped over to the village church. A couple of candles flickered on the altar. Spontaneous and spirit-filled, we began singing – until we stopped, standing in the darkness, holding hands in complete and voluntary silence.

***

Friday evening, we prayed around the cross – kneeling, touching the wood, remembering the death of Jesus. The Saturday evening candlelight service was brilliant – joyful prayers, beautiful singing and the light of God.

Much of the theology and music of Taizé centers on the images of light and darkness: *Do not let my doubts and darkness speak to me. . . Within our darkness night, you kindle the fire that never dies away. . . Our darkness is never darkness in your sight, the deepest night is clear as the daylight. . . .*

Afterward the candlelight service, nearly sixty people gathered in the brothers' dining room for a time of sharing with Brother Roger. The room was dark but warm; candles were lit on the table.

Someone asked him, *From where does the source of hope come?*

Perhaps his answer was simple; perhaps it was profound. I found Brother Roger and Taizé to be both: *The source of hope is placed into each of our hearts by the Holy Spirit.*

***

We celebrated the Sunday Eucharist this morning. People came together from countries, languages, and traditions from all over the world.

The good-byes have come quickly – Sabine, Jane, Petra, John, Emily and then Karine. Fittingly, Paul and I are the only ones left.

In the afternoon, I went on a beautiful walk, down country lanes adjacent to winter fields. The sun was golden, warm and invigorating.

***

Having said good-bye to all of my friends, I was ready to be by myself for my final day at Taizé until I started meeting the new people who began to arrive.[53] Winnie, born in Hong Kong, has just flown over here from Toronto. Jezebel, from Belgium, and Pasquel, from France, both study in Saarbrucken, Germany.

At Bible study on Monday, I met Gaia, an Italian with deep, dark eyes. *You're from America!* She exclaimed when she met me. She is studying Indian languages at university in Venice.

I went to mid-day prayer, had lunch, and then washed up dishes with Gaia and Winnie. After song practice, I went to read and journal. In the evening, I packed and headed to Barrack 10. There, I spoke with Jezebel in German about religious signs– at least, I think we did – and then I began to say good-bye to my new friends.

Gaia and Winnie insisted upon walking me to the bus stop. I had only met them that morning, but it felt like we had known each other for ages. Eventually, the bus came, and I got on.

I said good-bye to Taizé and to new and old friends. Strangely, I was not sad. Rather, I felt surrounded, warmed by peace and love. I left in the cover of the night, slipping away just as I had slipped in exactly the week before.

***

Lourdes was never more than a word to me, so I had no idea what to expect. My first impression was the beauty of its surroundings – a small town nestled in the foothills of the Pyrenees. Early on a November morning, the town was empty.

I walked to the church and then to the grotto – a small cave beside a beautiful river. A small spring. Water taps. The Virgin Mary. Thick, smoky candles. The church is built high on the bluff, on top of the grotto, overlooking the river.

The Stations of the Cross ascend up a steep hill, hardly accessible to the handicapped. A sign reads: *Approach only on your knees.* I thought this was slightly absurd in a place like Lourdes that attracts

---

[53] It is recommended to arrive and leave Taizé on a Sunday. I arrived and left on a Monday, giving me one day with a new group of people.

thousands of wheelchair-bound people. The stations have larger-than-life gold figures. A soldier welding a large axe is in every scene. He annoyed me. Higher and higher the stations climb. Christ is whipped, stripped, and crucified.

In the visitors' center, I watched a video on the history of Lourdes and the life of Bernadette, the fourteen-year-old girl who saw the Virgin Mary over a span of two weeks in 1858. For a century and a half, pilgrims from all over the world have crowded to Lourdes seeking healing and spiritual peace. Photos showed the hoards of summer pilgrims, and I confessed to myself as I got on a train heading towards Spain that I was glad that I had come in the winter. Leaving Lourdes, I briefly reflected upon the injustice of casually visiting a sacred place that is the life-long destination of somebody else.

Spanish Steps

(Spain: November 26th – December 5th)

James, the son of Zebedee and a disciple to Christ, was a leader in the Jerusalem church. Tradition suggests that he had a brief missionary journey to Spain, before becoming the first disciple to be martyred (Acts 12:2-3), decapitated by Herod between the years A.D. 41 and 44.

According to legend, a group of disciples gathered up his remains and took them to the coast where an unmanned ship lay waiting. There, they placed the apostle's body in a marble sepulcher, laid him in the boat, and an angel guided the ship across the seas to the distant land of Spain.

The apostle's body remained undiscovered until the ninth century when a supernatural light appeared in a field (Compostela means *star of the field*), revealing James' burial place to the hermit Pelayo. In turn, Bishop Theodomir identified the tomb as that of the apostle. A church was soon built, and the pilgrimage to Santiago de Compostela was launched.

St. James has two very distinct images. First of all, he is *Santiago Peregrino*, the gentle and devout pilgrim. His second role, however, is quite different. During the tenth and eleventh centuries, the Islamic Moors controlled most of Spain and threatened to overtake Western Europe. Christianity was at a crucial point in its history. The image of St. James as *Santiago Matamoros* – St. James the Moorslayer – developed, playing a major role in the Reconquest of Spain. This James is depicted on a white horse with a sword in hand, leading his armies into battle.

In the twelfth century, a French priest, Amerique Picaud, wrote five volumes of a travel guide to Santiago, which included miracle stories and practical information for pilgrims. By this time, churches, abbeys, hostels, and hospitals had been built along the way to give care to the pilgrims. Of the thousands who started the journey trusting in the protection of St. James, hundreds perished, killed by man and beast, overcome by disease and climate, or drowned crossing rivers and seas.

While the pilgrimage to Santiago has been continuous for over a thousand years, as is true with other pilgrimage sites around the world, Santiago has become increasingly popular over the last generation. Perhaps more than any other Christian pilgrimage, Santiago provides the modern pilgrim with a sacred journey as well as a holy destination. Hundreds of miles of the *Camino de Santiago*, the Road to Santiago, remain open for pilgrims traveling on foot, bike, and horseback.

Today, yellow arrows and scallop shells mark the route. Modern pilgrims receive a *credential,* a passport of sorts, which is stamped along the way verifying the pilgrim status of its holder. The passports allow admittance to *refugios* – hostels offering free overnight accommodations. Pilgrims who walk, bike, or horseback ride the last one hundred kilometers (sixty miles) – officially for spiritual or religious reasons – may present their passport to the cathedral for a *Compostela,* a special pilgrim certificate.

***

Jos, a Dutch friend, lives with his Spanish wife, Mercedes, in Burgos, one of the major Spanish cities along the *French Way* of the *Camino de Santiago*. I had hoped to spend a week visiting Jos and walking a few days on the *Camino.*

Unlike my previous weeks at Bossey and Taizé, I was mostly alone in Spain, left to my own thoughts and emotions. It was a week of reflection rather than conversation, an individual rather than a communal journey. In the end, my pilgrimage to Santiago was incomplete. But rather than leaving disappointed, I left determined to go back. Santiago, more than any other place I would visit, would beckon me to return.

After a slow train ride through some beautiful Spanish mountains, I finally arrived in Burgos where Jos was waiting for me at the station. We stopped by the Burgos *refugio* and were told that over 5,000 pilgrims had come through Burgos the summer before. Burgos is located about one-third of the way between France and Santiago, approximately 300 miles from Santiago.

My first full day in Burgos, the home of legendary El Cid, an eleventh-century Spanish hero, was spent exploring the city. Scaffolding hid most of the supposedly beautiful Burgos Cathedral. A picturesque river runs through the center of town. From the top of an old fortress, I could see the vast plains that surround Burgos.

I began exploring the *Camino*, following it through Burgos. After just 400 meters, I had already gone the wrong way. It's difficult to always stay on the path. Even when you know where you want to go, it's easy to get lost. I wound my way back, found the *Camino* again, and followed it to the river.

To see the yellow arrows – and the shells – marking the route and to know that I'm on the Road to Santiago was exhilarating. Seldom on my pilgrimage did I have the emotion of arrival, but the first time that I realized that I was on the *Camino,* I sensed a special energy, and I perceived the irony – I had arrived to a journey.

That night, around Jos' dinner table, I was confronted with the reality that I wouldn't be able to walk any of the *Camino* to Santiago. The weather was bad; I was poorly equipped, and the logistics were inconvenient. One of the lessons along the pilgrimage is that now is not always the right time. Some things must wait; other things will never be.

But what are the lessons?

God is in the facts.[54] His presence is found in what you do, in what happens – not in what you didn't do or what could have been.

God is in the facts. His presence is found in reality not in regret. Sometimes the time isn't right. My plans were put on hold, but strangely, I was content. I was not disappointed but rather expectant of the future. I was surprised that I felt such peace.

Contentment is a gift.

---

[54] This phrase comes from Hughes, *In Search of a Way.*

Bettina Selby, in her book, *Pilgrim's Road*, describes a middle-aged Belgium woman named Sophie, who lives with the dream of making the walk to Santiago. This was Sophie's second attempt; she suffers from bronchitis. No one in her family expected her to make it to Santiago.

Selby writes: *I thought Sophie too would probably never quite achieve her goal, but that the urge to walk to Santiago would always be there, adding something special to her life, something big to look forward to, to plan for, to set out towards year after year. As many have discovered, it is not the arrival that matters, but the journey itself.* [55]

***

My second full day in Burgos was Thanksgiving in America, and I spent the day walking through the countryside. I followed a wooded path adjacent to the river, and within an hour, I came to a monastery. Unfortunately, it was closed, due not to open for another hour. I left, walking back down the lane, when, about two hundred meters away, I turned back around and saw that the monastery gate had been opened by a monk who was now standing beside it.

I walked back up the lane and spent about twenty minutes sitting in the choir of the church. Sometimes, we turn our backs on something only to be surprised. We are delighted when our disappointment disappears. I was pleased to have seen the church.

Four kilometers later, I came to a small, desolate village. A lot of construction was going on, replacing drabness with drabness. From there, I set off up an inclining road, and soon I saw the large monastery of San Pedro to my left, nestled below in a valley, a kilometer off the road. I walked down the lane through the beautiful monastic grounds to the church where I sat in silence for half an hour before venturing back out. Surprisingly, there was a pub on the grounds, and I went inside to try to order something. The man behind the counter said something in Spanish a couple of times, and then he disappeared into the kitchen. I think he said that he wasn't open yet,

---

[55] Bettina Selby, *Pilgrim's Road: A Journey to Santiago de Compostela* (London: Abacus, 1995), p. 77.

and so I slipped out when he wasn't looking, wondering as I walked back up the lane, if I had, in fact, ordered anything.

I began retracing the journey back to Burgos. Now and then, the sun came out, but otherwise, it was cloudy and breezy. The openness of the Spanish countryside is almost eerie. It is vast and rolling, stretching into the distance. Unpopulated.

Early on, I noticed that my shoes weren't very comfortable. Later, I was to discover four nice-sized blisters. The pain reminded me of the obstacles, the time commitment, and the single-mindedness that pilgrimage requires.

I stopped in the village of drabness to warm up with a cup of coffee, which I drank while sitting in the corner of the bar watching television. In the news, a gunman from a nearby village had apparently killed a couple of people in Burgos and then turned the gun on himself. The news flashed scenes of a Spanish man and a couple of women in the small village grieving in anguish. Whatever their world, whatever their faith, it has just been brutally shaken. Grief is a common denominator.

The remaining walk back into Burgos was very pleasant. It was now sunny. My feet ached some, but I still had enough energy to explore. Suddenly, though, I began to feel uneasy. I had taken a lot of photos during the day, but I couldn't remember the last time that I had changed film. The counter on my camera was broken, so I never knew how many exposures I had left. My suspicion proved correct – I didn't have any film in my camera! I quickly tried to figure out when I had taken out the last roll. How many other days of film had I lost? Since I was mailing my film home, I wouldn't know for another six months. I was surprised that I wasn't more upset, and I realized that even photos aren't mine to possess. Photos are extremely important; photos aren't important at all. Life is a constant journey of losing things along the way. However, the day was sunny, and I rebounded. I loaded my camera, and I started taking a few more pictures of Burgos.

Back in my cold room, I had one of my most thankful Thanksgiving meals ever – my usual backpacker's meal of bread, cheese, chocolate, and yogurt.

***

The next evening, Jos picked me up from my hotel, and we went over to his house for dinner. He told me about the murders in Burgos that I had seen reported in the news: A man, fifty-five, unemployed for fifteen years, wanting a relationship with a twenty-two-year-old woman, went to her flat where he killed the woman's mother and her two brothers. He then went to their village and killed her grandmother and an aunt before turning the gun on himself. The young woman and her father were the only survivors. The man had actually withdrawn money that morning from Jos' wife, Mercedes, who works for a Burgos bank.

***

I walked through a light mist from my hotel to the train station where I caught a train heading towards Santiago. A couple of hours into the trip, just outside of Astorga, the train broke down. We sat motionless for three hours. The weather was gorgeous, sunny, and warm. It was not a bad place to break down, but it kept me from seeing other parts of Spain in the daylight. Moreover, I would be arriving late into Santiago.

They eventually brought in another engine, and we finally started moving. The ensuing landscape, the Montes de Leon, was beautiful, but soon it was all lost in the darkness. Eventually, around eleven, we pulled into Santiago. It's a long trip to Santiago, even by train.

I had mixed thoughts as I arrived unceremoniously into one of Christianity's most famous pilgrimage cities. It was late. I couldn't speak Spanish, and I needed accommodations. I ascended a large set of stairs leading out of the station to the city streets above. There, a short, middle-aged woman was soliciting. *Pensión? Pensión?* I was wary, but I hovered near her enough that she noticed me. *Pensión?*

Sí, I said, and I began following the woman.

We walked towards the center of the town, trying to communicate along the way. I could tell her that I had come from Burgos. She mentioned the murders. We passed the Galician parliament building and then turned down a side street. Up in her apartment, I was given a large room with two beds where I soon jumped into one for a long, wonderful night's sleep. My guardian angel, maybe St. James, was looking after me. I liked Santiago already.

***

Appropriately, my first morning in Santiago was a Sunday. I set off for the cathedral to attend Mass, coming into the city by way of the *Camino*. The cathedral was very chaotic; people were scurrying around, coming in late. Finally, halfway through the service, everyone began to settle in. After communion, two men brought out the *botafumerio,* a special tradition of the Cathedral of Santiago dating back to the ninth century. The *botafumerio* is an overgrown incense burner, three feet in height and weighing over one hundred pounds, which is suspended from the ceiling by a gigantic pulley. Once lit, it is swung back and forth from one end of the transept to the other while thick, smoky fumes trail behind. It takes two men just to carry the *botafumerio,* four strong men to control the rope. The remarkable tradition, a symbol of spiritual purification, got started in a most practical way – to air out the cathedral from the stench of smelly pilgrims.

After Mass, I went down into the crypt to see the silver casket, which holds the remains of St. James, and then I climbed up the narrow steps behind the altar to embrace the thirteenth-century statue of St. James. The architectural gem of the cathedral is the *Portico de la Gloria*, the original western façade of the Romanesque cathedral, carved in 1188 by Master Mateo. The whole company of the heavenly host is assembled in the work – Christ, St. James, the apostles and the prophets. Near the base of the central pillar, deep grooves have been worn into the work as pilgrims for hundreds of years have placed their hands on the stone in a prayer of thankfulness for safe arrival.

Back outside, I began exploring the streets of Santiago as the sound of bagpipes, native to the local region of Galicia, filled the air. I ate lunch over-looking the cathedral as scarf-clad soccer fans began to appear, waving pennants, their voices echoing through the narrow pedestrian streets. It was game day. My homage to St. James complete for the day, I began a new pilgrimage, joining the thousands making their way to the soccer stadium. At the game, I tried asking the man beside me how good the Compostela team was. I thought he said that they were usually pretty good but that they just weren't playing very well that day. I later found out that they were in last place – they were actually lousy all of the time and lost 2 - 0 to Real Betis. As long as Compostela continued to wear their light blue uniforms, I didn't exactly see them inciting fear in any of their opponents.

After the game, I explored a large, modern mall, noticing Andi McDowell's photo on the cover of two Spanish magazines. It was comforting to see a familiar face. On my way back home, I bought some cheese, bread, and yogurt at a storefront bakery. *No hablo español*, I told the woman working behind the counter. She grabbed her throat, smiled and whispered, *No hablo español*. She had laryngitis.

***

The luggage lockers in the Santiago train station have directions in several different languages, including both English and American!

English

Deposit:
Put your luggage in
Push the door and keep it closed

Removal:
Type your code

American

To Use:
Find open door
Put in luggage
Close and hold door

To Remove:
Type access code indicated on ticket

I wondered what that was all about.

***

I woke up in Madrid after taking the night train from Santiago, and an hour later, I emerged from the subway for thirty minutes of sightseeing in the Spanish capital before catching a train to Barcelona – in order to catch another train to Italy. The trip through Spain was beautiful. We passed desert mountains, castles, churches, and several poor and desolate villages.

Once in Barcelona, I took the subway to the city center. The medieval streets were lined with Christmas lights, and a warm breeze blew in from the sea. I stepped into the Basilica by the Sea and then walked among medieval buildings and old city streets to the main cathedral. Inside, a warm advent excitement permeated the air. A small, private wedding was taking place in a chapel. I went out into the cloister, a tropical garden full of palm trees and large plants. Afterwards, I ducked into a bar across from the train station and ordered some chicken and chips, using up the last of my Spanish money. When I was finished, I crossed the street and walked right onto the train.

An alarm went off in a bag on the luggage rack above me. An eccentric, though attractive, Italian woman suddenly appeared, grabbed her bag, reached inside and turned off the alarm clock. She then sat down beside me, looked at me with a wide smile and dark eyes and asked, *Spanish or English?*

I speak English.

Hi, I'm Lucia. She was thirty and also from Padua, where I was going to visit Gaia and her family for the weekend. Lucia was getting a master's degree in art history from Bologna and has a grant to study religious art in Spain.

She is single and lives at home with her parents. She had been in Barcelona for two weeks. *I'm lonely. I'm ready to go back to Italy.* We spoke a while about loneliness.

Lucia felt alone, on the fringe, as if she did not belong. *Back home, all of my friends are married, and now they are having kids. That's not what I want for my life. My interests are different; I don't fit in. So far, I am a disappointment to my family.* She paused and then looked me in the eyes, *If I had lived 400 years ago, they would have burned me.*

Umm, I muttered, moving back a bit.

After some silence, I told her about my travels. She called me courageous, although it struck me that we had a lot in common. She gave me a postcard of a seagull. On the back, she wrote her address. I asked her about the card. *Well, I bought the card because the seagull reminded me of someone, but I choose not to give it to him. Now, you remind me of the seagull. I want you to have it.*

I showed her Gaia's address. *She's twenty-two, isn't she?* Lucia said, correctly guessing Gaia's age from her handwriting.

That's right, I said. *Maybe, she is a witch,* I thought.

We continued to talk until we were ready to go to sleep. Throughout the night, Lucia would wake up, look deeply into my eyes and smile.

The next morning, the couple across from us got off at Tortino. Lucia slipped across to the other seat, and we sat in silence for the remainder of the trip. It made me sad. It was like we were all talked out – or that we had shared too much the night before. Columbian author Gabriel García Márquez writes in *Strange Pilgrims*: *I realized that like old married couples, people who sit next to each other on airplanes do not say good morning to each other when they wake up.*[56] I guess that holds true for people on trains as well.

---

[56] Gabriel García Márquez, *Strange Pilgrims* (London: Knopf, 1993), p. 61.

The House with a Mother's Heart

(Italy: December 5th – 18th)

Immediately upon arrival into Milan, I began to feel the symptoms of a cold, which got worse throughout the day. I wore myself out exploring the city and was doubly disappointed that the church housing *The Last Supper* was closed both times I dropped by. Long before I caught an evening train for Padua, I felt miserable.

Gaia, whom I had met ten days earlier at Taizé, met me at the train station, and she drove me to her house where I met her parents Mara and Paulo and her brother Francisco. Francisco was busy preparing my first home-cooked Italian meal. My cold ran its course, which meant that I had it for most of the next two weeks. Mara, mothering me as she could, gave me a bottle of nose drops with a handwritten label on it: *31 Herbs*. Whatever was in it certainly cleared my sinuses.

***

Gaia had lectures on Friday, and so, along with her mother, we took the train to Venice. After a quick coffee together in a sidewalk café, Gaia ran off to class, and Mara briskly escorted me, arm in arm, through the streets of Venice, crossing bridges and canals. We arrived in the Plaza of San Marco, which in the early morning hours was empty but for a group of Japanese tourists.

I have visions about my past lives, Mara said, clutching my arm tightly as we maneuvered our way back through the narrow streets. *Once, I was a monk. Some of these same qualities – the pursuit of the spiritual life, for example – are very strong in who I am now.* We crossed a bridge, stopping to take photos. *But I was also an alcoholic, which ended up destroying my life. I died in an alcohol-related fire that I started in the chapter house.*

We took some more photos, visited an art exhibit, and then woke up Mara's sister, who lives upstairs in a quaint Venetian flat in the midst of a maze of pedestrian alleys, for our second cup of morning coffee. I savored the caffeine, unsure of who or where I was.

***

On Saturday, Gaia escorted me through the streets of Padua, the home of St. Anthony, a Franciscan monk born in Lisbon in 1195, who is now the patron saint of lost articles. In a downtown cafeteria, Gaia and I talked about the moments in our lives when we had seen *glimpses of God. I want to spend my life pursuing God,* she told me over a bowl of minestrone. We then continued walking around Padua, content until Gaia realized that she was missing a glove, and we searched in vain, unsuccessfully invoking the help of St. Anthony.

***

Early on Monday morning, I said good-bye to Gaia as my train rolled slowly out of the station. I was on my way to Naples, with a short stop planned in Florence. I once took a graduate class on the history of Florence. We studied the plague, *The Prince,* Dante, commerce and trade, arts and science, and politics. Now, in four hours, I was attempting to cover the semester.

However, as I started down the first street, I saw a familiar person walking past on the other side – a woman with short hair wearing a red jacket. It was Jane from Taizé, an American in Florence! We stumbled down streets, catching up on the past couple of weeks, as I tried to take in the sights around me.

Jane was tired of traveling. The day before, she had changed her flight and would soon be returning to Houston. *I cried myself to sleep last night. I was cold. I haven't been eating very well.*

Travel is a sponge, an opportunity to experience new worlds and to absorb new thoughts and ideas. But, travel is also an opportunity to reflect upon one's life – to see the old from a different perspective. At the end of the day, change needs a context in which to grow. New dreams and new directions cannot sprout until they find a home, a foundation. Now is Jane's time to reenter. Mine will come soon enough. Eventually, we all need to return home. After lunch in a small restaurant on the Ufizzi Plaza, Jane escorted me through the San Lorenzo market to the station, and I boarded the train for Naples.

***

Bob Bronkema, the chaplain of Casa Materna, drove me through the crowded streets of Naples before we entered the gates of Casa Materna. *We have just entered paradise,* Bob said, alluding to the fact that life on the streets is hell for many of the kids. While most of Casa Materna's children are not orphans in the traditional sense, all of the resident children come from very difficult family situations.

***

Buy some matches, signore?

Riccardo Santi, a Methodist pastor, looked down at the two poor children selling matches. Angelo was six; Rosetta was four. Their father had recently died; their mother worked long hours as a house servant.

Riccardo seemed to hear the voice of God as clear as the children's cry: *These children belong to me. Take them and love them. I will bless you.*

Riccardo grabbed their small, dirty hands and took the two children home where his wife, Ersilia, was preparing tea. The day was June 12, 1905, and Riccardo was celebrating his thirty-fourth birthday. As Ersilia made room for two hungry guests, Casa Materna – *the house with a mother's heart* – was born.

Riccardo and Ersilia soon found many more unwanted children who lacked decent food and shelter living in the streets of Naples. As their crowded home grew, their needs were always answered through the generous help of others.

In 1920, thanks to the support of the Methodist Church, Casa Materna moved into a seven-acre villa on the coast, which still serves as their home. Incised on stone above the façade of the old villa are the words of Jesus: *Lasciate i fanciulli venire a me* (Let the children come to me). Riccardo often described his own compassion: *When I see a child suffer, I do not ask who that child is. I become that child.* Today, Casa Materna is home to over forty children. Another two hundred children come through its gates to attend the primary school.

***

On my first morning, I went with Bob to the auditorium for chapel. Afterwards, several boys dragged me upstairs to their room where there was a map and a chalkboard. I showed them the United States, and using the chalkboard, I drew several of my interests: the Kansas City Chiefs, the Ozarks, camping, and canoeing.

It reminded me of the time when I visited a foreign language school in Minsk, Belarus (former USSR). Igor, my host, took me up to the third floor to show me his English classroom. There, written on the chalkboard were the words: *There was an old lady who swallowed a fly.* I thought then that perhaps we were taking the Soviet Union a little too seriously.

During my visit, I participated in the day-to-day life of the home, attending some classes and taking my meals with the children. Each of the three meals begins with the Casa Materna prayer:

> *Padre Santo, Padre Buono,*
> Holy Father, Good Father,
> *Questo cibo e il tuo dono.*
> This food is your gift.
> *Danne anche ai poverelli,*
> Give it also to the poor ones,
> *Perche siamo tutti fratelli.*
> Because we are all brothers and sisters.
> *Amen!*

***

I went with the kids to the NATO Christmas party – a bus ride through rainy Naples, a private reception room with a small military band playing *Frosty the Snowman* and *Jungle Bells*, a beautifully decorated Christmas tree, a gift for each kid, an abundance of refreshments, a professional photographer, and, of course, Santa Claus.

A boy named Ralph, who wears a New York Mets baseball jacket, has taken to me. I was with him as he slowly opened his gift. He quietly inspected a sweatshirt and then gently put the cover back on the box. He displayed no emotion; he was neither excited nor upset. He seemed to be living with a heaviness of heart that I couldn't understand, that couldn't simply be covered up with a sweatshirt.

Our group was then rushed through the rain to the bus, which took us over to the officers' club for the lighting of the Christmas tree. It was hot and crowded with other school children. Adults, full of Christmas cheer, were pushing and complaining. The program – songs, prayers, the lighting of the tree, Santa Claus, and tons of candy – was remarkably uninspiring.

I thought about the day on the long bus ride back to Casa Materna. A lot of what I saw was full of good intentions, yet much of it seemed so incongruent – one world trying to help another without really taking the time to be present. We try to feel good about ourselves without ever leaving our own world; we import people so they can see what they don't have, and then we give them just enough to remind them.

***

Where there is charity and love, God is found.

***

Stephan, twenty, a conscientious objector from Germany, is fulfilling his national service by volunteering at Casa Materna for a year. Jesse, eighteen, has just finished working six months and will return to Wisconsin to begin university studies. Stephan and Jesse are adult caretakers who provide the kids with much needed love and discipline.

Every night Stephan and I talk about the kids, said Jesse. We talk about what they did, their progress, what is going on in their lives. With some strong, loving guidance, we believe that each of these kids has a great chance to turn out for the best.

In the evening, I went to Stephan's wing – untidy and full of strange smells – and played hockey with some of the boys; others ran around crying. They all needed fathers. My presence represented something that they lacked, and they weren't afraid to hold the hand of a man who couldn't speak their language.

***

On Wednesday, the kids played musical chairs and other games at the Sunday school Christmas party. After a Bible story, we served them Christmas cake and juice. The kids were simply out of control.

I ate supper at the head table with another male worker. When the kids were finished eating, they came by the head table to kiss the adults goodnight. I was uncomfortably humbled. Their kisses were wet and slimy, and I tried not to imagine the germs now swimming on my cheeks.

Afterwards, I followed the boys back up to their rooms. It was a chaotic, human zoo, full of non-stop noise, screaming and crying. One small boy, an epileptic, was running around naked, constantly coughing and occasionally spitting up. To add to the confusion, the lights shorted out three times, giving the kids yet another reason to scream. I was exhausted and realized that Stephan was seeing far more action here than any of his peers were in the army.

***

At morning chapel, I taught the kids *Deep and Wide*, and then I remained in the auditorium to watch the rehearsal of the Christmas program. After lunch, I visited outside with some of the kids before they had to return to class. Some girls kept repeating, slower and slower, the Italian words for: *Send us gifts.*

In the evening, I went with Bob and his wife, Stacy, to the town of Salerno, where Bob is also the pastor of a Waldensian/Methodist congregation.[57]

---

[57] The Waldensians, one of the oldest Protestant churches, was founded in the late twelfth century by Peter Valdez (or Waldes), a merchant and wandering preacher who dedicated himself to poverty and preaching.

The Italian Waldensian/Methodist Church, formed in 1979, has around 100 pastors and 300 churches. In 1984, a treaty was signed between the church and the government, whereby the state now recognizes Protestant weddings and no longer requires all churches to promote Catholic teachings.

In the car, Stacy asked me, *How do you relate pilgrimage to people living stationary lives?*

The storefront church in Salerno looked like a pizza parlor. Four children came for Sunday school. They made mobiles and then practiced for their Christmas program. Afterwards, four couples, each in a Protestant/Catholic marriage or engagement, met with Bob to discuss religious, cultural, and familial issues affecting their relationship. When they were finished, we all went out for pizza. Sabine, an energetic Italian with black, curly hair, engaged me in conversation. She told me that she had become a Methodist while living in England.

Sabine on giving: *Giving and receiving are the same. We receive when we give.*

On priests: *Priests have to renounce their private life. I don't think that's fair. I think the Protestant way for pastors is better. When and how did you decide to be a pastor? What did you have to renounce when you became a pastor?*

***

I told Ralph and Nadia, two of my favorite kids, good-bye at breakfast and left for Rome to meet Emanuela, a friend of Gaia's. I had an opportunity to see Rome with a Roman – not an opportunity to turn down.

I asked Emanuela to tell me her thoughts about Mary, the mother of Jesus. *Mary is love, nurture, and protection. She is very important to me*, Emanuela shared.

We walked through the Vatican and then spent a beautiful day hitting the high points of Rome. Throughout the day, Emanuela pointed out the unique and colorful Roman doorways, and I listened to her ongoing poetry.

I love doors. . . . I do not like gates.

Doors! They are so beautiful, warm and prodigious! I have taken hundreds of photos of them, 'cause I love them all. I really do! I have met some doors that I didn't like, but they were exceptions.

Every door has a personality. Some of them look like old whores (I learned that English word from reading Shakespeare. Culture is not always polite). Some look of Victorian brothels. Others seem as severe as German tutors. I love them all, even the tiny, whiney doors you sometimes find; they are rare and precious!

In Morocco, doors are painted blue; it's a color of hope.

Doors incessantly keep secrets and reveal worlds. That's why they open and close, open and close, open and close. I love when doors open, and they let you see – second by second – what is kept behind them.

Doors enchant me by their various woods and ornamentation. They tell me: 'Come, come and touch us.'

What does your door look like? Mine looks like a doctor: frosty and imperturbable!

Gates! Ugh! I don't like gates. They are vigorous, high and made of iron. They are smashers of beauty. They allow you to see through them, but you cannot break them down.

I love to close my door and put my forehead on it, just for a short moment, just to have a little rest! Could I ask for anything more?

I love when a friend appears from behind a door. You ring the bell, you wait for a while, and suddenly a smiling, familiar face appears.

When at last the day was over, I put Emanuela on a night coach bound for Padua, and she waved good-bye to me through the open door of the departing train.

***

I rang the bell of Casa Papa Giovanni in Assisi as instructed. *Hello. We've been expecting you.* It was Sister Giovanna. Bob Bronkema, chaplain of Casa Materna, had insisted that I go to Assisi to meet a sister pilgrim.

I was in time for the end of lunch, and I joined a table full of people for a wonderful Italian meal before Sister Giovanna took me across the lane to the International Franciscan Center for Interreligious Dialogue, where I had a room waiting for me. I would meet my host, Father Mizzi, in the evening.

I spent the afternoon walking the streets, taking in the quaint hill town, which was enveloped in an angelic, advent mist. In the late afternoon, I ascended above the fog, and I watched an incredible sunset over a sea of clouds. I returned to my room where I struggled to stay awake, aware, however, that my host would be arriving at any time. Finally, someone knocked on my door. It was Father Mizzi, a short, gentle man from Malta. He apologized for being late – he and the other brothers had just been in a car wreck, but everyone was okay. He gave me a quick tour of the center, introduced me to a couple of the brothers, showed me the chapel, and invited me to come to Mass in the morning.

***

I rose early for morning Mass. There were four brothers plus myself. By the time the Eucharist was consecrated, I was the only one not behind the communion table. I was uncertain what to do. I certainly wasn't bold enough to approach the table, but I hated to be denied the Eucharist. After all, I had been invited to attend. Then, just when it seemed like they were finished, Brother Peter, a Franciscan from California, looked up at me and mouthed these words of grace: *Would you like to partake?*

I was invited by the brothers to eat lunch in the Sacred Convent. It was an indescribable thrill, equal – I have been told – to eating at the

Vatican, Buckingham Palace or the White House. The cook is a Franciscan who used to be a chief at a prominent restaurant in the region, so the brothers are well fed. We sat around the outside walls of the large refractory, facing each other, while we were served a gorgeous three-course Italian meal. Father Mizzi then gave me a tour of the convent, which included both the mailroom and the grave of St. Francis. We went out into the cloister, pausing to take a couple of photos of each other. Then, entering the adjacent church by a special entrance, Father Mizzi showed me the two sanctuaries, built one on top of each other, both full of priceless relics and frescos.

***

I joined Giovanna and five other people in the small, quaint chapel at Casa Papa Giovanni for evening Mass. There were only seven people. This morning there were only four. Fortunately, God's atoning sacrifice is not dependent upon our presence. There weren't many people at the cross.

After dinner, I sat down with Sister Giovanna:

I worked many years with the mentally ill, and for many years, I gave hospitality to traveling pilgrims. Then I asked God to allow me to be a pilgrim. I have been a pilgrim ever since. I used to go on pilgrimage throughout Italy, hitchhiking without any money. But now hitchhiking is illegal, so I carry enough money with me for a bus ticket.

The streets are such good teachers. . . . There are a lot of poor people in Italy, a lot of refugees. People living on the streets. By being a pilgrim, my heart learns to hear the cries of those people who have no choice but to be pilgrims. As a pilgrim, I become more attentive to God – and also more aware of the conditions and needs of God's children. This is what I call the 'third eye' of the pilgrim.

Did you know Carlo Carretto? I asked. His book, *Letters from the Desert*, was formative in my decision to make this pilgrimage.[58]

Yes, Carlo and I were very close friends. I worked with him for many years at Spelo. Carlo was fond of quoting St. Francis in saying that

---

[58] Carlo Carretto, *Letters from the Desert* (New York: Orbis, 1972).

there are three great moments in life: the hermitage, the street, and the community. In the hermitage, one is completely alone with God. Then one goes out into the streets as a pilgrim. Here, one learns about the world, hears its cries, and helps a brother or sister. Back in the community, everyone shares with each other his or her faith experiences.

I asked Sister Giovanna if she had ever been to Medjugorje, a small village in Bosnia-Herzegovina, where, since 1981, six young people have seen daily visions of the Madonna.

I have – incidentally. We went through Medjugorje and spent a night outside the church sleeping on the ground. We were actually on our way to Sarajevo – twenty-seven hundred of us on a peace march during the war. We walked carrying our rucksacks and flags with rainbows on them. For ten straight nights, we slept under the stars. Many of us were over seventy years old!

We were eventually rerouted away from Sarajevo because of the heavy fighting. Still, our destination city was in the middle of the war. When we reached the city, all twenty-seven hundred of us were walking single file carrying our rainbow flags. We could see soldiers and snipers in the streets and up on the buildings. The day we entered the city was very hot; we were all very tired. All of a sudden a huge thunderstorm came up, soaking everyone of us.

Then the rain stopped. As the clouds rolled away, the sun came back out, and there, in the middle of this war-torn city was the biggest, most beautiful rainbow any. of us had ever seen. We all cheered, throwing our hats and our flags up into the air. Enemy soldiers stood looking at us and at the sky in amazement. The peace that prevailed for those few hours was beautiful. For a moment, God had stopped the war.

She looked at me with a sparkle in her eye. *Now, tell me about your journeys.*

***

I went to say good-bye to Father Mizzi and found him alone, working in his office. He had a photo of himself with almost every political or religious figure of the world – including Clinton, Arafat, and the Pope. Many of these same people have given him notable gifts, which he proudly pointed out to me. My host then graciously placed a tau cross around my neck. He gave me a hug, and I soon slipped outside into the darkness of Assisi's fog-shrouded stone streets.

A Swiss Interlude

(Switzerland: December 19th – 21st)

I gave Ursula and Simone, friends from Taizé, tau crosses that I had brought from Assisi, and we walked in the dark rain from the Lucerne train station to Ursula's apartment where I spent a couple of nights en route to Germany. In the morning, we took to the streets window-shopping, before walking over the restored fourteenth-century *Kapellbrücke*, an historic wooden bridge recently ravaged by fire, which led us to a couple of large churches. Ursula and I sat praying in the Jesuit church. She likes the Franciscan church better. *It is more intimate.* The Jesuit one is white and spotless. *I feel too alone here,* she told me.

We spent a cozy afternoon inside, sheltered from the gray, wet December day. We read, drinking tea while the radio played softly in the corner of the room. Later, I played the guitar with Simone and simple board games with Ursula. I love rainy day companionship. I had no expectations for the day, nor any strong desire to do anything in particular. Culture is a cup of shared coffee, not necessarily a museum of fine art.

***

Ursula asked me in the morning if I wanted to see the sun. I didn't understand her. It was foggy and cloudy outside. On top of the mountain, she meant.

During the ascent, Simone drew cartoon frogs on the windows of the gondola. *Do you know who this is?*

It's the breitmund frosch! She said. I smiled. It was one of my favorite high school jokes:

> Wide-Mouth Frog: *Momma Cow,*
> *What do you feed your babies?*
> Momma Cow: *I feed them milk.*
> Wide-Mouth Frog: *Momma Horse,*

What do you feed your babies?
Momma Horse: *I feed them hay.*
Wide-Mouth Frog: *Momma Chicken,*
              What do you feed your babies?
Momma Chicken: *I feed them worms.*
Wide-Mouth Frog: *Momma Snake,*
              What do you feed your babies?
Momma Snake: *I feed them wide-mouth frogs.*
Wide-Mouth Frog (mouth puckered): *Is that so?*

The wide-mouth frog is alive and well in Switzerland, but the Swiss version has a different punch line. Instead of saying, *Is that so* (mouth puckered), he says, *There are a lot of wide-mouth frogs over there.* That response drastically changes the character of the frog. In the version I know, the frog adapts to the situation; in the Swiss one, the frog deflects attention away from himself, endangering others. How do we react to situations? Do we change, adjusting to the circumstances, or do we divert attention to others, potentially endangering them?

At last, we ascended above the clouds. The peaks of Pilatus and other distant mountains rose above the lake of fog. The sun, unseen for several days, shone bright and clear. Like God, the sun is always there, even when we can't see it. Often, God is hidden from our eyes, covered in clouds.

We started walking down the mountain, sliding on the ice and enjoying the landscape. At the fog line, we turned around and retraced our steps. A man was riding his bike on the snow. Others were walking; people stopped and said hello. From a cable car above us, a group of Japanese shouted, waving at anyone who would wave back.

During the descent, I sat facing the top of the mountain, watching other cable cars passing us on their way up and then disappearing into the fog. Like life – like my pilgrimage – each new experience appears, comes into focus, and then disappears again into the fog. The memories and emotions of the recent past fade away until they are not recent at all. The only constants – and even these are temporary – are the people in the car with me.

We hurriedly grabbed a bus back to the station, and Simone and Ursula put me on a train bound for Germany. Soon, I was leaving Lucerne and my friends far behind. While I traveled, they were getting on with their plans for the day while other friends were preparing to receive me that night. In the meantime, I felt secure, comfortable, and mildly excited. Enjoying the train ride, I felt the irony – God was carrying me even in my good times.

The Twelve Days of Christmas

(Germany: December 21st – January 2nd)

Those preparing to receive me were Torsten and Ines, friends I made when I studied theology in Bonn. Torsten is a Lutheran pastor and was serving a church near Rosenheim, south of Munich. I arranged my visit over a Sunday in order to attend Torsten's church, which I did on Magnificat Sunday. We commemorated Mary's advent song of praise:

> *My soul glorifies the Lord*
> *And my spirit rejoices in God my Savior,*
> *For he has been mindful of the humble state of his servant.*
> *From now on all generations will call me blessed,*
> *For the Mighty One has done great things for me.*[59]

God helps us in reality; he answers our prayers.

We spent the afternoon on Fraueninsel, a small island in a large alpine lake. The day was raw; the wind was unrelenting. We visited the cloister, walked around the island, and then stopped at the hotel on the island for a cup of coffee. In the evening, we went to the Christkindmart in Rosenheim. Using hot holiday drinks as hand warmers, we milled around the festive Christmas market until the cold night sent us home.

***

It was snowing when I arrived in Heidelberg. Julia, an acquaintance from Iona, met me at the train station, and we spent a snowy afternoon walking through the streets. We took a coffee in a very ugly coffee shop, and then back outside Julia showed me her university before we took a train to her house near Ludwingshafen.

It snowed heavily throughout the night, and we spend the evening visiting with her parents and sitting around the fire. Around midnight, we went walking in the snow. The snow fell thick and fluffy. It was

---

[59] Luke 1:46-55.

going to be a white Christmas.

***

The next morning was Christmas Eve. I changed trains in Frankfurt, spending a one-hour layover hanging out in shops near the station. Some familiar music caught my ears, and walking over to an electronics store, I found a monitor showing *Lebenskries,* or *Lion King.* Setting my backpack down, I stood outside in the cold for a few minutes listening to the German lyrics of *Circle of Life.* An hour later, the train continued north to Giessen, but, unfortunately, the snow chose not to follow. White fields gave way to browns and greens. I wasn't going to have a white Christmas after all.

Manfred Schmidt and his wife, Ilsa, were hosting me for a couple of days over Christmas. I had met Manfred a few years earlier while researching family history in the area. Describing genealogy as a ministry, Manfred has discovered, starting with my grandfather's grandfather who left Hessen in 1842, over forty of my direct ancestors. I spent Christmas Day with the Lauchts, my cousins. Our most recent common ancestor was born in the 1500s but that didn't stop us from celebrating the day as family.

***

A forty-nine-year-old lady, attending a Christmas Eve service in Frankfurt, detonated a grenade that was strapped to her, killing herself and two others during the worship service.

***

On the second day of Christmas, Manfred, Ilsa and I attended worship in their village church. We sang *Er ist ein Ros* and *Stille Nacht.* Church bells rang during the Lord's Prayer, letting the housebound know when to pray along with the gathered congregation. After lunch, we went to Ansburg, a former Cistercian abbey, now a romantic set of ruins. The grounds were beautiful, and several people were out in the cold, raw day.

***

It's not even so much about the number of people, reflected Michele, whom I had met in August at family camp in Minnesota. *Rather, it is all about God. I mean, when you pray alone, you find God. When you share in the small group discussions, there is God. And when all 80,000 people are worshipping, singing and praying together, there's no doubt that God is present. It's absolutely amazing.* Michele and I, together with Amy, another friend from camp, gathered in Stuttgart, Germany along with 80,000 other people to attend the Taizé European Meeting of Young Adults.

While the primary components of the Taizé experience were integrated into the European meeting – daily prayer services, Bible study, work, simple meals – the sheer size of the gathering necessitated an incredible amount of planning (e.g. feeding 80,000 people in an hour). Several of the brothers had been in Stuttgart for over four months. Thousands of young people arrived two days early to serve as volunteers.

The focal points of each day were the two worship services held in the Messe, Stuttgart's large convention center. Four separate halls – each accommodating twenty thousand people and decorated with the orange banners, live greenery, candles and icons of the Taizé church – served as the venues for worship. Additional worship services took place in local churches throughout Stuttgart, which served as hosts for the gathering.

***

Upon arrival in Stuttgart, I found the English registration site, where I received maps, a meal ticket and a transportation card. I was then assigned a host parish – the Brenzkirche, a Lutheran church, and I traveled there with Junto and Midori, two women who had come all the way from Japan. At the Brenzkirche, I grabbed some food and began mingling. Most of the adults were in their twenties; however, I noticed an older man with a beard who looked a bit out of place. Feeling obliged to talk to him, I introduced myself to Kevin from Ireland.

I have noticed the presence of the handicapped here. They are visible. It must be terrible to be an invisible person in this world. Kevin seemed to be referring to himself more than he was to the physically handicapped persons around him. I asked him what he did. He was retired.

What did you do? I asked him.

I was a psychologist. He replied. *Often a depressed one.*

***

I was assigned, along with Nicole from Bavaria, to the sub-freezing apartment of a university student named Michael. Nicole, physically attractive and prone to overpack, had more stuff with her for the weekend that I had for the year. Michael, friendly but a bit eccentric, did not have a shower in his apartment. When he chose to take one, he used the showers at the train station.

***

I went to the Messe to look for people I knew. I found Taco from Holland. When I had left Taizé six weeks earlier, Taco was beginning a week of silence.

How was your experience?

It was beautiful. The silence made me take time to discover that God has been with me all of my life. When I discovered this – that God has always been there – it was a beautiful thing.

***

Brother Roger, founder of the Taizé Community, spoke each night. In his message, translated into over a dozen languages, he encouraged everyone to discover the light of Christ. His special edition of *Letter from Taizé*, entitled *From Doubt to Brightness of Communion*, was used in the Bible studies and group discussions.

We live in a world in which there is both light and darkness . . . but through Christ, we are moving from doubt to community, he writes. *In 1 John 1, we read: this is the message we have heard from him and proclaim to you – God is light and in him there in no darkness.*

The Gospels tells us that God has a calling for each person. Jesus said, 'You received without charge; give without charge' (Matthew 10:8). There is a call for each person – a call of going to the point of giving one's self.[60]

Brother Roger is an example of a person faithfully living out a vision. His initial vision did not include the thousands of young adults who now visit Taizé; rather, he dedicated himself to living a life of prayer and reconciliation. However, when someone lives a genuinely faithful life, people respond.

***

I can only imagine the actual discussion.

Guten Morgen, I began.

Guten Morgen, they replied. I was off to a good start.

I was extremely nervous. I had been asked to lead a German-speaking small group, something that I knew I couldn't do. We were supposed to discuss the story of the adulterous woman (John 8:3-11) and Jesus' command to forgive (Matthew 18:21-22). I had sample questions in front of me in both German and English.

What message of hope do you find in the story about Jesus forgiving the woman? How does Jesus help you to discover love? I stumbled in German.

I waited for someone to speak. I waited a little longer.

Someone began talking. I followed the first sentence, and then with each passing sentence I became more and more confused, until I was completely lost. Then others joined in.

I think Jesus awakens in me an attitude of compassion because I know that he hasn't condemned me either. This humbles me and allows me

---

[60] *Letter from Taizé,* Special Issue, 1997.

to be open to love and serve other people.

Yes, I agree. Jesus has helped me to discover love and has led me in turn to love others.

That's right. But who made this American moron our group leader? There's only one of us who can't speak German, and he's our leader! Jesus, help us.

Catching the last bit, I thought that the group must still be on track. Pretty soon, however, I was going to have to throw out another question – one that would advance the discussion without letting them know that I was unable to follow it. I tried to listen carefully.

I bet if we all smile at the Yank and tell him that he needs to take a shower, he'll think that we are just being friendly.

Somebody tried it, smiling at me, *I think your German stinks – and you're an illiterate fool.*

But how do we love others like Jesus did? I jumped in, sensing that everyone was looking for me to say something.

We learn to forgive others. Someone spoke up.

Yeah, he forgave the woman; he forgave the disciples. He forgives everyone, even every one of us here. Slowly, but surely we were coming to the end of the hour. *Jesus said that we should always forgive people, and God gives us the love and the power to do that.*

I thought I'd end by changing the subject. *So, what does Jesus say about forgiveness?*

Someone looked at me and said, *I think you're an idiot.*

Great, I said, apologizing again for my German but thanking everyone for helping me.

Afterwards, a man in the group came up to me. He handed me a gift; I was flattered – a kind gesture to let me know that everything was fine.

Then I realized that he had given me a Bible tract. *I've come to Taizé to tell people about Jesus . . . so they won't go to hell,* he offered.

I met Nicole, who was in another small group, and we walked over to the Messe for worship. On the way, we talked about options for the afternoon. *Do you want to go to a swimming pool?* She asked me. *I brought my bikini in case I met an American man whom I wanted to go swimming with.* She sort of stunned me, but she did succeed in getting my mind off the events of the morning.

We entered the large conference center to the sound of Taizé music. The musicians were already practicing for the service, which was to be live on German national television. There was a growing excitement in the air as we all felt that we were a part of something big.

***

A New Year's Eve service was held in the Brenzkirche. Around midnight, we could see fireworks through the windows. The service abruptly stopped, and we passed the peace, giving New Year kisses, it seemed, to anyone we could find.

New Year's Day was on a Sunday, and Nicole and I walked to the Brenzkirche for worship. Afterwards, a hot lunch was served in the basement, and I spent a final hour meeting new people. Elena, a Romanian, was studying to be an English tour guide. Her father was an Orthodox priest. She and her fellow Romanians had spent two days and two nights on a bus to get to Stuttgart. Within the hour, they were returning home.

Time was quickly drawing to a close. We said our final good-byes to people at the Brenzkirche, and Nicole and I returned to Michael's. At the house, I collected my bags, said good-bye to Nicole, and walked back out into the snowy street.

***

Michele, Amy, and I found a hotel near a streetcar stop. We talked and laughed for hours, recovering from the grimy freeze of the week.

We threw all of our extra army rations onto the coffee table, letting the small mountain of uneaten goulash and chili-mac thaw before throwing it all away and going back out into the cold for a memorable New Year's dinner.

In the morning, we went downstairs for coffee, and then Michele walked me to the stop – just outside the café window. I said a quick good-bye to her and got on the streetcar, reminded once again that all human relationships are incomplete.

***

I flew back to Scotland where I spent a long weekend visiting friends and finally getting my shots for Africa – yellow fever, diphtheria, typhoid, and hepatitis – one of them was headed for my rump.

Can I make an eight-hour bus trip? I inquired, concerned about being sore on my bus ride to London later on in the day.

Well, I'd lean over on one side.

You can get ready, another nurse told me. *And if you need to, you can hold the teddy bear.*

Why? Because it'll hurt, or because I'll be embarrassed?

I don't have any comment, she said, jabbing the needle into my buttock.

The bus to London was fairly full. I gave up my window seat to a couple with a baby, later noticing that the baby had a huge, swollen upper lip. I tried to sleep some, but the large-busted woman serving the refreshments keep brushing up against me every time she walked up and down the aisle. Occasionally catching my attention, some young women in leather sat talking a few rows ahead of me.

***

I arrived at Gatwick International Airport three hours before my flight. I checked-in and then called home. . . .Two days after

Christmas, my mother had fallen at work and had broken her wrist and her pelvis. She did not sound too bad considering that she had just had surgery on her hip. She was in a wheelchair and was receiving home help three times a week. We spoke for a while and then wished each other well.

***

Leaving Europe . . . destination Africa.

Another week has gone, but more significantly, I'm entering a whole new world. I am turning a big corner, and I feel myself wanting to go very, very slowly. I am suspended in my thoughts and emotions. I'm lingering.

I have not found it necessary to spent a lot of time preparing myself for the next adventure. I trust my ability to adapt to new worlds, to absorb essential details, and to quickly make myself at home in new surroundings.

If I went to Africa directly from America, I know that my emotions would be different. I'd be more excited, and the preparation would have preoccupied me for weeks. Even so, I have learned that certain things are simply impossible to understand until they happen.

Kenya will soon sweep me away, and my focus will be that which I can see and touch. The world of the pilgrim is the world he or she wakes up to.

Harambee

(Kenya: January 8th – 27th)

Nicolas, an accountant in the Methodist conference office, met me at the Nairobi airport. A young man, smartly dressed in a suit and a tie, Nicolas was married with three daughters.

You will experience much friendship in Kenya, Nicholas told me in the car, striking up a warm and easy conversation. *Here, you are not just a person named Rodney. You are a special guest, and you will make many connections. You will need a pick-up truck to take back all that you will learn.* He told me about his daughters. *Their names mean 'tree,' 'it's mine,' and 'small hill.'* I commented that names seldom have meanings in English. *I believe that cultures that use names with meanings are more intimate,* he replied.

At the Methodist conference office, I met Dr. Stephen Kanyaru, the conference secretary, who had arranged my visit to Kenya, and an hour later, I was with him and two other pastors in a Land Rover heading towards Kianjai, a village four hours north of Nairobi. We drove along the main highway, through villages and towns, past lines of people walking up and down the road. The air was warm, and I kept falling asleep. As I did, my head would suddenly jerk forward, waking me back up. I wanted to absorb the drive, but I couldn't open my eyes without them closing again.

We arrived into Kianjai at dusk, and we drove straight to Bishop M'bogori's house, where the retired bishop and his wife were expecting us. After a couple of plates of food and some initial conversations about Kenya and Kianjai, I was shown my room and quickly drifted off to sleep.

***

I wanted to stay in bed, hidden, for at least a few more hours, but I reluctantly emerged to a breakfast of toast and eggs. In the afternoon, I went with Rev. Solomon, the circuit pastor and my daytime host, to the market in the middle of the village square – four dirt roads lined with wooden storefronts and an occasional permanent brick building. The produce was on the ground, spread out but organized. Here were the tomatoes; there were the roots. Potatoes and beans then gave way to bikes and sewing machines. Women were dressed in colorful market clothing, and as I strolled around with Rev. Solomon, I was greeted with stares, salutations, and sodas. Everyone I met offered to buy me a pop, and refusing to refuse, my kidneys were soon floating in Fanta and ginger soda. The day was warm and invigorating. A gentle breeze full of market smells stirred through the crowd while generalizations about America – a land of professional wrestling, porno movies, and throw-away babies – reached my ears.

***

Gerald Mwithia, whom I began calling *Uncle Gerald*, was my transportation for the week – he hauled me and sometimes up to a dozen people in the back of his covered pick-up truck. Dr. Kanyaru had given them strict orders not to let me walk anywhere, and as it turned out, the only time I tried it, an elderly man picked me up on his bike and peddled me home.

Almost everyday, I spent some time drinking tea at Uncle Gerald's house, where his young elementary granddaughters, intrigued by me, would peek in and out of the room.

Bishop M'bogori and Uncle Gerald were best friends: *We feel that we are living on borrowed time now. The life we knew is gone. People are living with different values. It is a difficult time for us.*

Bishop M'bogori began to share stories of his life and ministry. *When I was a young pastor, I learned to get on with the missionaries. I had to if I ever wanted to get a ride home.* He told me a story of being assigned by white missionaries to a flea-infested hut. *I had to leave. The fleas didn't speak my language.*

The old missionaries were shortsighted. In many ways, they lied to us. For one, they didn't think that Africans would ever visit Europe. When we did, we realized that the religion that they taught us was not the same one that they were practicing at home. For example, they preached that alcohol is a sin, and that attitude has always been a part of the Kenyan church. Once, a few of us were in Switzerland for a meeting, and alcohol was being served everywhere. When we abstained, they looked at us as if we had somehow offended them.

They also taught us that politics is a sin, and they didn't allow us Africans to question their authority. They told us that Nairobi is a sinful place and that we must never go there. They wanted to help us, but often their motives and attitudes were very condescending. Missionaries must always remember that all people are thinking people.

The old missionaries, however, couldn't have acted any other way. They threw out both the form and content of old African culture and replaced it with a new religion, because there was no way for them to know the difference. For them, it was simply a question of Christian worship versus ancestral worship. But now, Africans are rediscovering African forms for Christian content. The old missionaries made several mistakes, but the problem with today's missionaries is that they let people believe whatever they want.

One problem that we sometimes get is people who think they have all the answers for the African church. A few years ago, there was an African-American missionary with a specialty in youth who was unwilling to serve where the bishop wanted him. With his superior education and Western background, he thought he could call the shots. Finally, we had to tell him that we no longer needed his services.

Bishop M'bogori continued, now referring to Gerald, who was a tea farmer. *Here in Kenya our tea farmers can barely afford to serve tea. They sell the tea to foreign companies who process it and then sell it back to us with a 100 percent mark up. There's something wrong when tea farmers can't afford to drink tea.*

Critiquing modern society, M'bogori gave me his analysis of polygamous cultures, maintaining that they took good care of women and children. *In today's monogamous culture, once a woman is divorced, there is no one to take care of her and her children. In the past, women and children never fell through the cracks.* Later he added, *In the past, we had natural family planning. We always made sure that the youngest child could work in the fields before having another baby.*

There was company all night at the M'bogori's house because of church matters, and they spoke with one another in Kin-Meru, their mother tongue. Later, the Bishop apologized. *It was not polite for us to speak in front of you in our own tongue. But it was an important church matter that we needed to discuss clearly. The matter itself is not very edifying. We appreciate you allowing yourself to be ignored.*

***

While spiritually the Methodist Church in Kenya is vibrant, daily life in rural areas like Kianjai is a constant struggle. In an area of subsistence farming, the success of the crops depends completely upon the rains. Coming out of the rainy season in a drought, there was talk of famine. The beans have failed; there was fear that the corn will follow. Consequently, the wealth of the circuit is dependent upon the weather.

If it rains, I think the house might be completed by August, said Rev. Solomon, referring to the new parsonage that was slowly being built. Currently, Rev. Solomon lived in a small, two-room structure with no electricity or running water. Solomon's family lived in another village several miles away; he returned home every other week.

***

I spent most of the day on the grounds of the Kianjai church. There, I met Richard, a new minister in the circuit, and his wife. They literally had just arrived on the night bus. In his early thirties, Richard liked to smile and quote scriptures. His wife, barefoot and in a purple dress, spent most of the day sleeping outside on a mattress in the churchyard.

We walked over to the Methodist-sponsored polytechnic school. There, we met the headmaster, a nice, welcoming man. The school taught tailoring, home economics, mechanics, woodworking, metalworking, secretarial skills, plumbing, and business accounting. We toured the classrooms, and the students stood up as we entered.

The classrooms had dirt floors, desks, chalkboards, and basic necessary equipment – e.g. sewing machines and model engines. In the toolmaking shop, graduates were making carpentry and metalworking tools. Students go into the work place already equipped with their own tools.

School starts each day with a prayer assembly after breakfast. On Sundays, students attend the Kianjai church. The headmaster spoke a number of times about the umbrella of Jesus Christ being over the whole school. *We help the students spiritually as well as vocationally.*

I was told about a nearby capped well capable of supplying water for 100 families. Unfortunately, no one had successfully administered a plan for collecting the money and distributing the water. Five years later, the well was still capped.

Later in the afternoon, we walked through the primary school grounds where throngs of beautiful kids with bright white eyes and smiling teeth greeted us. I waved at one kid, winked at another, accidentally stepping in a pile of cow dung as I did so.

Inside an old classroom, Rev. Solomon and I met with the primary school teachers, and as we gathered, I felt the eyes of the teachers looking over their unannounced guest. I took a few minutes to return the favor. We introduced ourselves, and then we had a time for questions. Several of the teachers raised their hands. *Is it true that there is devil worship is America? Is it true that churches are being sold in America?*

***

The plains are vast and beautiful. There are mountains on the horizon. In the flat valley lands, there are fields of struggling beans and corn. The tea farms are higher up in the mountains. People here believe that the landscape is a manifestation of the spirit world – a world, though, not always in cooperation with its inhabitants.

***

Mrs. M'bogori was very friendly, motherly and caring. She worked hard on the family farm, picking beans and digging potatoes. One afternoon, Mrs. M'bogori showed me the land around the house. *This is my office,* she told me. *Over here is where the elephants destroyed our mango trees a few years ago.*

***

Prayer is a big part of family life in Christian Kenyan. Group prayers were always said before meals, before traveling, before going to bed, and sometimes even before drinking a cup of tea.

On the M'bogori's wall was the same saying that I saw in the dining room at Casa Materna:

> *The Lord is the guest of the house.*
> *The silent listener to every conversation.*

Beside it was a copy of the Prayer of St. Francis: *Lord, Make Me an Instrument.*

***

I ate breakfast, and then at the Bishop's suggestion, I paid a quick visit to a young circuit minister who lived on the grounds. He was having difficulties; there were allegations that he made inappropriate advances to one of the M'bogori's servant girls.

***

It is a beautiful, sunny day; a gentle breeze is blowing. Several shrubs and trees are in bloom. In the front yard, there are some clothes on the line; a couple of goats are eating beans. A large cistern, half-full of water, is in the middle of the yard. I can see mountain peaks off in the distance. Various birds are singing, occasionally interrupted by the intrusive sound of the barnyard roosters.

***

Later in the morning, after journaling for a couple of hours on the porch, I began to feel sick, a loss of energy, an ache in my legs. After some lunch that I didn't want, we began a long trip, deep into the back roads, to attend a wedding presentation. I rode in the back of the truck, bouncing along dirt roads for several miles, passing villages that seemed to be in the middle of nowhere; yet, there were always scores of people walking the roads and gathering in the market squares.

My memories of the wedding presentation are clouded by the sudden unwelcome illness that overtook me throughout the day. For a while, I sat under a large tree in the front yard with M'bogori's son and two of his friends. I was brought a bowl of porridge and then a huge, disagreeable plate of food. I nibbled on it, feeling that I was obliged to eat it. My legs ached. I wanted to throw the food away and go to sleep. After the meal, we all gathered in the backyard, and for the next several hours, we heard speeches and blessings directed to the bride and groom. The sun 'was strong, and I developed a terrible headache.

At last, we started home. The road was bumpy, and I sat in the back, just trying to hold on. I was conscious of each passing second; each one meant that I was closer to my bed. Eventually, we arrived back in Kianjai, and finally, we were back at the house. I went straight to bed where I spent a long, restless night alternating between strong stomach cramps and bouts of diarrhea.

***

The diarrhea intensified in the early morning, but miraculously, it was never a problem while I was at church, which was surprising, since the service lasted three hours. Over 500 people gathered from all over the circuit to attend the New Year covenant and communion service on the front steps of the Kianjai church. Afterwards, Solomon told me that many things were disturbing him. Of his two pastors, one had gone astray, and the other one was unwanted.

***

Do you see that mountain over there? Beyond it lies my farthest church. I have to leave the house by six in the morning in order to be there for a ten o'clock service, said Rev. Solomon, the superintendent of the twenty-one church Kianjai Circuit, whose only means of transportation was a bicycle.

I was riding on the back of Rev. Solomon's bike to visit parishioner Dickson Kabubani, a teacher who recently had been in a car wreck. Inside his house, we drank tea, while Solomon and Dickson discussed some of the conflicts that had arisen in the circuit. Solomon shook his head. *The Lord's work is very difficult. We have our problems like any other church.*

Dickson added: *It's hard to follow God in a confused world.* The people didn't want the new pastor. What they wanted was an apology from the bishop. Dickson continued: *People aren't respecting the rules of the system.*

We walked down the road to the newly built Mutionjuri church. *We moved here from next door,* said lay leader Francis Michoko pointing to an adjacent structure. *The old building has been turned into a local dispensary – the only one in the area.*

Inside the dispensary, while Rev. Solomon was offering a prayer for the mothers and children crowded into the small waiting room, a young girl had a malaria seizure and was immediately taken in for treatment. Later in the day, we heard that she was okay. Everyone here has had malaria at one time or another.

Back at the church, Michoko continued, *Our main problem is communication; the people in the back of the church cannot hear. We need a sound system. So far, we have not been able to afford one.* Dedicated a year ago, the Mutionjuri church was already too small. The Sunday morning crowds were overflowing; several people had to sit outside.

We had lunch in a nearby house – beans, vegetables, and some stewed meat that I couldn't quite swallow. Religious wall plaques and mix-and-match furniture filled the room. The final visit was to a poor farm, where we sat inside a dark, grass hut and had yet another cup of tea. We rode the bike back to church and lay outside on mattresses napping. I had made it fairly well throughout the day, but when I woke up, I felt sick again.

Near dusk, someone on a motorcycle came to the church to pick me up, and I rode in the dark on the back of the cycle over bumpy, dirt roads passing people carrying water, firewood, and potatoes. I held on tightly to the bike, closing my eyes, trying not to let the chilly air, the bumpy ride or my aching body bother me.

After visiting educators, farmers, and retired villagers, I spent the evening in the home of a local merchant, a family with slightly more wealth than the other families that I had visited throughout the day. I was clearly welcomed – an honored guest from America – which alone made me feel bad, since I was in no shape to be good company. Likely, they will never forget the occasion. I was too sick to remember it.

The food looked wonderful, but I was just too sick to eat much. I tried to absorb as much of the evening as I could, but really, I just wanted to go home. I felt better once I got engaged in conversation, but with my last cup of tea, I started sweating again. After an evening prayer, we finally left. I was sick and a bit scared.

***

I got up for breakfast and then went back to sleep, never stirring again until almost five in the afternoon. I got up around six, stayed awake for a few hours, and then returned to bed.

***

I came to Kenya, and I got sick. The last few days have been most difficult – living through an unknown illness in a strange, foreign country. Each day has been a pilgrimage of endurance and perseverance, letting time slowly tick by until at long last, I'm alone in my room.

My digestion is far from normal. A sleepy, sickly fatigue pervades my body, especially in the evenings after a full day. I have a slight cough.

Such a meaningful experience, but what an awful time! Above all, it's been a time of prayer, feeling vulnerable due to forces outside of my control, calling upon an external source – God – for help. More than anything, I have longed for water – simple, ample drinking water.

I am learning as much about myself as I am about Kenya. My pilgrimage of faith continues – a daily journey into the unknown. I'm being stretched, emptied and humbled. I am learning to live on prayer and to be thankful for the blessings of each day.

Being sick challenges my pilgrimage reflection that the present is of the most importance. We journey toward the future, but we should always be aware of God's presence in the now. It takes a present to make a future; we have to be here to get there – it's just that we often wish that the present wasn't so painful.

We journey to God; we journey with God.

***

Communication and transportation – these are our two greatest needs, echoed Miathene Synod Bishop Peter Mukuccia, whose modest office was next to the Kianjai church. A simple phone, a few books and files, educational posters on AIDS and other African issues filled an otherwise bare room. *I look around my office, and I ask myself, 'What is essential for a bishop's office?' I answer, 'Only those things that can help empower people for Christ.'* Unfortunately, the closest copier and fax machine were twenty miles away.

We spoke frankly about the relationship between the African and the Western churches. *In South Africa, they move twenty tons of rock in order to find one ounce of gold. Often the Church works very hard but forgets its purpose; we must always remember what our focus is – the Gospel of Jesus Christ,* the bishop said.

We in the African church are often frustrated, because we find the Western church less and less interested in evangelism and more and more involved solely in developmental projects. Various organizations will help provide water and food or help us build roads. But it's becoming harder and harder to equip our ministers with bicycles, our school children with Bibles, or to find money that will assist with the building of churches or parsonages. We should never forget what is essential – our primary task is transporting and communicating the Word of God to individual people.

I am disturbed, he continued, *that our Sunday schools do not have enough Bibles [in our own language]. Each Bibles costs only six dollars or three hundred shillings, but that's over a half-month's wage for most of us.*

We are all on a journey and as brothers and sisters in Christ, we must ask each other, 'What do you need? How can I make your journey with God easier?' There are many ways that the African and Western churches can help each other, but everything we do must first of all have the spiritual journeys of people in mind. We must be in solidarity with one another. We are not to carry but rather to enable one another.

The West thinks that Africa is spiritually rich, but the African problem is one of material resources. We are like Peter who said, 'We have no silver and gold.'[61] *The problem in the West is how to spend money, but the West is losing spiritual strength. If all this is the case, then we should share our physical and spiritual resources with each other.*

What do people who live according to the weather do when the weather is bad? The West thinks that Africa is lazy, but now you know differently. You can tell your people to come and see with their own eyes. Unfortunately, we have so much working against us. We live in a harsh and unpredictable environment. We seem endlessly trapped in a viscous economic cycle that we can't get above. Our economy is a still slave to our environment. As long as that is true, we will continue to struggle.

The West is relaxed. In the meantime, Islam is taking over, and Christianity is being swallowed up. The oil-rich Islamic countries are pouring money into Africa. They are sending missionaries and putting up mosques all over the country – even in small villages. The West is a mature church, and we are afraid that it lacks energy for the future. However, the Church must remain evangelistic. We are called to go and make disciples, not to go and build buildings and water systems. Our enemy is strong, aggressive, and confident.

---

[61] Acts 3:6.

We must take care of our pastors, and we must equip the soldiers of God with shoes, food, transportation, and housing. Cows are very useful. They give milk for a long time. However, if the cow is dead, it is good only for its meat.

He ended by saying, *the Methodist Church in Kenya doesn't belong to us – it is the Church of Jesus Christ. Whatever happens here affects the Church around the world.*

***

Uncle Gerald took Rev. Solomon and me to his tea farm high up in the mountains. Unlike the plains, the vegetation there was lush and green. Laborers were in the tea fields picking leaves; their bright, colored clothes stood out against the glossy, light green of the mountain fields.

***

We sat outside under makeshift shelters watching the Kianjai Primary School graduation ceremony. Each song, dance or poetry reading was introduced, usually by a young girl who would say, *I hope you will enjoy it,* and then she would curtsy. Children came by with pitchers, washing our hands with warm water, while others began bringing out plates of food. Two bulls had been killed for the party. I was looking at more food that I didn't want to eat.

Suddenly, it began to rain, and we all ran for shelter. Bringing the plate of food with me, I was taken with other VIP's to the headmaster's office to wait out the twenty-minute rain. The food was now cold and looked even less appetizing than when I first got it. Inquiringly, I looked up at Rev. Solomon, asking him with my eyes what to do with the food. When the rained stopped, I left the plate of food in the headmaster's office as we returned to our seats.

Twenty minutes later, it began to rain again.

This time, we were ushered into another building, a dark one-room classroom. The only illumination was the gray outdoor light, which came in through the open doorway. Students, coming in out of the rain carrying platters of meat, continued to serve us. Sitting on benches around the room, we passed the plate of meat to one another. I took a couple of pieces. It was tasty and tender. I was surprised that I had an appetite for it. I wanted some more.

Soon, another young boy came in carrying a second platter. This time, I took a huge chunk of meat – only to be disappointed that it actually didn't have any meat on it at all.

While I struggled, looking for a dark corner to spit out my wad of gristle, a nauseating odor began to fill the room. I saw the silhouette of a young boy standing in the doorway, holding yet another platter of food, apparently tracking in something dead on his shoes. I tried holding my breath, waiting for someone to tell him to go back outside and scrape it off. He handed someone the platter, turned around, and then ducked back into the rain. He was gone, but the smell was as intense as ever, and I suddenly realized that the stench wasn't coming from his shoes but rather from the platter of food. They were passing around a tray of boiled cow guts, intestines, and other digestive organs. I wanted to retch. Someone handed me the platter, and I sat staring in disbelief at the warm, shadowy mound of cattle parts on my lap, fortuitously shrouded by the darkness of the room. Rev. Solomon leaned over and nudged me, *Don't look at it, just eat it!* I passed the platter on, catching yet another warm whiff of the entrails as I quickly began figuring up how many more days I had left in Kenya.

***

Sitting in the churchyard shade, I met with the women and youth of the circuit, mostly fielding questions about America and the American church. Their questions centered on marriage, divorce, abortion and homosexuality. I was asked if pastors ever got divorced in America. *Are they allowed to remain as pastors?* When I said *yes*, one young man looked me squarely in the eyes and asked, *How can you say that you follow the Bible?*

They also asked about churches closing in America, something unimaginable in Kenya where church buildings cannot be built fast enough. Others asked about the role of women in the American church.

Uncle Gerald came by to pick me up, and I said my final good-bye to Rev. Solomon, my gracious and gentle host. He was noticeably animated. *You have come here, and you have listened to us; you know our needs. You have been honest in your answers and open in your attitudes. You are very transparent; my people have connected with you.* Then Rev. Solomon looked down at his feet. *I have not said anything before, but I would like to ask you for something. You must decide, but I would like a black robe – and a large cross.* I said that I would see what I could do. Then Rev. Solomon looked me in the eyes. He was smiling.

Go well. He said.

Stay well. I replied.

***

Bishop M'bogori woke up feeling bad. It was something that he had eaten. I felt bad that he felt bad, but I was somewhat relieved to know that I wasn't the only one who gets sick from eating the food.

I had learned a lot from the retired bishop, and I believe that he understood more than anyone what had brought me to Kenya. His wife, Mrs. M'bogori, had been like a mother to me, hosting me in health and nurturing me in my illness. After ten days together, we had a simple, though tender, good-bye.

***

I spent a couple of days visiting the Maua Methodist Hospital, where I had a room in the former nurse's dorm. I took a much-welcomed cold shower and shaved for the first time in several days.

The next morning, I sat in on the doctors' report – a post-mortem was being done that day on a patient due to some anesthetic concerns. Afterwards, I was given a tour of the hospital. A huge new maternity ward was being built in the middle of the campus.

Judith, a Kenyan nurse, invited me to her house for lunch. Around noon, we left the hospital complex, stopping by the butcher for a large piece of warm meat on the way home. Judith was a single mother, took care of a niece, and had several Western friends whom she had met through work. Judith was taking a Bible correspondence course from Dallas, and she mentioned her need for money to pay the girls' school tuition. She told me that she liked being a nurse. *I am able to do God's work,* she said, and then she added, *Life is good if you know how to fit into it.*

***

In the late afternoon, I went on a walk with four female medical interns through the village and up a long, steep hillside. The village children started following us as if we were Pied Pipers. We heard multi-voiced echoes coming from the woods and fields as if a choir of katydids were singing with human words: *Hello. . . hello . . . hello.*

The children were intrigued but easily frightened. Some kids wanted to shake our hands; others would come up close to us, only to run away. Occasionally, I heard the word *muzungu* mixed in with the *hello*s. *Muzungu,* or white person, literally means *one who goes around.*

The pathways were beautiful; the dust was thick, and the roads were steep. At a tea factory, we turned around and headed back down. We met dozens, if not hundreds, of people on their way home, carrying tea baskets, firewood, bananas, water, and beans on their backs and heads, steadily climbing the long, steep mountainside. Even in the growing twilight, the colorful bandanas, skirts, and blouses of the women were a sharp contrast to the dusty road. A man with big green hair, resembling Dennis Rodman and carrying a jam box on his shoulders, stood out in the crowd.

***

Passing an occasional *Cattle and Children Crossing* sign, we arrived in Nairobi in the late afternoon, and I was taken immediately to a hotel where the Methodist conference staff had gathered for a planning retreat. I joined the staff for the remainder of the day, attending the evening devotion. As they processed their experience of the retreat, Nicolas, the conference accountant, said, *I have learned that change is not an event but rather a process – and that God is always creating opportunities to allow us to make the transitions.*

***

Rosalie, the conference secretary, handed me a fax. It was news from Dad – Pa-Paw was in ICU. He had fallen on the ice, and his leg was broken in several pieces. I immediately felt the news. Pa-Paw would never recover – I had made all of the memories with him that I would ever make.

At the Air Malawi office, I bought a ticket for my flight to Zimbabwe. As the travel agent was making my reservations, I asked which route the flight took. *The long way,* the travel agent said. *Well, okay,* I thought, *I'm a budget traveler. I don't mind going the long way.*

Which city does it stop in? I asked again.

Lilongwe, he repeated, referring to the Malawi capital. My African geography could be improved.

***

I spent a night at a Methodist guesthouse while the conference retreat was finishing up. Waking up with nothing to do, I asked the front desk if anyone could show me parts of Nairobi. James, a young porter just getting off his night shift, took me into the city where we walked around for about two hours. James, nearly twenty years old, shared his faith with me throughout the morning: *You can live life to the fullest when you trust in God full stop. If you depend on him, everything is okay. It doesn't matter if you haven't got a shilling in your pocket. Life is good when you rely on God.*

Later in the afternoon, I watched the second half of the Kenya - Gabon football game which Kenya won 1 - 0. The Kenyan side is called *Harambee*, which is an African custom of pulling together and sharing resources. When someone is in need, an *harambee* is called, and everyone donates gifts and money to help support the cause.

I spent the evening with Dr. Kanyaru and his family, sharing with him my experiences in Kianjai and Maua. He confessed that he had intentionally placed me there, because being on a major highway, it was relatively accessible. *There are places much more remote that Kianjai.* As we sat down to eat, Mrs. Kanyaru looked at me and said, *Eat. The food is delicious.* Her simple, self-confidence was beautiful. Indeed, her food was outstanding – a full Kenyan spread. Afterwards, around a cup of tea, we continued our conversation. Mrs. Kanyaru talked about her twin daughters – one was disabled during delivery and now attends a special school. *I was sick during my pregnancy. The doctor told me that it was malaria; instead, it was twins.*

***

Bishop Maureen, the Methodist bishop of Nairobi and the first female bishop in Africa, picked me up at Dr. Kanyaru's house and took me to the church where she was preaching. Worship began with the youth leading some praise songs in Swahili. When they were finished, we sang the obligatory English hymns, which brought any previous worship momentum to a screeching halt. When the service was over, the congregation convened outside for a cup of tea. Several local street children, dirty and dressed in rags, joined us, making tea puddles in the mud and playing on the swing sets.

After church, Bishop Maureen and I went to a restaurant at the Karen Blixen House for a long, relaxed meal, speaking often about pilgrimage. *Pilgrimage people are always on the move,* she said. *We are always trying to be closer to God. Each year we must ask ourselves, 'Are we better? Do we love more, understand more, and give more than we did last year?'*

Bishop Maureen recently had her purse stolen in the cathedral, and earlier in January, while driving to the airport, her car tires were punctured. She was held at gunpoint and robbed. *I could hear people yelling, 'Kill her, kill her!'*

I was fine at the time. But when I was safe again, I began shaking all over. Afterwards, I couldn't believe all the support and encouragement that I received. I learned that if you acknowledge God in all circumstances, he can turn any situation into a blessing. My people helped me see this.

She talked about being a bishop. *It was a shock to me. I was ready to return to England. I don't like being bishop, but I have always reluctantly followed where God has called me.*

***

I have just left Kenya. Out of the left side of the plane, I can see Mount Kilamanjaro.

Grateful for the experience and for my health, I leave with no regrets, and I am thankful that the journey continues. I must let the experiences germinate within me, but in the meantime, I pray for rain.

The Power of Tea

(Zimbabwe: January 27th – February 13th)

Since Iona, I have been better able to accept my position in life, said Joan, referring to being widowed. Joan and I met as fellow pilgrims on the island of Iona. A resident of Harare, Zimbabwe, Joan hosted me before and after my visit to Africa University. *For me, Iona was a place where I could heal my wounds, and I found the worship services to be very meaningful. Iona has given me a strength and a resolve, which I can't quite articulate, but I know is there.*

***

I caught my first glimpse of Africa University in the distant valley. The view was magnificent, and yet, as we drove up, my first impression of the campus was that it is no different from other schools in America. Opened in March 1992, Africa University is the only United Methodist university in all of Africa and the first private university in Zimbabwe. A pan-African institution, Africa University has students from over seventeen different African countries.

The dream of Africa University began as early as 1898, when Joseph Hartzell, a Methodist bishop, stood on a nearby mountain and envisioned hundreds of African young people with books in their hands, running to the school in the valley below. In 1984, two African bishops – with the support of thousands of African Methodists – issued the call to create Africa University. In 1988, the United Methodist Church accepted the challenge, and the groundbreaking ceremony took place on land across from the Old Mutare mission site in April 1991. Africa University was officially opened a year later.

The purpose of Africa University is to train Christian leaders for African churches and societies, and students are engaged in various aspects of African life. Several students were spending the next ten weekends with a professor, visiting orphanages and studying the impact of AIDS in Zimbabwe.

During my visit, Africa University was experiencing its share of problems – protests against the cafeteria food, confusion concerning student fees, walkouts during student government meetings, and complaints about the lack of sporting facilities. Another big problem facing student life is the isolation of the campus. Built ten miles away from the town of Mutare, the campus rests in a beautiful but remote valley in the Eastern Highlands of Zimbabwe.

Spiritual life at Africa University centers around chapel services held on Wednesday and Sunday mornings. Also impacting the spiritual life on campus is FOCUS, a student-led prayer group that meets twice a week. The hour-long gatherings include spontaneous singing and prayer, which focuses upon the needs of the university.

***

I spent the first day breaking into the Africa University community, beginning a routine of eating meals, attending classes, and visiting with students. Rev. Randy Flanagan, a Methodist pastor from West Virginia and leader of a one-week work team of volunteers from the same state, preached during chapel – *Africa University is on holy ground.* After lunch, I spoke to the spiritual formation class about pilgrimage, and then I spent the remainder of the afternoon in the library. Heavy rain fell throughout the day, and I enjoyed the refreshingly cool weather while talking with a few students about the relentless rains that had been falling on Zimbabwe. *God doesn't do anything in small ways*, they said. Meanwhile, I thought of the drought that I had left in Kenya.

In the evening, I went by to visit Rosalyn, an African-American student from Illinois. Even though things were not going well for her here, she felt a call to stay another semester – a decision that postponed her graduation back home. Rosalyn wanted to be a teacher and had a passion to minister in the inner city. Later, a student came by my room, hoping to sell me something. Reluctantly, I bought a small stone sculpture of a father, mother, and child. It was entitled *The Abstract* and was apparently carved by a friend of his. I really didn't want to carry a rock around with me; yet, it was easier to help him. *The Abstract* reminded me of my Scottish friend, Andy, and his family, Rhonda and Robert. I planned somehow to give it to them.

***

Frank, a native of Portuguese-speaking Angola, told me about his first trip to Africa University. *I got off the plane in Harare with a hand-scribbled note in my hand that a friend in Angola had written for me, and I gave it to somebody in the airport. The note read: 'I do not speak English. I am going to Africa University. Please can you help me take a bus to Mutare?'*

***

I went with the West Virginia group on a day tour of the area. Everyone began asking questions of our guides, and many of the questions were about the day ahead. While we should be engaged with our world, there are some questions that are better left unasked – some answers that are better experienced than verbalized. It's the wait, the surprise, and the disclosure of the journey that contains the joy. A pilgrim, while not wanting to be ill informed, practices patience and waits for things to be revealed in their own time.

We stopped for a view overlooking a large valley. Walking along a path, we could see for miles, and back near the van, we rested on the porch of a small store, drinking sodas and visiting with some locals who sat near us while a young boy brought a herd of cattle down a mountain path. We loaded back up, and I sat, cramped in the van, forced to listen to Madonna as we drove for miles along a dirt road. Soon, it became apparent that our tour guides didn't know where they were going, and our confidence in them began to wane as they consulted maps and hesitantly turned down more dirt roads.

We eventually found the entrance of a national park, but the ranger denied us access because our tour guides did not have the proper permits. Randy went outside, spoke to the ranger himself, and in spite of our guides, we proceeded to the car park where we hiked a half-mile path to the second highest waterfall on the African continent. The scenery was spectacular, and we climbed rocks, and took photos of one another. Miscalculating the time, we missed lunch. We had planned to eat at a restaurant, but by now, the lunch hour was long over. People were tired, hungry and irritable.

On the way home, we stopped at a gas station. *Be careful,* the tour guides said as we unloaded. *There are thieves here.* I wondered why we even had guides. Is the job of a tour guide to warn us about thieves or perhaps to take us someplace where there weren't any? Perhaps I was asking too much. Still, throughout the day, our tour guides had no clue what they were doing, made bad choices, and had never been to the places where they took us. *Lesson of the Day:* Don't go with inexperienced guides.

***

That night, there was a dance in the student center, and several of us went over to check it out. During the dance, Randy remarked, *What is so special about Africa University is its vision and the speed in which this vision has become a reality. Other than that, it is just like any other university.*

I walked outside to get some fresh air, and a young student, gregariously drunk, began talking to me. He quickly covered the subjects of God and religion and then insisted that I come over to his house the next week. I didn't decline; rather, I just figured that he'd forget about it when he sobered up. Another group of drunken students was dragging a large, ten-foot snake that they had killed during the day along the sidewalk. It was a Saturday night on a college campus.

***

I went into Mutare to worship at St. Peter's United Methodist Church. Daniel, a student at Africa University, gave the sermon. He asked: *What is your destiny and where are you going?* Daniel used an interesting African proverb: *The power of tea is in the boiling water. When everything is easy, you can't distinguish between the strong and the weak. But when things get difficult, and boiling water is poured upon our lives, we are tested. Life is difficult. But with God's power, we can become strong in adversity.*

***

My job is to help students to actualize dreams and to solve problems,

Rev. Tsiga, the university chaplain told me. *Of course, this is best done through a relationship with Jesus Christ, which I try to get the students to develop. Many students come by my office to share their problems. The two most common problems concern finances and family. Most of the international students do not have money to travel back home during breaks, and so they are away from family – spouses and children – for several years. Many of our students face loneliness and separation here and wars and social unrest back home. It is a very difficult situation.*

I have found that I have had a richer response with non-theology students, who are genuinely struggling to live a Christian life and who realize, unlike some of the theology students, that they don't have all of the answers. I began, hoping to create a religious atmosphere on campus. But I soon realized that the students are here to seek an education not to be converted. With a shock, I quickly shifted gears. Religion can be mixed with the curriculum, but it can't be forced upon them.

***

It's not perfect, but it's happening, said Andra Stevens, director of information for Africa University. *The honeymoon stage is over; we are now in a consolidating phase – fine tuning things that have previously been ignored. However, our priorities have not changed. Our main focus is still making education accessible to students who otherwise would have no chance. In Zimbabwe, there are only university spaces for 2,500 people, yet 9,000 students graduate each year from high school. That is just Zimbabwe. As a pan-African institution, we are committed to taking students from many countries that have no university infrastructure at all. What we are doing here is vital for the future of Africa.*

I was at the first graduation in 1994, continued Stevens. *I can remember all of the dancing and jumping and crying going on. Graduation is not an individual thing, but rather it is owned and shared by the entire family and by the whole village. I was overwhelmed. I knew that working here was the chance of a lifetime.*

There is a unique spirit here. Africa University will be what it will be

– in spite of us of all!

***

I preached this morning during chapel – *Africa University is on a sacred journey.* It was a wonderful, unexpected privilege. Afterwards, a male student named *We know* said that he was going to name his first son *Aist.* I tried not to discourage him.

Lately, I have been falling asleep and then suddenly waking up with a weird sensation that chills my spine: *I am alive. Where did I come from? How did I get here?* Strange dreams as a side effect of malaria tablets.

***

In the afternoon, I walked with Calenge, a student from Angola, to the Old Mutare orphanage where wet, dirty kids begged for our attention. The facilities were simple and unsanitary. The kids were precious but with little hope.

Calenge: *I came here to study theology, but what has been so wonderful about Africa University is the opportunity to study with students from so many different countries, cultures, and languages.*

My initial sleep produced another psychotic-type experience. The face of a little boy was looking at me. I think that I was trying to catch him and then he disappeared, fading into a black veil of nothingness, confusion and despair.

***

Joan's son, Richard, lived in Muture, where he is the headmaster of a nearby prep school. I spent the day with the family – his wife, Fiona, and their five kids. We drove to Lake Alexander, passing a couple of gold mines on the way. The scenery was beautiful; everything was green and lush. At the reservoir, we had just begun a cup of tea under a picnic hut when the rains set in, interrupting our tea party. The day went by quickly, and they soon drove me back to the university.

***

Rev. Tsiga gave the Transfiguration Sunday sermon in the chapel.[62] He said that humans are transfigured but often by despair and stress rather than by the radiance and glory of God.

***

I said my good-byes at breakfast, and I left the campus in the pouring rain. While it was sad to leave the comforts of a room, to say good-bye to friends, and to face the unknown again, I knew that my visit was complete. In Muture, I walked around town for a couple of hours, passing a few beggars on the sidewalks. For some reason, I didn't think they were my problem, and I ignored their pleads for assistance.

***

Joan picked me up at the bus station in Harare. While I was in Muture, Joan had attended a talk by one of the Medjugorje visionaries. I asked Joan what she thought about Mary: *She was, after all, Jesus' mother. She must have been an incredible woman. I don't think that we Anglicans acknowledge her enough.* Mary's message is to pray, fast twice a week, repent and turn to Christ.

***

In the morning, Joan hosted an *Alpha* group, an evangelism program of the Church of England, for a group of *WOW*s, or *Worn-Out Whites*, as they call themselves. I was asked to open in prayer, and as soon as I finished, one of the ladies said, *I hope you don't speak that fast when you preach.* I didn't say too much after that.

The illustrations from the *Alpha* video included:

* *They say that the Japanese have two stomachs – one stomach for rice and another one for all of the other foods. They can eat all the food that they want, but if they don't eat rice, they will still be hungry, because their second stomach will still be empty. Jesus said, 'I am the living bread that came down from heaven.' People fill their lives with*

---

[62] Matthew 17:1-13, Luke 9:28-36, Mark 9:2-13.

all sorts of food, but they will always be hungry until they fill themselves with Christ, the bread of life.

* *Many people simply go from one thing to the next because whatever they have found in the present doesn't satisfy. There is always something missing until one finds God.*

Rumors were going around that God was leaving the Church of England. 'Well,' said one man. 'It will certainly be a blow; but we'll just have to go on.'

* *Faith is like standing on the edge of a swimming pool longing to get in but afraid to jump.*

Richard was in town and came by the house. Talking about school: *Youth romanticize suicide. The worse thing you can do is to give them sympathy. I drag them into my office and make them read 'Twenty ways to kill yourself.' We had three attempts last year at the school. Fortunately, none of them was successful.*

***

I ducked inside the Harare cathedral for a time of prayer and then went into the cloister where one black and three white women were having a cup of tea. The black lady wore white clothes and white gloves. *She thinks she's a messenger from God,* said the three whites. *She's a shouter; she's always coming here preaching against jewelry and makeup. We just put up with her.*

I have four children, the lady told me, ignoring the three white women. *But since my husband died, I have become the bride of Christ.*

We could hear organ music coming from the chancel. *My mother played the organ. Whenever I hear organ music, I start to weep,* she said tearing up. Her eyes lit up when I told her that I was a pastor, and she smiled when I called her an angel.

***

It feels strange saying goodbye to the African continent.

God prepares you for the goodbye, for the departure. Still, God doesn't take all the sadness away, and a lot of the emotion is simply suppressed. I thought about Hilary, an Africa University student from Kenya, who had told me: *Good-byes are like death. We know that they're inevitable, yet they're always a surprise. We are going to miss you.*

I walked out onto the dark tarmac and looked back into the airport floodlights. My journey into Africa was over but not finished. Pilgrimage is a call to service and action. We can change the world, but first, we have to listen to the voices of others. Once the cries are heard, though, the church must take a no-nonsense approach to helping others.

We took off and had a quick touch down in Johannesburg before flying in the night towards the western coast of Australia. I drank coffee, listening to *Easy* and *If You Leave Me Now* on my airline headphones.

Voices

Reveka, as she was called, had discovered at an early age that there was a voice within her which in spite of its being hers was nevertheless not hers at all.[63]

***

(Australia: February 14th – March 3rd)

I got off the plane in Perth and walked right into a bad haircut. Even so, I fell instantly in love with Australia.

My first full day was spent on the beach. The water was beautiful; the sun was hot and intense. I unintentionally fried the back of my ankles.

I took the train into Freemantle, a beautiful coastal town and a past host of the America's Cup. The streets were lined with renovated nineteenth-century buildings housing trendy shops and restaurants. Darkness fell as Valentine couple emerged, taking over the streets on the warm evening. I returned to Perth where the Perth Festival was going on, and I sat outside listening to the free concert in the park and watching the fireworks that followed.

***

I wasn't buying souvenirs; I was buying books. At one time, I had seventeen of them with me. Books from Europe. Books from Africa. Now books from Australia. They only added to my journeys. More narrative. More content. More voices. Gerard Hughes, Carlo Carretto, Paulo Coelho, Achebe, and Ng~ug~i. Women authors like Sally Morgan, Sheila Cassidy, and Kathleen Norris.

***

My morning worship experience in downtown Perth was just short of

---

[63] Quote from *Peasants and Masters* by Greek-Swedish novelist, Theodor Kallifatides, used in introductory page of Chenjerai Hove, *Ancestors* (London: Picador, 1996).

unbearable. The pastor was absent, which should have been a clue. Usually, parishioners know not to attend when the pastor is away. It's only the die-hard and the unfortunate guests who have to endure the pulpit substitutes.

The guest speaker donned white trousers and a white button down shirt. Inside his front pocket was a plastic pocket sleeve, the kind my grandfather used to wear when he ran a general store in Arkansas. My grandfather kept cigars and black wax pens inside his. The speaker's held a pair of glasses, an assortment of colored pens, and other basic office equipment. Some sort of social worker, he read a scripture which he never referred to and drew on overheads the whole time introducing us to the lives of his clients. You'd have thought that their tangled-up and triangulated lives would have been of some intrigue, but he droned on for ages, and he was so awful that I began to feel nauseous.

I can remember seeing *Funny Car Summer*, a drag racing movie, when I was in elementary school. It was so bad that Tate Williams was supposedly throwing up in the parking lot – not because it was gross or anything, just because it was bad. A few steps past aggravated boredom is a nausea that makes you want to hurl just because something is so totally inane. It's a bad scene when elementary kids throw up over a drag racing movie or when pastors lose it in worship.

Tea in the fellowship hall followed the service, and although I was inclined to hightail it out of there, I realized that it would be the only free food I'd get all day.

I have never in my life seen members of a church so aggressively seeking out visitors. Nearly taking my arm off, a middle-aged lady came up to me and said, *Oh, dear me. We do so apologize for our speaker this morning. Why, he was absolutely dreadful.* She wasn't finished before someone else caught my other arm and started, *I can't tell you how utterly embarrassed we are this morning. I don't know how anybody lets that man in the pulpit.* I looked around and saw small clusters of people around the room, members passionately apologizing to the few visitors on how awful the morning service had been. *Quite right, quite right,* I mumbled between sips of tea.

I left the church and entered the scorching mid-day heat; the sun was already torturously hot. I walked through Kings Park and climbed a large hill for a wonderful view of the Perth harbor. I then walked through some bush trails before catching a train back to the beach, where I swam for another hour. In the evening, I returned to Freemantle for evensong at an Anglican church.

The service was just beginning as I entered the church, and I joined about a dozen people in the choir, where we sat in two groups facing one another. *Deja vu* – another absolutely awful service. We sang the Lord's Prayer *(Did Jesus' disciples really ask, 'Lord, teach us to sing, just as John taught his disciples'?)*[64] And then the Apostle's Creed – same melody. The service was long and felt ancient – dead – I struggled unsuccessfully to find signs of life. I was probably still recovering from the morning and should have known not to over do it.

Finally – though abruptly – the priest gave the benediction. I took a deep breath. The service was over. *That was lovely,* I heard the woman in front of me say. *Too bad more aren't here; they don't know what they are missing out on.* I returned my hymnal and headed outside to join those to whom she was referring.

The sunset over the Indian Ocean was both beautiful and brief. I was reminded again of what Hilary had told me: *The departure is always a surprise.*

***

I prefer recommendations to options.

I asked the lady selling tours for Ayers Rock – or Uluru as it is called by the Aborigines – for suggestions. She just repeated the options. *Well, there's the sunset tour, the sunrise tour, and the tour to the Olgas.*

Thank you, very much. I can read the brochure, I grumbled. *What's your recommendation?* I asked. *What's the best value? What's the most popular tour?*

---

[64] A paraphrase of Luke 11:1-4.

Well, she snipped. *I'm not going to tell you what to do.*

I am looking for mentors in my life – people who have been there, people who can share their wisdom with me. I'm well aware of most of my options.

Well, I'm not going to tell you what to do. That's not very helpful.

***

There are signs everywhere asking people not to climb Uluru – asking people to respect the sacred grounds of the Aborigines: *Respect Aboriginal wishes and do not climb the rock because of its religious significance.* Nonetheless, there is a daily procession of human ants ascending the largest rock in the world, just something else to be conquered.

He who has ears to hear let him hear.[65]

The Aborigines are also tired of the human sacrifices – too much blood is being spilled on their altar. That week, a Japanese man died of a heart attack on his way up.

What is solidarity? Is it not listening to and obeying the voices inside us and around us, paying attention to voices that aren't ours? What are the reasons for climbing? The problem is that people don't think they need a reason to climb. *He who has ears to hear let him hear.*

The night before, I attended an Aborigine dance performance, *Mind Wanderers.* They shared their journey of the past, present, and future. *We now journey together,* they intimated, addressing a multi-cultural audience. We are given the freedom – and the choice – to listen, to share, to respect, and to obey. The voices in this world are not always ours.

The evening walk through the Olgas was beautiful. At the pavilion, I had some grilled kangaroo while talking baseball with a Japanese couple. Back in the youth hostel, I began packing for my early morning flight. After laying everything out on my bed, I unwrapped

---

[65] Quoted several times by Jesus. See Luke 14:35 as an example.

the rock, the family hug of Andy, Rhonda, and Robert that I had been carrying with me since Zimbabwe. It was now it two pieces – Andy's head had broken off. I bowed my head, said a short prayer and then regretfully threw it into the garbage can.

***

Paul had been the stranger on the bus to Taizé. Now, he was my host in Melbourne.

We had dinner together at his house before going to the Carmelite monastery near his high school for a Taizé-style prayer service. A room full of silence, incense and prayer greeted us, and I immediately found myself at home and at ease. The Friday night Carmelite service, Paul's first introduction to Taizé, contained all of the familiar elements. After worship, Paul and I sat in the common room, drinking tea and conversing with a few of the brothers.

Stop by the Breakwater Community in Geelong; it is right on your way to the Great Ocean Road, said Brother Daryl. *It was formally known as the Community of the Holy Transfiguration, and it was founded by four Baptist ministers and an Anglican priest. They did their spiritual formation in a Russian Orthodox monastery in England. Their spirituality is an interesting mix of Protestant Baptism, Russian Orthodoxy, and Celtic Christianity all set in an Australian context!*

***

Paul and I pulled off the main highway in Geelong and found an old bluestone church surrounded by hedges. A sign identified the building as a Baptist congregation and as the home of the Community of the Holy Transfiguration. A few minutes later, Paul and I found ourselves sitting on the verandah, sharing breakfast with the fifteen members of the community.

The Community of the Holy Transfiguration is an urban, integrated monastery – a community of people, male and female, married and single, couples and families. All of the adults have outside jobs – e.g. at the local Ford plant or with the social services. One woman is a seamstress; another man is a stained-glass worker. *We all have incomes, and we share everything in common,* said one member. *We have one common purse with two treasurers, a male and a female.*

Founded in 1972, the community is nearly thirty years old. *At first, we were given this old Baptist church which was about to close – mostly because the Baptist church didn't know what to do with us! All this land behind the church was a garbage dump. We have cleaned it up, built new buildings, remodeled the old ones, and we have been able to purchase some adjoining land.*

Over breakfast, the members shared their experiences:

* *We seek to know God through community – through our communal life of worship, work, silence and contemplation. Primary, though, is our relationship with Christ. Christ is the focal point of all that we do.*

There is a cycle in both our worship and community life that we are constantly repeating. First is the process of dismantling or stripping away that which is not of God.

This is followed by a period of liminality when we realize that we are not yet who God wants us to be. It is a time of waiting, a time of becoming – often it can be a desert experience, and so this period can be terribly frightening. In these moments of our darkness, all we can do is hold out our hands. God places a piece of bread in them, and this is the only way we survive.

The period of liminality is very long and difficult, but during it, we learn to participate in the victory that Christ has already won for us. This victory is the resurrection – which is the third aspect of the cycle. Through the resurrection, we share together with Christ the glory of our own transfiguration.

Our community has learned to deal with anger and with each other better than it did twenty years ago. We have learned to be angry, to deal with our rage, but we have found that violence cannot be a part of that. We try to give each other room to be angry, to learn to wait – both on ourselves and on others – during the growing times. This can be terrifying, yet unlike other communities, we cannot be content with accepting that so-and-so just don't get along.

*We take the words 'working out our salvation in fear and trembling' very seriously. We pray for peace in the world, for the release of hostages; yet, if in our little microcosm, we are holding each other hostage, then quite frankly, we find that God laughs at our prayers.

*Sometimes members must leave the community to break their destructive patterns – sometimes up to six months. I was one of the people who had to leave. Later, when I realized in my terrible loneliness the deep love and concern that others had for me, I was able to change my behavior and attitudes and rejoin the community.

*We have found that the greatest enemy to community life is obedience without understanding. Our greatest anger over the last twenty years has been with those who would not take responsibility for their own actions, usually through apathy not inability.

*I have found my own individuality only through community. Before, I had sacrificed myself on the altar of fundamentalism. Fundamentalism uses knowledge to suggest that it has the whole truth – fear, ignorance, and static absolutes to suggest that it has the authority to justify its own manipulation and control of others. Through the order and discipline of community life, I have been granted the freedom to obey the Gospel and to be safeguarded from fundamentalism. We regard fundamentalism as 'the noonday demon' – the 'pestilence that destroys at mid-day' (Psalm 91).

*One of the greatest enemies within and without is this noonday pestilence – the hour of no shadows. It appears only when the sun has reached its height, and we can no longer see our shadows – when we think that we are living in the truth. However, we should never lose sight of our shadows. Our shadow side is the enemy that must be recognized, owned and transfigured for our own good. We have mid-day prayer every day in order that we may take heed during the hour of no shadows and protect ourselves from our own piety and overconfidence.

After breakfast, two of the members gave Paul and me a tour. The baptism font in the church is formed in the shape of a cross and is set a few feet into the floor with steps on both sides. During communion, members receive the elements by walking through the baptism font – a ritual reminder of the connection between baptism and communion and of St. Paul's words of dying to self and being raised to life in Christ.

We then met back with the community in the prayer house for a service of *Blessing for Travelers* where Paul and I received prayers of protection and an anointing. As Paul and I said our good-byes, we received hugs, a book of prayers, and a little pocket change for our travels. *You couldn't have picked a better time to visit us,* they told us.

We were overwhelmed. *Thank you . . . for everything. We have received such a blessing from you.*

You have received as a result of what you have given, someone replied.

Paul and I got back into the car and headed for the Twelve Apostles, one of the most spectacular formations along the Great Ocean Road.

***

On my way to Port Arthur (Tasmania), the site of the worst mass murder in modern history, a news story broke over the radio – an assassin was loose on the top of the Empire State Building; one person was already dead. Three days earlier in Melbourne, I saw a magazine cover featuring the upcoming anniversary of the Dunblane (Scotland) tragedy. Voices of grief, death, and tragedy are all around us.

Port Arthur was a large self-contained prison settlement and is now a giant open-air museum. At the entrance gate, a sign greeted me:

The Port Arthur Tragedy
April 28, 1996

This event has touched us all and causes us great pain.

Written information is available from our staff.

However, we ask you not to discuss the incident with us.

General Manager and Staff

As written information was available, I intended to secure a copy for my journals. However, by the time I left the park, all of the offices were closed. Now, I am glad that they were. Sometimes solidarity is being aware of someone else's story without having to possess it. We sometimes confuse understanding someone with understanding the details of their stories – it becomes a question of respect rather than of knowledge.

Port Arthur was completely convict-built. At its peak, there were forty-one fully functioning trades, including shipbuilding. The prison grounds consisted of a cricket pitch, a hospital, barracks, officer houses, a granary, an asylum, and various trade buildings. Of special interest to me was the Port Arthur church. The convict church, built so that the worshipping prisoners could not see one another, was never consecrated. Instead of church pews, long rows of open-faced solitary booths faced the chancel. Prisoners were led one-by-one into the church. The first prisoner would go all the way down the row through a series of booths. He would then close the door and remain standing, facing the front of the church, waiting in silence until every prisoner had come in and had taken a booth. During the service, the preacher could see all of the prisoners, but not a single prisoner could see a fellow inmate. How contrary to the essence of Christianity!

I took a twenty-minute boat tour around the Isle of the Dead, the final resting place for the convicts. It began to rain during the peaceful ride, and when we returned to the dock, a rainbow was over the island. The rainbow hung around for a while, a reminder of God's promise of life in the context of death. I spent the last hour walking the grounds in prayer and reflection. Although its history is one of despair, brutality, and murder, I don't think that I have ever been in a more serene, tranquil setting in my life.

Heading north from Port Arthur, I found a dirt road, which I took as a scenic short cut. I stopped along a fencerow to take some photos of the pastureland in the late evening sun. Farther up, after I entered a forest, a kangaroo jumped out of the woods in front of my car, hopped down the road for a few seconds and then disappeared back into the woods.

***

Driving in Tasmania introduced me to a lot of new animals. About every hundred yards, I passed some form of road kill. Often sticking out of the flat furry mess was a tail that I know I had never seen before in my life. In the news, a man was caught with a frozen koala and twenty-seven other illegal animals in his freezer.

I drove to Coles Bay, gateway to Freycinet National Park. Wineglass Lookout, a large wooden balcony in the midst of huge granite outcroppings, gave me a magnificent, breathtaking view of the white sandy beaches of Wineglass Bay, to where I descended for a cold but refreshing swim.

After dark, I drove to a lighthouse, where I sat on the cliff watching an incredible moon rise over the ocean as a sky full of southern stars emerged. While I was driving, *The Land Down Under* came on the radio. Back at the youth hostel, *Crocodile Dundee* was on national television. My visit to Australia was already complete.

***

I spent five days in Sydney, visiting Australian friends that I had met at camp in Minnesota. Rose, a former camp nurse, and I spent a day in the Blue Mountains, about an hour or so outside of Sydney, looking at waterfalls and making short hikes. We stopped at Sublime Point, Echo Point, and the Three Sisters before taking the world's steepest incline railroad down into the valley, walking through the woods for a while and then riding it back up to the top. At the Hydro-Majestic Hotel, we sat on the porch drinking coffee and looking out over the huge valley.

***

The largest annual tourist event in Australia is Sydney's Mardi Gras, which took place the weekend I was there. We walked along the parade route, passing outrageously dressed people and creative floats assembling in the streets before finding the Koala Best Western where a party was waiting for us on the twelfth floor. Our balcony overlooked the parade route. I could see the Sydney Opera House off in the distance. The parade, though long and extravagant, ended way too quickly. Finally, we left, stopping in at a coffee shop below on Oxford Street where we sat drinking coffee until five in the morning.

***

The noise of the neighbor's weed whacker drove me out of bed a few hours too soon. Brett and Nikki, other friends from camp, came over to Rose's and then took me back to their house for the night. On the way home, we traveled back down Oxford Street, which had been dramatically transformed back into a sleepy Sunday afternoon city street.

But back in Arkansas, tornadoes were ripping through the state, taking the lives of twenty-three people.

Thinking Hearts

(New Zealand: March 3rd – 12th)

My around-the-world ticket gave me passage to places that I had not previously considered visiting – namely, Australia, New Zealand, and Fiji. While I was centrally based in most other countries, I chose to travel fairly extensively throughout Australia, maximizing airline destinations as well as I could. Fiji, as I discovered in my planning, was the home of Pacific Theological College, a Pacific Council of Churches seminary serving all of the South Pacific. For contacts in New Zealand, however, I turned to the Internet, where I found the home page of St. Paul's United Methodist Church in Auckland. Rushan Sinnaduray, the youth director, responded, extending a week's invitation to me and offering to arrange opportunities for me to visit with local church leaders.

***

If things continue as they are, in a few more years the Church [in New Zealand] will be dead, said Jan, a lay leader at St. Paul's Methodist Church. *How do you get people to see that Christianity is a life worth living?* She continued, nearly in tears. *I don't know; maybe it's good. Maybe it's time for the Church, as we know it, to die and for some other form of Christianity – from Africa or Polynesia – to take its place. Maybe it's time for the Church to regroup. We, as Christians, must understand exactly who we are. What do we mean by 'God'? What do we mean by 'Christian'?*

Jan was asking the right questions. However, she was on the verge of despair. She felt unequipped and unresourced. *I have taken some theological classes, but they haven't held any answers for me.* She is searching for her place in ministry, but hasn't found it. *I was a lay preacher, but I quit preaching because of the tension I felt between being honest (truth) and providing pastoral care (tact).*

***

The Community of St. Luke Presbyterian Church, pastored by the

Rev. David Clark, is one of the few churches currently growing in Auckland. *What we are doing at St. Luke's is trying to rekindle the liberal flame. Our slogan, 'The Thinking Heart,' expresses our desire to integrate intellect and emotion with the spiritual dimension. Too often liberal theology had been very rational and had lacked spiritual depth. Worship is still at the core of life at St. Luke's*, said Rev. Clark, who has visited both Iona and Taizé.

We are a baby boomer church – and baby boomer theology is very cerebral. We are trying to move from the cerebral to the affective.

We recognize and value the diversity of all people. We want to stand alongside other belief systems and journeys of exploration. There is a Maori word, 'mawa,' which means 'a deeper presence.' That's what we strive for. We seek to be an inclusive community; however, I admit that when you try to be inclusive you are always going to exclude somebody.

I asked him why his church was growing.

I don't know. . . . We don't have an evangelism plan. Rather, we are slowly puttering along, and to our surprise, we are growing. Sometimes I ask myself, 'What are we doing that is so right?' Maybe we are offering an alternative to mainline churches.

We are trying alternative worship styles as well as worshipping at various times throughout the week, although our primary service is still on Sunday. However, if we are serious about the family, then the Church has got to stop worshipping on Sunday mornings which, quite frankly, is the most ridiculous time of the week – splitting up families during the only time they would otherwise have together.

***

Wesley Jeyaseelan, a native of Sri Lanka, has recently been appointed to St. Paul's Methodist. He describes his ministry as *the lifelong pursuit of making the Christian faith meaningful and relevant in a secular and pluralistic society.* His understanding of ministry was recently depicted in a painting that he had commissioned. In four different scenes, a minister is described equally as a stranger, a guest, a partner, and as an unearther of treasures.

First of all, the minister is a stranger – a traveler in time – moving from place to place, Jeyaseelan said. *The minister is a prophet, pointing out new and unnoticed aspects of life. Secondly, a minister is a guest – a receiver – welcomed into people's lives, homes, and communities and receiving their love and hospitality. The minister is also a partner, journeying together with people – carrying and sharing the load with others. And lastly, a minister is the unearther of treasures, helping people to discover qualities, gifts, and abilities that lie within them. In short, the minister helps people to discover the Kingdom of God, which is like a treasure buried in a field.*

I was surprised by the many references to journey in Wesley's understanding of ministry.

The Christian life is one of journey, Wesley said. *God is always feeding us along the way. . . . A family was preparing for a picnic. They were ready to leave when, all of a sudden, a storm came up, raining out the picnic. The family sat down at their kitchen table and began eating the picnic food when one of the children started complaining that the sandwiches didn't taste very good, although the child would have loved the same food in the park. The child was right. The food wasn't meant to be eaten at home. So it is with the Christian faith: the Christian life is much more rewarding when we are on the road – helping, serving, discovering, and sharing. God's food tastes better on the journey.*

***

In the parking lot of Pitt Street Methodist Church, I met Jioni Langi, a Fijian minister who seemed eager to make some arrangements for my trip to Fiji.

***

The Rev. Percy Rushton, a retired Methodist pastor, currently works two days a week at St. Mary's, a Methodist-Anglican cooperative parish. *Each denomination is responsible for providing pastoral leadership,* he explained. *For five years, the Methodists appoint a pastor; the next five years, the Anglicans appoint someone. If a cooperative church is also Presbyterian, then for five years, the congregation is allowed to call someone.*

All Methodist ministers in New Zealand earn the same salary; raises are based on inflation. The Methodist Church in New Zealand does not have bishops but rather presidents who serve one-year terms. Additionally, there is a stationing committee, which together with the president, the past-president, and the president-elect makes the yearly appointments of pastors. Rev. Rushton served as president in the late 1980s.

I believe that evangelism is not just personal transformation but rather social transformation as well, said Rev. Rushton. *During my year as president, the Methodist Church began the 'Bi-Cultural Journey' with the native Maori people. In 1840, the Treaty of Waitangi was signed between the English and the Maori. While it was supposedly based on equal partnership between the two groups, the Maoris have always been treated as second-class people. The Methodist Church in New Zealand has led the way in re-establishing a partnership between the different cultures. In the 'Bi-Cultural Journey,' the Methodist Conference has committed itself to being ruled by consensus – with the Maori delegation, approximately ten percent of the conference, and the non-Maori delegation both having to agree for a decision to be made.*

Rev. Rushton believes that the Methodist Church has been on the forefront of many issues in New Zealand, including pacifism. *When I was an exchange pastor in Tennessee, I gave a sermon against nuclear weapons. I was quickly surprised to find out that the topic had never been discussed from the pulpit. Here in New Zealand, if there was a World War III, I believe that many people would not fight.*

***

My time in New Zealand was not always fun. I found myself often reacting against the mundane – and sometimes boring – work of day-to-day church ministry. Throughout the week, I encountered a struggling Church drowning in a post-modern society.

I said good-bye to Rushan at the Hertz office, and I immediately went up a one-way street on my way out of Auckland. I spent the next two days with a couple of friends who just happened to be backpacking in New Zealand. Together, we went blackwater rafting – donning wet suits and spelunker helmets, we grabbed inner tubes and made for the glowworm caves. While floating on underground rivers, we turned out our flashlights and looked up at the thousands of tiny, miniscule lights on the roofs of the caves.

Back in Auckland, I called Jioni Langi from the airport. He had been trying to arrange something for me, but Cyclone Gavin had just hit Fiji, and all of the phone lines were down. He couldn't get a hold of any of his family. Discouraged, I hung up, further upset that my flight was delayed, not due to arrive until nearly midnight. Both anxious and apathetic about my trip to Fiji, I began killing time in the airport lobby.

God of Surprises

I was reading *God of Surprises* by Gerard Hughes when I saw the Rev. Jioni Langi walking towards me. Just two hours before, Rev. Langi had told me regretfully on the phone: *The cyclone has hit Nadi and the western side of the island very hard. All the phone lines are down. I still can't reach my brother.*

Although I understood the situation, I was not looking forward to arriving in Fiji at midnight, 120 miles from the Pacific Theological College in Suva where I was to spend the next week. So I was shocked but pleased when I looked up and saw Langi. He had come all the way out to the Auckland airport to find me.

I remembered my cousin, Samuela. He's also a Methodist pastor. He lives in the next town north of Nadi. He'll be at the airport to pick you up. You'll spend the night with him and his wife, and they'll put you on a bus for Suva in the morning.

The God of surprises was still in control of my pilgrimage, reminding me who had put the trip together and who was going to finish it!

Having previously visited with Rev. Langi for only ten minutes in a church parking lot, we spent an hour together in the airport. Jioni Langi is from Rotuma, a tiny island located three hundred miles from the two main Fijian islands. Racially and culturally different from the Fijian people, the Rotumans were politically united with Fiji by the British many years ago.

Over the last fifteen years, Langi has worked with Fijian and Rotuman congregations in Australia and New Zealand, helping his people to retain Christian community amid the individualism and materialism of modern society. *I am trying to bring back to life people who have gone astray, who have forsaken their Christian roots, and who feel lost or alienated from our culture and faith,* he said. Rev. Langi studied at Pacific Theological College, and most of his family lives in the Suva area. *When you get to Suva and PTC, make sure you look up my family; they will want to get together with you.* He told me that he likes to help people. *A lot of people would say this was all a coincidence, but I know that it's not. God has brought us together.* Eventually, we said good-bye, and I watched him as he walked out of sight – extremely grateful for my worries that he had just taken with him.

***

(Fiji: March 12th – 18th)

Samuela's wife fixed me a big breakfast, and after showing me his church and pointing out some of the local damage caused by Cyclone Gavin, Samuela put me on a mini-van headed for Suva. I sat in the back seat listening to the radio – *If I Could Change the World, Staying Alive, Afternoon Delight,* and *Lying Eyes.* It was a beautiful coastal drive, ending up at the doorstep of a quiet and empty Pacific Theological College.

In fact, the school was closed; all the classes had been cancelled because of the funeral of a stillborn child of a Samoan student and his wife. The college community was now away at the cemetery. I walked over to the Lighthouse, a nearby café overlooking the ocean, and had a chicken pie and an *America's Choice* lemonade made in Australia exclusively for Fiji. An hour later, I returned to the college, where everyone was now present, attending the funeral reception – an odd but appropriate setting, as it turned out, for the introduction of their new guest.

***

The Pacific Theological College, located on sixteen acres of oceanfront land, was founded in 1966. The college, currently the home of sixty-seven students and families representing thirty different churches and eighteen nations and territories from throughout the South Pacific, is the largest Protestant seminary on the Liquid Continent. While I was there, many of the faculty members were attending a Pacific Council of Churches conference in Tahiti, which was celebrating the two-hundred-year anniversary of Christianity in the South Pacific.

The most notable difference between the Pacific Theological College and other seminaries is the visible presence of families living on campus. While a growing number of its students are female, PTC offers a special Women's Programme to assist wives of PTC students in the development of personal growth, practical leadership, and biblical and theological knowledge. In 1980, a children's preschool was started, and in 1992, the Women's Centre, which has facilities for craft making, cooking, typing, sewing, and other skills, opened.

While the many families live in apartments throughout the grounds, the few single students live in dorm rooms on the second floor of the main building. Organized by Lupe, a female master's student from Tonga, the students share a common meal every evening. Lupe looked after me as well, inviting me to the meals, showing me around the campus, taking me to the market, and including me with the Tongan delegation, which paid a pastoral visit one night to the grieving Samoan couple.

***

I had breakfast upstairs with the singles, attended chapel, and then spent the day sitting in on classes – one class spent the hour talking about alcoholism; the pastoral care class addressed violence and gender issues in the South Pacific; AIDS was the topic in the afternoon.

I watched the sunset while sitting on the ocean wall with Lupe. *I've got English blood,* she said.

Really? I asked.

Oh, yeah, my grandfather ate white people.

She continued, *Now don't get me wrong. We didn't eat whites because they tasted good, but because we believed that by eating them, we could possess their spirits.*

Well, I said, too scared to move. *As long as you ate them for the right reasons.*

***

Tui is a huge, but gentle young man from the Cook Islands. All week, he wore the same T-shirt of a large Cook Islander stirring a boiling cauldron: *Send more tourists. The last lot was delicious!*

***

Lupe and I took the bus to the market, where we bought some dalo, a basic root plant, for the evening meal. While walking the streets of Suva, we decided on the spur of the moment to see *Ghosts of Mississippi,* a movie about black civil rights leader Medgar Evers, who was shot to death in June 1963 while standing in his driveway. After successfully sneaking the large bag of dalo into the theatre, we found our seats just as the previews for violent American movies began. I sat through the film – watching a movie about colored relationships in America with a Tongan woman in Fiji – and I wondered how we Americans ever explain ourselves to others.

Back on campus, I watched a rugby game in the common room with some of the students. The Waitoko Chiefs were playing the Auckland Blues. A couple of remarks by the commentator created quite a reaction by the Pacific Islanders in the room: *He is a former Fijian* (Can someone ever be a former Fijian?) and *The Samoan is a piano remover. He doesn't play one; he just removes them.*

***

I went to a Rotuman Methodist worship service with Rosa and her daughter, relatives of Jioni Langi. After the service, I was invited home with Aggie and Freddy, more relatives, where we hung out for an hour and then went over to Aggie's parents' house for breakfast – fish, dalo, yams, beef, and fruit. After another worship service in the afternoon, I went home with Kafaa, yet another relative of Langi. She has a son about my age named Christopher; Lincoln is her two-year-old grandson. I relaxed, trying to get comfortable in a sulu, a one-piece skirt worn by South Pacific men, and watching rugby on the television before eating another huge meal – dalo, fish, and coconut chicken. Jioni Langi was right – his relatives wanted to get together with me, and I enjoyed some of the best hospitality in the world.

***

There was a campaign for women's rights in Fiji. A television advertisement showed two welders with the same qualifications: the female makes $5000 while the male makes $8500.

***

On my last morning in Fiji, I spent some time with Wesis, a Methodist student from Papua New Guinea where in many places Christianity is only one generation old. In 1968, the Methodist Church joined with the Congregational and Presbyterian Churches to form the Uniting Church of Papua New Guinea, which has nine regions with a total of 400,000 members.

Born to one of a dozen wives of his father, a tribal chief, Wesis has around twenty-four brothers and between thirty to sixty sisters. Wesis is the first person from his region of 68,000 church members (a population of two million) to be educated at the master's degree level. Having already been the principal of a small Bible college and a tutor in a theological college in New Guinea, Wesis said that there would be great expectations from his denomination upon his return home. *The denomination would like me to teach at the main theological school of Papua New Guinea,* he told me, *but I feel that my call is to work in my own region with my own people. I'm the first person from there that has gone so far, and I think that I should return home.*

***

I had lunch with Lupe at a Chinese restaurant, and then she walked me to the station where I boarded my bus, which left fifteen minutes earlier than scheduled.

On Top of the World

(Korea: March 21st – March 31st)

From the Sodaemun subway station, I walked straight to the Methodist guesthouse. Unfortunately, I did not know it, failing to recognize either of the two landmarks that I had been told to look for – a giant tree and a Chinese church. How was I supposed to recognize a Chinese church in the middle of Seoul, Korea?

I spent the next hour walking around the area, carrying a heavy, broken backpack. Back and forth, up and down, becoming more and more confused. When you leave where you are supposed to be, things can only get worse. Finally, I came to a police station, and they pointed me back in the direction that I had started.

This time, with more deliberate investigation, I found a gate next to where I had stood an hour before. I pulled the bolt; it was unlocked. Inside the yard was a set of apartment houses; the middle one had on a light. Next to the door, a rock was holding down a note with my name on it. Beside it was a key. I let myself in, crawled up the steps and slipped into my room.

***

I set out in the crisp Saturday morning air to explore Seoul, wandering this way and that, letting my curiosity lead me. I walked up overhead bridges, down commercial alleys and small streets, and along busy roads until I came to the walls of the Kyongbokkung Palace. Inside, the gardens were beautiful. Statues, ponds, and bridges covered the palace landscape. Mountains formed a backdrop in the distance. Couples were having their photos taken. A man from Japan introduced himself, giving me his card. *Call me if you are in Osaka!* School children were looking at me. *Hello! Hello! Hello!* Back on the streets, soldiers were stopping people, mostly students, asking to see their IDs.

In the afternoon, I found Taeksukong Palace and walked into a free outdoor concert of the Seoul Pops Orchestra. The concert included

Strauss as well as a soprano soloist, some traditional screaming, and a young male pop talent. After the music was over, I walked around the grounds, taking photos of people taking photos of each other. Occasionally, groups of Korean school children would ask to be in a picture with me. Wedding couples in traditional outfits were abundant, as were families with kids.

Eventually, I left the park and began wandering downtown where I stumbled upon the commercial pedestrian streets full of Saturday night shoppers. Minutes later, I walked into a small student protest, which soon attracted the presence of dozens of riot police. At first, it was all very interesting – even a bit unnerving – but before long, I became bored, and I left, seeking the comforts of my bed.

***

It was Palm Sunday, arguably one of the most celebratory Sundays of the church year, and so expectantly, I went with David, an Irishman who ran the Methodist guesthouse, to one of the largest Methodist churches in the world. I had visions of palm branches, children's bands, hallelujah choirs, joyful music, perhaps even a play or a cantata. I couldn't wait to see the church and to be carried away in joyful worship with thousands of others.

David and I found the twelve-story educational building and four-story sanctuary tucked off a main city road. Five minutes after we entered the lobby, a little lady finally rushed over to greet us. Expecting us to follow her, she ran up three flights of stairs, tripping only once, leading us to the upper balcony where signs that read *FOREIGNERS* greeted our arrival. We were given headphones to follow the translation of the service, and as I sat down, I looked out over the sanctuary, riddled with scaffolding.

The sanctuary was old, colorless, and unremarkable. Down below, the choir was squished into a small side transept of the sanctuary; a small orchestra was positioned in front of them. The service began with an unimpressive start and only got worse.

To my displeasure, a white American preacher was giving the sermon. To my horror, he gave the most gruesome sermon on the death of Jesus that I've ever heard. The preacher went into detailed descriptions about the acts of brutality, the pain and suffering, and the medical causes of death. Every joint, tendon and ligament were pulled apart, and just to make sure that he was dead, the preacher gave Jesus a final, fatal stab which broke everyone's heart. I wondered if throwing up was a part of repentance.

Instead of palms on the altar, there was scaffolding in the sanctuary. Instead of Jesus riding triumphantly into Jerusalem, he was dead. And I had been given way too much information.

During the offering, though, the pastor apologized for the remodeling. It was *progress at work, our church is on the move*, he assured us. Then he further comforted us by saying that only the finest of exported materials were being used – he was confident that everyone would like it. The result, he promised, would be more inspiring worship.

I was emotionally crushed. I only wanted to wave a palm branch, but they had just killed Jesus. After the benediction, I sat in silence for several minutes wondering what I was going to do the rest of Holy Week now that Jesus was dead. My Friday had suddenly become wide open.

I didn't know what to do. Jesus was dead – dead before he even had a chance to say good-bye. Isn't that life? Not only are our celebrations turned into mourning, but it all happens so abruptly, with such finality.

I vowed to do something about it if I could. Even if it was for purely selfish motives, somehow, God willing, before the sun went down that night, I was going to bring Jesus back from the dead.

I met a Korean friend in the afternoon; we walked through a couple of parks and palaces together before going our own ways, and I was on my own with a couple of hours of daylight left. Walking past antique shops and carnival booths, I spotted a church. An evening service was about to begin.

I slipped inside the sanctuary and found a pew appropriately distant from everyone else. I couldn't understand a word of Korean, and considering that, the sermon seemed kinda long. But there, on the altar and handed to me as I walked in were branches of the palm tree – branches that seem to be shouting as loudly as they could, *He's alive. He's still alive.*

I was in a Korean Catholic church, but I felt right at home. I sat in prayer, reflecting upon my Psalm Sunday emotions. In the midst of joy and celebration, it rains on our parade; somebody crashes our party. Faced with pain, disillusionment and despair, we look everywhere, anywhere for a sign of hope, for a sign of life. The palms tell us: *Jesus is still alive.*

But the branches have been cut from the tree, so they also tell us that we are given but a short reprieve. The palm is green and beautiful, but it has lost its connection to life. It's going to die, and soon it will wither and return to dust. The palm is only a temporary sign of a temporary celebration. Yes, Jesus is still alive. But he only has one week.

I left the church, going out into the night lights of Seoul. Walking down a busy city street, I passed a bus stop, equipped with a sing-a-long karaoke monitor in the corner of the small shelter. It was playing Karen Carpenter's *On Top of the World.* I chose not to sing, but I took a moment to reflect upon the good news that Jesus was still alive – if only for just a couple of more days.

***

In my dreams, I was playing kickball.

***

After a relaxing morning at the guesthouse, I went to see the Rev. Gene Matthews, a Methodist missionary in Korea, and my contact person for the week. Gene Matthews believes that a lot of the success of the Korean church is superficial. *Unfortunately, the message has been attend church faithfully, pray without ceasing, and perhaps, most importantly, give generously to the church, and you will prosper.* For an alternate perspective, Gene suggested that I visit Holy

City Foreign Mission Church, an English-speaking congregation comprised of migrant workers from the Philippines, Bangladesh and other third world countries.

Gene was preparing for retirement. As I left his office, he handed me an open letter:

Dear friends in Christ,

As our time in Korea slowly begins to wind down, I increasingly find myself saying to guests from abroad, 'When I first came to Korea . . .' Well, things really were different then. U.S. Ambassador James T. Laney recently pointed out that the economic and political development achieved by the Republic of Korea in the past forty years is unequaled anywhere else in the world. That period of time almost exactly parallels my time in Korea as a missionary. I have observed and participated first hand in the transformation of this nation from one of the poorest in the world, its population essentially rural and destitute, to its current status as one of the emerging economic giants. Democracy has finally begun to take hold in this land after decades of political chaos and harsh military dictatorship.

The church in Korea has pretty much paralleled the development of the country. At the time of my arrival in this tragic land, I found the church debilitated, congregations had been scattered by the war, and the vast majority of the church buildings had been wiped out by war's devastation. Pastors ministered to their flocks in unheated tents, with the parishioners sitting on the barren, cold ground. The serious struggle in those early days was the struggle to survive. Food was scarce, and death by starvation was common. Much of our work consisted of the most basic kind of relief. Funds and relief goods were needed to feed the starving, clothe the naked and rebuild the bombed out churches.

Somehow, it all came together. God blessed the people of Korea. They did much more than just survive. Korea ranks near the top of the world's nations in many economic categories. And the church in Korea may well be the most exciting and vigorous in the world today.

Or at least that is the perception. Westerners have always tended to see what they want to see when observing Korea. The devastated, impoverished image which Korea conveyed to the world in the 1950s and on into the 1960s was one with which the Western nations and churches seemed comfortable. The popular and skillfully performed M.A.S.H. television series created and fostered an image of Korea which persisted long beyond the time it may have had any validity. Visitors to Korea today gape in wonder at the modern, bustling, urban society in which they find themselves. Korea is constantly on the move. People are in a great hurry. Signs of abundance and prosperity are everywhere. Incredibly, this crowded little peninsular nation about the size of Indiana, void of any natural resources, has clawed its way out of abject poverty to material splendor.

The progress and accumulation of wealth have not taken place without cost, however. Seoul boasts some of the worst traffic in the world. It led the world in traffic fatalities until recently. Now, the permanent traffic jams are so bad cars are seldom able to move fast enough to kill people.

And much of the progress now appears to be superficial. A whole series of disasters has struck the nation in recent months. A bridge has fallen down during rush hour. Two major gas explosions, one in Seoul and one in Taegu, have killed hundreds. Most recently, a major department store, noted for its stocks of luxurious goods, collapsed in fifteen seconds, killing several hundred people. Investigations in each case reveal the same sordid story of massive bribes to the authorities in order to obtain approval of the most shoddy kind of construction. Investigators into the department store collapse say the construction was so bad the mystery is not that it fell down but that it survived for six years.

Where does the Church stand in relation to all of this? Internationally, the Korean church has become a model to be copied. Numerical growth during the two decades just past has been phenomenal. The Assemblies of God-related Full Gospel Church in Seoul is the largest church in the world with participation recently reported to be in the range of eight hundred and twenty thousand! Seoul also boasts the largest Presbyterian church in the world and several Methodist churches in Seoul with memberships in the tens of thousands are also vying for the number one position in that denomination.

Forty years ago when I first arrived, most of them were meeting in boarded up piles of rubble or tents 'borrowed' from the U.S. Army. The growth of the churches has echoed the growth of the nation. Unfortunately, much of the 'success' of the churches is as superficial as that of society in general. Riding the wave of prosperity, which has rushed over this nation, the churches have evolved a pragmatic theology of success and prosperity. Jesus' admonition about worshipping either God or Mammon has been rendered meaningless because Mammon has become God. Attend church faithfully, pray without ceasing, and perhaps, most importantly, give generously to the church, and you will prosper. In the revealing glare of the judgment of New Testament Christianity, the theology comes across to me as heretical in the extreme. But it works. People have flocked to church, and they have prospered, and the church has grown to the extent that it is now the envy of the world.

Recently, a young pastor came to my office. He is a missionary to a group of illegal immigrant laborers working in factories. These people are a recent phenomenon in Korea. They have swarmed into the country to fill the vacuum created when Korea's laboring class became sufficiently prosperous that they were no longer willing to engage in the 'three D's' of Korean industry: the Dirty, the Dangerous, and the Difficult. Young men and women from various Asian nations are employed on assembly lines and construction jobs. The government overlooks their presence, because they are necessary. They are grossly underpaid and overworked and have no fringe benefits of any kind.

Accompanying the pastor was a young man from the Philippines. His right arm had been cut off between the hand and the elbow the previous week while he was cleaning a machine. He was immediately fired without pay because he was no longer able to work. He was trying to return to his home in the Philippines for medical treatment, but he did not have money for the trip. The pastor had visited a number of the large wealthy churches seeking a donation of the few hundred dollars needed for the flight home. The amount would not have dented the petty cash amount of most of the churches, but none would help. The theology of success provides no room for such an 'unsuccessful' person.

Yes, we helped him, and he made it home, but I heard Jesus weeping that day, not only over the thousands far from home being chopped up in the factories but over the church which is too busy 'succeeding' to care for the 'least of these'.

There is one more thing, which must be said with great reluctance. The owner of the recently collapsed department store, dispenser of generous bribes to the building inspectors, according to the media, was a Christian, a devout and faithful member of a prominent church. He believed with all his heart that if he faithfully attended church, prayed without ceasing and gave generously to the church, he would succeed. He did. He got all that the church promised and was wealthy beyond belief.

– Matthew 25:35-46

In faith,

Gene Matthews

*** *** ***

I stood outside KFC, waiting anxiously and nervously for Ju-Jin, who never came. I waited and waited, walking up and down the street, hoping that each dark-haired Korean woman in the distance would be her. The day had turned warm and beautiful, and I wanted to be exploring the city with my Korean friend from Bossey. Finally, an hour later, I left, feeling physically sick with disappointment. Back at the guesthouse, I took an hour's nap, disgusted at the day, and then woke up to give Ju-Jin a phone. She, too, had waited at KFC for over an hour, but unfortunately, I had waited at the wrong one.

I realized that it was now up to me to make something of the day, so I decided to go to the Seoul Tower, a popular tourist spot. The weather was still gorgeous, and I left the guesthouse, hoping to salvage the day. I took the subway for a few stops, and back above ground, I zigzagged up several streets until I finally found the base of the cable car, which ascended Seoul Tower Mountain.

Up top, I slowly meandered, checking out the kiosks and other tourists. I spotted three young Korean college students, a male and two females, stopping a group of Westerners. I saw the Westerners shake their heads, and the two parties broke up. The students wanted to speak English, but they had just approached some Germans. I wandered close to the students until I caught their attention. Surrounding me, they began to speak English. I tried to ask them if they were doing an assignment – or if they just wanted to meet some Americans. They just grinned and nodded. We began speaking, and then after talking among themselves in Korean, they invited me in broken English – and with a lot of hand motions – to go with them to a restaurant.

The students ordered for me, and we continued a lively conversation, which had only a limited amount of actual communication. Somehow, the conversation turned to dogs, a delicacy in Korea. *We eat dog in July and August. When it is hot. It makes men more strong,* the male student said, pointing down toward his crotch.

Okay, I said, ignoring that last comment, but always agreeable to talk to Koreans about dogs. *I know you all eat dogs. But how does this work? Do you also have dogs? I mean, do you like dogs as pets?*

One of the girls nodded her head. *Yes, we have pets.* She paused for a second and then looking at me, she said, *I like eat dog; I like pet dog.* I nodded my head with her, aware more than ever, that I wasn't an animal lover.

They started suggesting that we get together again, asking me to go with them on Saturday to visit a home for the mentally handicapped. At least, that was what I think he was gesturing. When I reluctantly, but firmly said *yes,* they all began to clap.

***

I had arranged to meet Hye-Jin, a contact I made at Taizé, at the Kyongbokkung Gate, and right around two o'clock, Hye-Jin appeared carrying a single red rose for me. We took a tour of Changdokgung Palace, quickly lagging behind rest of the group. *My mother told me that I couldn't bring you home,* she said abruptly, confirming our conversation about the reserved nature of Korean society.

Hye-Jin is Catholic, but her boyfriend is not. Her dream, though, is to have a Christian family.

We passed the antique shops of Insadong on our way to visit Chongmyo, a large park with a nice forest and two large shrines. At the far end of the park was a sign that read: *Phone 147 Meters.* Nearer to the entrance, we walked passed an automated pop machine that was dispensing liquid upon itself. We finished the day at a nice Korean restaurant, sitting on the floor under a small table, covered in various Korean dishes.

***

As I was walking down the streets of Seoul, Korea, I fell down a manhole.

I stepped on the cover, and it gave way before catching me between the legs. I sat dazed and confused, straddling the manhole cover, half-buried beneath the street.

A short Korean man ran up to me and asked, *Are you okay?*

He looked at me; he looked at the hole. Then he looked at me in the hole, and pointing, he exclaimed, *It is very dangerous.*

***

I went to the Assemblies of God-related Yoido Full Gospel Church, claiming the largest congregation in the world, with participation reported to be near eight hundred and twenty thousand. Even at 11:30 on Holy Week Wednesday morning, the sanctuary was full of several thousand housewives who had been bussed in for the service. Again, an American was the guest preacher. The service was already in progress when I took a seat up in the balcony.

The sermon was on the seed of God; the theology was congruent with the Prosperity Gospel that I had been told characterizes the Korean church – *The seed of God will grow, and there's no limit to the fruit that will result*. The preacher finished his sermon by talking about a list of forty countries that he was praying for. Korea, of course, was the list, and in a good used car salesman voice, he pointed to the congregation saying, *I will be praying for you. Will you be praying for me?*

An intercessory prayer time followed. One of the ushers, seized by the Spirit, came down the steps of the balcony where I was sitting and fastened his opened palm to my forehead, attacking me if he was one of Hitchcock's birds. I sat their motionless, holding my breath, until he had his fill and moved on to other prey. After the benediction, I quickly slipped outside, taking photos of the church, while busloads of Korean housewives sped away, eager to get home for lunch.

***

I met Ju-Jin, this time at *her* KFC, and we walked a few blocks before going into a lunchroom. I told her to order for me. I had already eaten out several times, and I had enjoyed everything so far. I didn't expect, however, that Ju-Jin would order the cow gut stuff that kept appearing in Africa. It was some kind of soup with large globules of congealed blood and bit and pieces of roughly textured digestive parts. After a couple of courtesy spoonfuls, I looked at her in disbelief, afraid that I was going to add my own undigested bits to the dish. *Well, most Korean men like it,* she offered, implying that she would not have eaten it either. Ju-Jin then took me by the Korean National Council of Churches, her former place of work, and then we took the subway to the Namdaemoon Market. After looking around the Myondong Cathedral for a while, we stopped at a nearby restaurant for a much better meal.

***

I waited for a ticket, afraid though, that I was in the wrong line. At the window, I had trouble pronouncing T'aebaek, my destination city. Some students helped me; others tried to tell the ticket man that I was in the wrong line. Fortunately, he sold me a ticket. I walked right on to the train and sat down in a window seat. Only then did I realize that I was sick. The energy in my legs was gone. I didn't have a fever, but I felt awful.

In T'aebaek. I bought a ticket for a bus leaving in a couple of hours, and feeling miserable, I began slowly walking the streets of T'aebaek. A few blocks later, off a side road, I found a church and sat down on the front steps. Soon, a man came up to me asking where I was from. He was the Presbyterian minister there, and he invited me inside the church for a cup of tea. He lived for fourteen years in Canada and just came to T'aebaek last year.

Visitation is a big part of ministry in Korea. We keep a regular schedule, and I visit every parishioner twice a year. I do a lot of counseling during those visits. I'm in each house for ten to fifteen minutes. I visit six to seven houses a day at times.

Korean pastors preach ten times a week. There's Sunday morning, Sunday night, Wednesday night, and 5:30 prayer services every morning, even on Sundays.

I walked back towards the station, stopping at a store to buy water and some cough drops. After a twenty-minute bus ride, I walked up the long hill towards Jesus Abbey, where I was given a tiny, frozen room and laid down on the floor for a few minutes, feeling awful and wishing to postpone dinner for as long as I could.

***

Ninety-nine percent of the churches today are organized in such a way that nobody knows whether anyone really loves anyone or not, remarked the Rev. Archer Torrey, founder of the Jesus Abbey, a small collection of rock and thatch buildings nestled in a remote valley in the mountains of Korea.[66] *1 John 3:14 says, 'We know we have passed from death to life because we love our brothers and sisters.' This is what Jesus Abbey is all about – loving each other.*

Rev. Torrey, who came to Korea in 1957 to teach at a war-demolished Anglican seminary, left after seven years, believing that theology should be taught in practice not in theory. *My wife, Jane, and I became convinced of the need for a Christian community where 'theology' – biblical principles for everyday life – could be taught*

---

[66] Quotations from Rev. Archey Torrey come from Reuben Archer Torrey III, *Letters from a Mountain Valley* (Seoul: Word of Life Press, 1992).

through the common life, he explained. Together, they came to the mountains, built a house, and devoted themselves to prayer. *The most basic form of spiritual warfare is not preaching but prayer. . . . This almost unseen work of prayer is the most important work there is.*

Beginning with a small, quiet group of people gathered for prayer, Jesus Abbey, known in Korea as *Yesu Won,* has become a retreat center for Christians of different nationalities and denominations who come for a few days of prayer, for a three-month training course, or for a lifetime.

Through the Holy Spirit, we are united with all people, continued Rev. Torrey. *We have a bond that transcends all divisions and differences. At Jesus Abbey, we are simply 'Christian' – on the surface, anyway. In a crisis, nationality, class, gender, race, and denominationalism emerge, and we have to deal with new problems over and over again. But we have found that for new problems, God always has new solutions. God never runs out of new ideas.*

Founded in 1965, Jesus Abbey currently has around thirty permanent members, thirty additional children, and approximately a dozen novices. Each year, thousands of visitors are welcomed to the simple life of the mountain retreat. Jesus Abbey is Christian family living in a Korean context.

Along with prayer, work is central to the life at Jesus Abbey. Chores are evenly shared, and the abbey is seeking to be economically self-sufficient through farming, raising livestock, and selling crafts and resource materials. Besides prayer services and meal times, work comes to a halt three times a day with the ringing of the Angelus bell, which shifts thoughts from daily labor to prayer for the poor and oppressed.

We try not to fall into the devil's trap of neglecting the work of intercessory prayer for something less important, Rev. Torrey said. *While we are doing the work of intercession and all the practical support work, which accompanies community life, God has sent the mission field directly to us! Suddenly, we are the missionaries for thousands of guests who come to Jesus Abbey seeking healing, comfort, guidance, faith, or to discover if God is real. They come to meet the Lord Jesus.*

***

I arrived at Jesus Abbey on Holy Thursday a few minutes before supper – the last food before a twenty-four-hour period of fasting, prayer, and silence – where I sat with Bernice, a thirty-year-old Korean-American from New York, and Joseph, the current director of the abbey. Bernice translated for me during the foot washing and communion service that followed. It was a beautiful service – more than fulfilling my wishes for a meaningful Holy Thursday. I left the service feeling somewhat better, going straight to my frozen room where I arranged my sheets upon the floor amidst body aches and shakes. Someone checked in on me to see how cold I was, and soon I was asleep.

***

A stroke of good fortune! Good Friday, the Day of Crucifixion, is the only day of the year in which the abbey does not have a 5:30 morning prayer service. I woke up feeling a bit better, walked around the grounds taking photos, and then went to the common room where the seven-hour prayer vigil – one hour for each of the last sayings of Jesus – was beginning:

> *It is finished.*
> *Into your hands, I commit my spirit.*
> *Woman, look at your son.*
> *Father, forgive them.*
> *I am thirsty.*
> *Today, you will be with me in paradise.*
> *My God, my God, why have you forsaken me?*

A thirty-minute meditation – and then thirty minutes of silence. I hung in there, sitting in a haze of sleepiness for seven straight hours. Praying with others in silence, I experienced the power and healing of fasting in community. Surprisingly soon, it was four o'clock, and we closed with a formal prayer. After feeling so terrible the day before, my health returned. I was drowsy – in prayer but not always focused. I was reminded that Christ died for me in spite of myself.

Jesus Abbey is a warm and welcoming place – yet another example of Christian community. Jesus Abbey was founded as a reaction against theoretical theological training. Faith must be practiced not just thought about.

I have worked for many years with youth in New York and Washington, reflected Bernice, who came to Jesus Abbey four months ago. *But for now God has called me to learn how to serve people. That's why I'm here.*

***

On Saturday, I met the college students as promised, and along with several of their friends, we went to a home for severely mentally and physically handicapped persons. One of the deformed young men, a high school student, told me that he was learning English. Another resident remained kneeling the whole time with his head on the floor A deaf and dumb man was playing with himself. Variety of odd laughter came from all corners of the room. I split my time between the residents and the visiting students. Occasionally, I looked over at a Korean soccer game on the television. One of the students told me that he comes here for himself. *This is something I need.*

***

On Easter Sunday, Ju-Jin and I went to the Korean Mission Church, a congregation of international migrant and factory workers – an English-speaking third-world church in a Seoul suburb. Located on the third floor of an office building, the walls of the makeshift sanctuary were covered with paper cutouts proclaiming *God is Alive.* People sat in folding chairs, crowding as close as they could to the front of the comfortably packed room. During the announcements, the pastor introduced me as a special guest. I shared some information about myself and then gave a short Easter message: *Mary Magdalene saw the risen Christ through her tears. . . . God is a God of surprises. . . . the resurrection happened on a workday.*

My life is so far removed from the daily situation of the lives of these worshippers. However, I could feel the presence of Christ among the struggling, disenfranchised people – people from various lands and languages having nothing in common except for their disadvantaged lives and their hope in Christ. *To such belongs the Kingdom of Heaven.*

We ate lunch, which is served every Sunday after church, and then the tables were cleared for English classes. On our way out, we were shown the shelter, a room of bunks for overnight guests – abuse victims, homeless individuals, and displaced immigrants.

Missions, missions, missions. That's all they talk about. But where are the church structures that will help change the situation? Ju-Jin wanted to know. If the body of Christ is truly effective, somebody will be fighting for systemic change while others – like this Korean pastor – look after the needs of the people. These people need to feel that God loves them, that he hasn't forgotten them. Here is a Korean man attempting through his own strengths and weaknesses, through his own power and vulnerability to be their pastor.

In the Seoul subway, deciding against a Western hug, I had an awkward good-bye with Ju-Jin, but, nonetheless, we parted, and I walked back to the guesthouse knowing that now even Korea was a closed chapter.

Wind is Invisible

(Japan: March 31st – April 15th)

It was as if God had yanked me off the plane. Osamu, who had just recently finished his own around-the-world pilgrimage, was there to greet me, ready to guide me through a two-week journey of Japan. Osamu knew what a Christian pilgrim should see and do in Japan; he provided me with an energy that I was beginning to lose.

Most of my pilgrimage in Tokyo centered on Sanya, an area of homeless day laborers. Each morning, the trucks come through hiring people for various menial and underpaid jobs which are vital to the Japanese economy. The Nihonzutsumi Church, in the middle of the Sanya district, was built in 1990 with the free, volunteer labor of the homeless people. Osamu and I arrived a few minutes late one night for a Bible study where the Rev. Fukuyama was teaching one of his parishioners from the book of Genesis.

The Bible is full of history, Rev. Fukuyama said later over a cup of coffee at the Café Bach. *It is very important, however, to understand the viewpoint of this history – a view written by the people in power. It is the same today. Nobody in power cares about the lives of the homeless people living here in Sanya. We must always question our own viewpoint.*

We are all saved, believes Fukuyama. *Through the cross, salvation has come to all people, and salvation is the work of God. The most important thing in life is to notice this essential truth. Our task as a church is to share the good news with people so they can be liberated and not live life in fear.*

I live in the midst of miracles – every day miracles, he continued. *The existence of this church building is a miracle. Ministering in this area and with these people is a constant realization of the miracle of life itself.*

***

The cherry blossoms in Ueno Park were in full bloom, producing a somewhat mystical effect as though there was a warm Spring snow. We ate at a small noodle shop and then headed to what Osamu called the *Protestant Vatican* of Tokyo, which houses the offices the United Church of Christ in Japan (UCCJ), the National Council of Churches in Japan, and other related organizations. Nearby, we ducked into the largest Baptist church in Japan, the Tokyo Peace Church, an international congregation comprised of Japanese, Koreans, and Burmese.

***

Osamu's mother fixed breakfast for us as Osamu went to work on the day's plans.

Do you want to see Mt. Fuji?

Yes, of course, I replied.

Osamu called around, trying to locate some discount train tickets, and we set off, taking a train into Tokyo. The train door opened, and we stood on the platform looking into a gigantic, multi-story hole in the ground, the size of a full city block, which was being dug out to make room for another skyscraper. *I'm shocked. . . . there used to be a discount ticket shop here,* said Osamu, staring in disbelief at the big hole.

***

> *Each time I see Fuji it appears changed.*
> *And I feel I view it ever for the first time.*
> *How shall I describe Fuji to those who haven't seen it?*
> *It is never seen twice alike*
> *And I know no one way of describing it*
> — Suzuki

***

Osamu Mimura and I stood looking at Japan's Mount Fuji. *Indescribable,* said Osamu. *I wouldn't know what to tell others,* I added. While in awe of the fabled mountain, Osamu and I joked about the connections that had brought us together to the slopes of Mount Fuji. A United Church of Christ in Japan minister, Osamu had recently completed his own year of pilgrimage. Besides visiting Iona (Scotland) and Taizé (France), Osamu spent four months in Bangladesh working in mission with Taizé brothers before studying at the World Council of Churches Ecumenical Institute at Bossey near Geneva, Switzerland. I met Osamu at Bossey during my week's visit in November. There, Professor Hizkias Assefa of the Nairobi (Kenya) Peace Initiative used the poem on Mount Fuji in his lecture on peace and reconciliation.

Life is an ongoing process, Dr. Assefa had stated. *Nothing is permanent; everything is in change. Therefore, every time we see something, we see if differently. It is new. That is what reconciliation is all about – learning to see one another always again for the first time.*

Five months later, Osamu and I were together at Mount Fuji, remembering Dr. Assefa's words and our friends from Bossey. *The earth is my home,* Osamu is fond of saying. *As a Christian pilgrim, I do not feel attached to any specific country or to any particular form of Christianity. I am at home in any Christian community as long as it is engaged in social justice and is moving towards ecumenical unity and understanding.*

***

We spent a couple of hours in Isao Uematsu's simple apartment, sitting on the floor sharing conversation, prayers, and lunch. Uematsu makes a modest living using his carpentry skills, and he has furnished his apartment with discarded furniture that he has found on the streets. Although he doesn't call any particular congregation or denomination home, Uematsu leads an informal, ecumenical prayer circle in Tokyo.

The first atomic bomb was dropped on Hiroshima on August 6th, the same day the Church has traditionally celebrated Transfiguration Day, Uematsu shared over a bowl of noodles. *Remembering Jesus' glorious transfiguration before his disciples and then contemplating the terrible transfiguration that occurs to victims of nuclear war makes me weep. It is a day full of despair and hope, destruction and ultimate redemption. Within this dichotomy is contained the entire story of humankind.*

God has given us the power to change the world either through love or hate, yet our most fundamental need is for God to save us from ourselves. Each of us will eventually be transfigured from our present condition. Through confession and repentance, our journeys can take us to the mountaintop rather than to the wasteland.

***

Osamu and I took Mass with the Missionaries of Charity, the male counterpart to Mother Theresa's order. Every morning, their downstairs lounge is open for the homeless. Lunch is served around noon. Osamu left me with the four brothers, and I spent the night, sleeping on the floor in the second-story living room while outside, on the street below, were the homeless of Tokyo.

***

Osamu and I sat belly-up to a large circular bar as a conveyor belt carried plates of sushi around to the diners. A sushi man worked inside the bar making up fresh plates of raw fish. If you wanted something that you couldn't see, you just yelled – the sushi man would make it. We stacked up our dirty dishes, paying by the plate as we left. After the meal, Osamu took me on what he called the *Prostitute Trail* – the dark side of Tokyo history, which led to a large Buddhist shrine in the middle of the city.

In the evening, Osamu and I volunteered at a soup kitchen held in an UCCJ church in Sanya. The one-room storefront church witnesses to the true banquet of God through its unique Eucharist table. Worship is held in the same room as the soup kitchen; the communion table and the soup table are literally one and the same.

***

Osamu's mother prepared me another Japanese breakfast of soup, tofu, and rice – there is no difference between Japanese breakfast and dinner foods – and I discovered as I was eating that she had prepared eggs and toast for herself. Apparently, she was tired of Japanese breakfasts.

I feel like I have had tag-team pilgrimage coaches over the last several countries. I feel like a runner who has paced himself fairly well and is coming down the last stretch exhausted and ready to see the finish line. I seem to have lost a physical energy that I can no longer regain with a good night's sleep. With Osamu as my guide, however, I will finish strong in spite of myself.

***

The Rev. Okura, pastor of the Tode Church in Kawasaki, leads a UCCJ congregation in the midst of an impoverished area of Korean immigrants. *The Koreans in Japan have long been discriminated against,* began Rev. Okura. *And this discrimination is still perfectly legal. During the years of occupation, the Japanese forcefully brought many Koreans to Japan for various reasons. Over the years, the Koreans have been refused jobs and denied entry into universities, schools, and day care centers. Most Koreans have lost their language and customs yet have no place in Japanese society. Even now the local council wants to remove the Korean houses in the area. Since they have lost their ties with Korea, they have no place to return.*

It is not easy work, but it is joyful, continued the Rev. Okura. *At first, our church was not accepted by the Korean community, but our relationship has continually improved. We are seeking partnership – not paternalism. We have helped the area to form human rights groups, which has empowered the community.*

The Koreans in the area are mostly Confucians and Buddhists, although some Korean Christians belong to our church. Most of our fifty members are actually educated Japanese – many come from far away to attend the church because they believe in what we are doing. After worship, we ate at a local noodle shop and then returned to the church for a few more hours of visiting with one another, playing with the children and drinking green tea.

On our way out of Kawasaki, Osamu and I stopped by an art exhibition of Tomihiro Hoshino. A physical education teacher, Hoshino had a gymnastics accident, which left him almost totally paralyzed. Learning to write and paint by holding a brush in his mouth, Hoshino's signature works are watercolors of Japanese flowers with short poems reflecting the depths of his struggle and the deep joy he possesses as a Christian:

> *Wind is invisible,*
> *Yet blowing through the trees it becomes a green wind*
> *And breathing on the flowers it becomes a flower wind.*
> *Now, the wind caresses my face.*
> *Well, then, I wonder,*
> > *what kind of wind will it become now?*

And

> *When I believed that life was the most important thing,*
> *I found it very difficult to live.*
> *When I realized that life is not the most important thing,*
> *Life became joyous.*

His text above a watercolor of a dandelion beautifully captures the pilgrim spirit:

> *I have seen you flying in the sky. When was it?*
> *Your way of traveling fills me with joy.*
> *You each carry only one thing on the wind.*
> *It is the only thing necessary for human beings.*
> *If I could throw away what I don't need,*
> > *Even I could fly in the sky.*

***

I said good-bye to Osamu and spent my final weekend in Japan with Kyoko, an old friend from my student days in Germany. On Friday evening, her husband, Shoshi, and I went to a baseball game between the Chiba Marines and the Seba Lion, fulfilling one of my biggest cultural dreams. They weren't exactly the Tokyo Giants – but still I had a great time. Both teams had a pep band in the outfield, giving the game a college football feeling. Male cheerleaders in long decorated robes led each section of fans. I took several photos of them thinking one day I'd go as one for Halloween. On our way home, we saw the Hale-Bopp Comet high in the Japanese sky.

On Saturday, I accompanied Kyoko's family – her parents and husband – to the local Shinto temple for the christening of her two-month old daughter, Karine. Allowed to go with the family into the temple, I watched the priest do his thing – the significance of which I couldn't follow. We were given some holy water to drink on our way out, and after a while, I asked a couple of questions about the meaning of the rituals. *We're not for sure*, they shrugged. *It's just something that we do.*

Sunday was my birthday. I didn't go to church. Instead, I spent the day riding in a car for seven hours with Kyoko's husband. After Karine's birth, Kyoko had spent the last couple of months with her parents near Tokyo while Shoshi continued his work in Iwate. Now, mother and child were moving back.

It was also Kyoko's birthday. She spent the day taking the train with Karine, a much easier trip for the baby.

The day was beautiful, and I actually had better views of Fuji than when I saw it with Osamu. We drove through the city of Nagoya, and an hour later, we were in Iwate, where we picked up Kyoko and Karine at the train station and then shopped for groceries before going to their apartment.

The next day, Kyoko arranged for us to celebrate our birthdays with a day trip to Nara, the ancient capital of Japan. To do so, she hired a babysitter through a professional service, and on schedule, an older woman arrived to look after Karine. Baby and babysitter were introduced, and then Kyoko told the older woman that Karine had been a little constipated. *The baby doesn't go to the bathroom because her mother is fat,* the old woman said. Furious, Kyoko ran out of the apartment, stringing together long phrases of Japanese that I seemed to be able to understand.

The day turned gorgeous, and in Nara, we spent our time walking in the parks and visiting temples and museums. Later in the afternoon, several high school kids approached me as part of their English lessons. *Why are you here? What do you like about Japan?*

Then, in the morning, I caught a train for Tokyo where I boarded a plane for LA, leaving foreign soil for the last time.

It's a Small World

(Los Angeles: April 15th – 19th)

I decided to ride *It's a Small World* one more time. I'd catch the next bus back to Manhattan Beach where I was staying. True freedom is being at Disneyland without your parents; however, I spent the day retracing the steps I took with my family when I was five. The spinning teacups still made me sick, but this time Uncle Johnny did not turn into a ghost at the Haunted Mansion – I did.

The pilgrimage is not always a trip into the unknown. Sometimes, it is a return to what is or was familiar.

The bus dropped me off at my connecting stop, and I began waiting in the dark for a bus that never came. Soon, a man came up to me and began to talk. I tried not to be afraid. Like me, he was waiting for the same bus. His car had broken down; he was returning from a Tae-kwon-do class. His wife was at a Clippers basketball game.

The more we talked, the more he befriended me, and eventually, he gained my trust. He bought me some coffee. He let me use his phone. Together, we waited – encouraged by uninformed bus drivers. Slowly, an hour passed and then another.

Yesterday, my brother-in-law was sentenced to life in prison, he unloaded. *He hasn't committed any hard crimes, but 'three strikes you're out,'* he said referring to California's law regarding three convictions. *He's thirty-two and has already spent ten years behind bars.* I discovered that I was speaking to Brother Ben, a local Baptist minister. *This has really shaken up our church. He's the son of our senior pastor, my father-in-law.*

Finally, Ben and I grabbed a different bus, one continuing on the original route that I had taken from Disneyland almost three hours earlier. As it turned out, we discovered alternate connections that worked well for both of us. Brother Ben got off at his stop, and I watched my guardian angel escape into the night. I arrived home after midnight thankful that the unexpected ordeal of my return journey was finally over. From Fantasyland to reality, it's a small world but a really big city.

***

I stayed in Los Angeles with the Clements – yet another family from camp. We went biking along the beach and caught a Dodgers game, but as the game went into the late innings, I became distracted, thinking about my ailing grandfather and the next day's flight home – the inevitable but successful end of my physical journey.

***

They would get there, they thought. Every traveler arrives somehow. Inquiring along the way, getting lost, finding the way again, singing happily or sorrowfully, they would get there. . . . A person who has a mouth cannot get lost. They would find the place one day. Walk on ahead. It is useless to think of the hills and fish and animals of the old homestead. Life or death is ahead. The cloud in the sky will be down on earth one day, as a mist or rain seeping into the soil. The eagle might fly high, but it will perch one day. It will surely perch. Walk on, plod on, to the very end. The journey never ends. It is the traveler who ends.[67]

***

It took two airlines and four flights to get home from LA. Unaware that my flight out of Kansas City stopped in Fayetteville, Arkansas, I enjoyed an aerial view of my new home – having learned while I was in Los Angeles that I was being appointed to a church there. In Fayetteville, all of the passengers disembarked, leaving me alone with the crew of two.

Looks like you're it! said the co-pilot.

Do I get any special privileges? I asked.

Sure, you can sit anywhere you like – just make sure your seatbelt is fastened when we take off.

---

[67] Hove. p. 169.

I spent the flight moving from one seat to the next – a pilgrim personally escorted to his final destination. Seven months ago, I had left Little Rock with two other passengers. Now, I returned alone. Before I knew it, we touched ground. I had just finished going around the world, and I was thirty minutes early. I grabbed my bags and sat on the airport curb waiting for my parents to arrive.

By the Banks of Roasting Ear

(Roasting Ear Creek, Arkansas: April 22nd – June 1st)

Two days later, I was at the hospital bedside of my grandfather, who laid alone, heavily medicated, hardly able to stay awake but aware that I stood above him. After an hour of holding his hand, I slipped away again, this time to the Ozark wilderness for forty days of reflection and prayer. Ever since high school, I had wanted to example Jesus' forty days in the wilderness. Now, I had the opportunity, ending my pilgrimage with time alone – and in one place.

Near a spring on Roasting Ear Creek, we broke bread – the Rev. Steve Johnson, Kay and Bob Burton, and I. They offered prayers of protection and consecrated the campsite and outdoor altar. The touch of their hands left my head and shoulders, and the three of them walked away in silence, leaving me alone in the wilderness. I was left in transition: from pilgrimage to hermitage, from visible to invisible community, from God to God.

I remembered Sister Giovanna in Assisi, Italy who had taught me: *The three greatest moments in life are the hermitage – being alone with God; the street, our pilgrimage journey into the world; and the community, sharing our faith experiences with one another through fellowship and worship.* My physical journey was over, and I now began a forty-day hermitage in the Ozark wilderness.

A few weeks earlier, Isao Uematsu, who leads an ecumenical prayer group in Japan, told me about a monk who wanted to spend a full year alone in prayer. *Although the hermitage experience was not a normal practice of this particular order, after a lot of prayer, the entire chapter decided to take this man to his hermitage site,* said Uematsu. *There, they held Mass and offered special prayer for the brother. A year later, the whole chapter went out again and brought the monk back to the community. It was a visible reminder that we are never alone. It's important that the community remains an integral part of any hermitage or pilgrimage experience. The community is always upholding us through their prayers and support.*

By the water of Roasting Ear, I sat . . . and sat . . . and sat. Forty days is biblical for a really long time. The experience itself shifted back and forth between the images of paradise and wilderness. The hours spent reading the Bible filled me with a timeless peace. Candle-lit eventide prayer, sunsets and starry nights, nightly campfires and the constant sound of living water produced moments of Eden's garden rapture.

At other times, however, the moments of peace quickly dissipated, and I become aware that I was living in a wilderness from which I needed God's protection. I saw dozens of snakes, hundreds of ticks, and I endured a severe storm that seriously damaged my tent. I managed to patch up a one-yard rip with eight Band-Aids and a fork. Similarly, I discovered that the Lord's Prayer comes directly out of Jesus' own wilderness experience: *Give us our daily bread . . . protect us from the Evil One.*

Handwritten notes of news from home sometimes accompanied my silent food pick-ups, which I gathered out of a large cooler on the edge of the Burton homestead. My cousin Liesel was killed in a car accident. Pa-Paw was expected to die any day. I felt the pressure to pray – but I also felt prayer's peace and power.

My heart beat with expectation on the eve of the fortieth evening. Candles were lit on the altar, and I sat meditating on the full-size cross erected at the foot of the spring. From the now grown-up path came sounds of the return. The community had arrived. I broke my silence, and I had my first human contact in forty days. We sang hymns and offered prayers of thanksgiving.

In the wilderness, I was able to reflect upon the past year. In many ways, the lessons of the woods complimented the pilgrimage.

Throughout the journey, age-old spiritual truths surfaced. The specific narrative of my faith journey became the teaching tool of the Holy Spirit. What I learned, I believe, is universally true: we discover God through the actual events of our lives. Through the eyes of pilgrimage, we can see how otherwise ordinary experiences are spiritual opportunities. The pilgrimage embraces not only the present and the future but also allows us to look back on our past and to discover God's presence in ways previously unnoticed.

As I take my faith memories with me into the future, the narrative stories of my journeys will remind me of spiritual truisms that I believe are operative for us all:

- God is in the facts. We should not look for God in what could have happened or in what should have happened. Rather, we find God's presence in what actually happens. The reality of life with God is always better than our imaginations.

- *All will be well, all will be well, all manner of things will be well.*

- We are in the palms of God's hands.

- We do not possess anything; rather, God possesses us.

- God is constantly revealing and unveiling his presence in new and unexplored ways.

- Now is always the most important moment of our lives.

- We must wait upon God and learn to see life through the *third eye* of the pilgrim.

- Everything is always changing; all things are temporary.

- Life is a constant experience of losing things along the way.

- The Christian life is one of continuous transformation.

- Regardless of the situation, our reaction to it is always our own choice and responsibility.

- And, of course, the journey is never over.

There is more, but there always is. John, a young Dutch doctor, reminded me of this at Taizé: *I am still learning from a year I spent eight years ago in a leprosy colony in India.*

I went in search for God, and God answered. I found more than I had ever dreamed about and more than I had bargained on. God is constantly calling us, challenging us with words that are both sweet to the ear and frightening to the heart. The spiritual mystery is that God's peace stays with us even as we are being called out of our comfort zone.

From my wilderness journal: *Into the future, God will show me the path that I am to follow. For now, his presence will light up my immediate path with peace and contentment, yet the future remains undisclosed, shrouded in a veil. Like the luminous glow of the moon before it actually rises so is our hope in the distant future – there is an assurance of its coming reality, yet now we are not able to gaze at it.*

God is a God who is perpetually revealing and unveiling something – to my surprise and delight. God's answers are not always to my questions. Yet the spontaneity of God in my God-relationship is wondrous beyond comprehension. So we wait upon the Lord – we wait for answers to our petty problems, for help to our cries of desperation, and for the consummation of our ultimate redemption. Yet as we position our spirits in quiet expectation, we can savor the fruits of gardens never before explored, and God embraces us in ways never before anticipated. To our surprise, we discover that crumbs have been dropped along our path, and we are allowed to indulge on bits and pieces of the Bread of Life all along the journey.

***

After a couple hours of conversation, Steve, Kay, and Bob left, and I spent the final evening alone by myself. At daybreak, I broke camp, carting all of my provisions back to the house, where Kay was busy preparing biscuits and gravy.

Around noon, I arrived at the hospital, where my grandfather had trouble recognizing me with my forty-day beard, but eager to remove it, I went through a half-dozen gift shop disposable razors, cutting myself only occasionally, and by the middle of the afternoon, my grandfather knew who I was. *I have always thought highly of you,* I heard him say as I left his room in tears.

***

My forty days ended as our annual church conference began, and as I drove to rejoin fellow United Methodist clergy and lay persons from around North Arkansas, I passed an Arkansas Department of Transportation pick-up truck pulled off on the side of the interstate. Its driver had a shovel in his hands, scooping up a dead dog, which lay on its back with all four legs pointing stiffly to the sky, and perhaps, for the first time, I realized that I was home.

Throughout my pilgrimage, several people asked me where I was going. *Arkansas* was the best answer I could give. It seemed strange. Few people from Arkansas have the opportunity to travel around the world – even fewer people travel around the world with Arkansas as their destination. But in most pilgrimages, we end up returning to where we started – it's just that we have become different people.

Pilgrim Companions

The following list includes books that were read during my travels. These books – of varying quality – provided me with additional content, images and narrative and became an inherent part of the pilgrimage experience.

Achebe, Chinua. *Arrow of God*. London: Heinemann Educational, 1964.

Achebe, Chinua. *A Man of the People*. London: Heinemann Educational, 1966.

Achebe, Chinua. *Things Fall Apart*. London: Heinemann Educational, 1958.

Anon. *The Way of a Pilgrim and The Pilgrim Continues His Way*.Translated by R. M. French. London: SPCK, 1963.

Borg, Marcus J. *The God We Never Knew*. San Francisco: HarperSanFrancisco, 1997.

Carretto, Carlo. *The Desert Journal: A Diary (1954-55)*. Translated by Alison Swaisland Bucci. New York: Fount Books, 1992.

Carretto, Carlo. *Letters from the Desert*. Translated by Rose Mary Hancock. New York: Orbis Books, 1972.

Carey, George. *Spiritual Journey: 1,000 Young Adults Share the Reconciling Experience of Taizé with the Archbishop of Canterbury*. Harrisburg, PA: Morehouse Publishing, 1994.

Cassidy, Sheila. *Audacity to Believe*. Glasgow: William Collins, 1977.

Coelho, Paulo. *The Alchemist*. Translated by Alan R. Clarke. San Francisco: HarperSanFrancisco, 1995.

Coelho, Paulo. *The Pilgrimage: A Contemporary Quest for Ancient Wisdom*. Translated by Alan R. Clark. San Francisco: HarperSanFrancisco, 1995.

Coelho, Paulo. *By the River Piedra I Sat Down and Wept*. Translated by Alan R. Clarke. San Francisco: HarperSanFrancisco, 1996.

Coelho, Paulo. *The Valkyries: An Encounter with Angels.* Translated by Alan R. Clarke. San Francisco: HarperSanFrancisco, 1995.

Dalrymple, William. *From the Holy Mountain: A Journey Among the Christians of the Middle East.* New York: Henry Holt, 1997.

Davey, Cyril. *Casa Materna: The Santi Story.* Tuckahoe, New York: The Casa Materna Society, 1982.

Di Giovanni, Janine. *Against the Stranger: Lives in Occupied Territory.* London: Viking, 1993.

García Márquez, Gabriel. *Strange Pilgrims: Twelve Stories.* Translated by Edith Grossman. London: Knopf, 1993.

Goldman, Ari. L. *The Search for God at Harvard.* New York: Times Books/Random House, 1991.

Halberstam, David. *Ho.* New York: Random House, 1971.

Hove, Chenjerai. *Ancestors.* London: Picador, 1996.

Hughes, Gerard W. *The God of Surprises.* London: Darton, Longman, and Todd, 1985.

Hughes, Gerard W. *In Search of a Way.* London: Darton, Longman, and Todd, 1994.

Hughes, Gerard W. *Walk to Jerusalem.* London: Darton, Longman, and Todd, 1991.

Lame Deer. *Lame Deer: Seeker of Visions.* New York: Simon and Schuster, 1972.

Lewis, C. S. *Miracles: A Preliminary Study.* New York: The Macmillan Company, 1947.

McKibben, Bill. *The Age of Missing Information.* New York: Random House, 1993.

Morgan, Marlo. *Mutant Message Down Under.* New York: HarperCollinsPublishers, 1994.

Morgan, Sally. *My Place.* Freemantle, Australia: Freemantle Arts Centre Press, 1987.

Norris, Kathleen. *The Cloister Walk.* New York: Riverhead Books, 1996.

Ng~ug~i Wa Thiong'o. *Matigori.* Translated from the G~ik~uy~u by Wang~ui wa Goro. Harare: Zimbabwe Publishing House, 1990.

Ng~ug~i Wa Thiong'o. *Weep Not, Child*. London: Heinemann Educational, 1966.

Paton, Alan. *Debbie Go Home*. London: Cape, 1961.

Peck, M. Scott. *In Search of Stones: A Pilgrimage of Faith, Reason, and Discovery*. New York: Hyperion, 1995.

Roger of Taizé, Brother. *No Greater Love: Sources of Taizé*. Collegeville, Minnesota: Liturgical Press, 1991.

Selby, Bettina. *Pilgrim's Road: A Journey to Santiago de Compostela*. London: Abacus, 1994.

Sheldrake, Philip. *Living Between Worlds: Place and Journey in Celtic Spirituality*. London: Darton, Longman, and Todd, 1995.

Torrey, Reuben Archer, III. *Letters from a Mountain Valley*. Seoul: Word of Life Press, 1992.

Twain, Mark. *The Innocents Abroad, or The New Pilgrims' Progress*. New York: The New American Library, 1966.

Weible, Wayne. *Medjugorje: The Message*. Orleans, MA: Paraclete Press, 1989.

Welsh, Irvine. *Trainspotting*. New York: W.W. Norton, 1996.

Zinsser, William K. *American Places: A Writer's Pilgrimage to Fifteen of this Country's Most Visited and Cherished Sites*. New York: HarperPerennial, 1992.

Printed in the United Kingdom
by Lightning Source UK Ltd.
9537600001B